Using Concepts in Medieval History

Jackson W. Armstrong · Peter Crooks ·
Andrea Ruddick
Editors

Using Concepts in Medieval History

Perspectives on Britain and Ireland, 1100–1500

palgrave
macmillan

Editors
Jackson W. Armstrong
Department of History
University of Aberdeen
Aberdeen, Scotland, UK

Peter Crooks
Department of History
Trinity College Dublin
Dublin, Ireland

Andrea Ruddick
Faculty of History
St Paul's School
London, UK

ISBN 978-3-030-77279-6   ISBN 978-3-030-77280-2   (eBook)
https://doi.org/10.1007/978-3-030-77280-2

Cover illustration: Bartholomeus Anglicus, Livre des propriétés des choses, BnF, Français 134, fol. 169r

This Palgrave Macmillan imprint is published by the registered company Springer Nature Switzerland AG
The registered company address is: Gewerbestrasse 11, 6330 Cham, Switzerland

PREFACE

This book sprang from a series of conversations, first sparked in the summer of 2014 immediately following the Harlaxton Medieval Symposium which considered the 'The Plantagenet Empire' (and which later resulted in the publication of that same name edited by Peter Crooks, David Green and the late Mark Ormrod). An exchange of post-conference reflections that summer and autumn between Peter Crooks and Jackson Armstrong identified a shared curiosity about how historians in our field, and more generally, select, critique and put concepts to use in their work. That exchange led to a joint interest in facilitating an organised discussion which would invite late-medieval historians of Britain and Ireland to reflect on and explore the raw conceptual work that is so often an implicit, rather than explicit, part of their craft.

In May 2015, the Research Institute of Irish and Scottish Studies at the University of Aberdeen funded a first scoping discussion led by Jackson and Peter into the shape of the topic to be explored, and how this might be most fruitfully achieved. That meeting involved the valuable input of Michael P. Brown, Amy Hayes, Jeff Oliver, Ana Jorge, Andrew Simpson and Patience Schell, whose expertise drew from the fields of History, Archaeology, Law and Literature. In May 2016, funding from the Trinity Long Room Hub Research Incentive Scheme, at Trinity College Dublin, enabled Peter and Jackson to convene a workshop of historians entitled *'Tyrannous Constructs' or 'Tools of the Trade'? The Use and Abuse of Concepts in Medieval History,* whose participants included Andrea Ruddick, Ronan Mulhaire, Lynn Kilgallon, Chris Fletcher, Sophie Page, Sparky Booker, Ali Cathcart and David Ditchburn. The meeting was given a certain gravitas, and its naming was duly justified, in being joined by Peggy Brown who offered concluding reflections on the discussion, and who contributed a paper on 'Feudalism and Periodisation'.

Following the Dublin meeting, which established a group of interested discussants, Andrea Ruddick joined Peter and Jackson in an organising capacity, and plans for a further meeting and potential publication began in earnest. In September 2017, a follow-up workshop on '*Tyrannous Constructs*' met at Exeter College, Oxford, funded by a British Academy/Leverhulme Small Research Grant led by Andrea. The participants included Andrea, Peter and Jackson; and Ali Cathcart, Chris Fletcher and Sophie Page joined again, with the addition of Ian Forrest, Eliza Hartich and Carl Watkins. John Watts offered a summative round-up of the discussions, posing a number of helpful questions about the aims of a possible publication.

We are grateful to all the various participants in this sequence of enriching conversations, to those who are now included here as essay contributors and to the editorial team at Palgrave and the anonymous reviewers of the proposal and the complete volume. We also wish to thank Áine Foley for her efforts in harmonising the footnotes. The editors would also like to acknowledge each other for their shared support, encouragement and commitment to this project over a number of years.

Aberdeen, UK   Jackson W. Armstrong
Dublin, Ireland   Peter Crooks
London, UK   Andrea Ruddick

CONTENTS

NOTES ON CONTRIBUTORS

Jackson W. Armstrong is Senior Lecturer in History at the University of Aberdeen. He is the author of *England's Northern Frontier: Conflict and local society in the fifteenth-century Scottish marches* (Cambridge, 2020) and the co-editor of *Cultures of Law in Urban Northern Europe Scotland and its Neighbours c.1350–c.1650* (Routledge, 2021).

Elizabeth A. R. Brown is Professor *Emerita* of History at Brooklyn College, City University of New York. She is the author of 'Feudalism: The Tyranny of a Construct' (*American Historical Review*, lxix [1974]) as well as numerous seminal works on the Capetian dynasty.

Peter Crooks is Senior Lecturer in Medieval History at Trinity College Dublin, the University of Dublin. He is the editor of (with Timothy H. Parsons), *Empires and Bureaucracy in World History: From Late Antiquity to the Twentieth Century* (Cambridge University Press); (with David Green and W. Mark Ormrod) *The Plantagenet Empire* (Tyas).

Christopher Fletcher is *Chargé de recherche* (Assistant Research Professor) at the Centre National de la Recherche Scientifique (CNRS), France, affiliated with the University of Lille. He specializes in late medieval political culture and the history of masculinity. He has published *Richard II: Manhood, youth and politics, 1377–99* (2008), *Government and Political Life in England and France, c. 1300–c. 1500* with Jean-Philippe Genet and John Watts (2015), *The Palgrave Handbook of Masculinity and Political Culture in Europe* with Sean Brady, Rachel E. Moss and Lucy Riall (2018) and most recently *Everyday Political Objects: From the Middle Ages to the Present Day* (2021).

Eliza Hartrich is Lecturer in Late Medieval History at the University of East Anglia. Her work explores political, economic, social and cultural relationships between townspeople in late medieval England, Ireland, Wales and France.

Her first book, *Politics and the Urban Sector in Fifteenth-Century England, 1413–1471*, was published by Oxford University Press (2019).

Sophie Page is Professor of late Medieval History at University College London. She is the author of *Magic in the Cloister: Pious Motives, Illicit Interests, and Occult Approaches to the Medieval Universe* (Pennsylvania State Press).

Andrea Ruddick is a History teacher at St Paul's School, London. She previously worked as a lecturer and research fellow at the University of Cambridge and the University of Oxford. She is the author of *English Identity and Political Culture in the Fourteenth Century* (Cambridge University Press).

Carl Watkins is Reader in Central Medieval History and Fellow of Magdalene College, University of Cambridge. He is the author of *History and the Supernatural in Medieval England* (Cambridge University Press) and *King Stephen* (Penguin).

John Watts is Professor of Medieval History and Fellow of Corpus Christi College, University of Oxford. He is the author of *Henry VI: The Politics of Kingship* and *The Making of Polities: Europe, 1300–1500* (Cambridge University Press).

Part I

Introductions

'Tyrannous Constructs' or Tools of the Trade? the Use and Abuse of Concepts in Medieval History

Jackson W. Armstrong, Peter Crooks, and Andrea Ruddick

> *Die ich rief, die Geister,*   (From the spirits that I called
>   *Werd' ich nun nicht los.*   Sir, deliver me!])
>   —Goethe, *Der Zauberlehrling* ('The Sorcerer's Apprentice').

Concepts are indispensable. They are 'the building blocks of thought'.[1] It is through concepts that humans seek intellectually to control and under-stand the disposition of the world they experience.[2] The etymology of the term—from the Latin *conceptum*, 'that which is conceived'—helps us under-stand the work that concepts perform: concepts enable us *to conceive* of the

---

[1] Quotation from Eric Margolis and Stephen Laurence, 'Concepts', in Edward N. Zalta (ed.), *The Stanford Encyclopedia of Philosophy* (Summer 2019 edn.), https://plato.stanford.edu/archives/sum2019/entries/concepts/.

[2] By way of introduction, John Wilson, *Thinking with Concepts* (Cambridge: Cambridge University Press, 1963), remains useful.

J. W. Armstrong
Department of History, University of Aberdeen, Aberdeen, Scotland, UK

P. Crooks (✉)
Department of History, Trinity College, Dublin, Ireland

A. Ruddick
St Paul's School, London, UK

3

world in our minds; *to apprehend* external realities, past and present.[3] As Iain
MacKenzie has put it: 'to think at all is to think conceptually'.[4] Consequently,
concepts are fundamental to humanistic research, both as an aspect of research
methodology and as a subject of historical investigation in their own right.

But conceptual history and conceptual analysis—as we shall see, the two
need not necessarily refer to the same programme of research—also pose challenges and have their attendant risks. Concepts conjured up in an effort to
bring order to the infinite complexity of the past have a bad habit of taking
on a life of their own. Rather as the apprentice sorcerer discovered—and as
Peggy Brown and Susan Reynolds famously demonstrated in the case of that
tyrannous construct, 'feudalism'—a tool of the historian's trade can easily turn
tyrant.[5] The aim of this volume is not so much to slay the tyrant as to explore
both the pitfalls and the pay-offs of working with concepts. In other words,
our shared goal is to offer a series of worked examples for a fresh generation
of medievalists—case studies that demonstrate how an alertness to concepts
can be used to enrich historical interpretation.

Tyrannous Constructs

A useful starting point here is the growing literature on tyrannous constructs in
medieval history. 'Feudalism' is only one of three master nouns in the professional vocabulary of medievalists that has been described as tyrannous within
the past two decades. In 1998, Tim Reuter picked up Peggy Brown's conceit
and applied it to a concept that was, if anything, even more fundamental to the
identity of medievalists *as* medievalists—namely the construct of 'The Middle
Ages' (and its adjectival running mate, 'medieval'). In setting up his argument,
Reuter offered a *précis* of what he understood to be the Brown–Reynolds
approach:

> On the one hand, there is the issue of, if you like, 'classification': is it helpful
> to see these phenomena, whatever their surface difference, as being linked by
> significant common characteristics? On the other hand, there is the issue of

[3] See Étienne Balibar, 'Concept', in *Political Concepts, Issue 4: The Balibar Edition*
(2018) http://www.politicalconcepts.org/concept-etienne-balibar/. The question 'What
is a concept?' is addressed directly and creatively in Adi Ophir, 'Concept', in J.M. Bernstein, Adi Ophir and Ann Laura Stoler (eds), *Political Concepts: A Critical Lexicon* (New
York: Fordham University Press, 2018), 59–86: 'A concept is neither given nor created
but, rather, performed or played in the act of conceptualization. This play both invents
and discovers the concept, both lets it appear and gives it existence, and in doing this it
also blurs the distinction between what is given and revealed, and what is invented and
created' (59).

[4] Iain MacKenzie (ed.), *Political Concepts: A Reader and Guide* (Edinburgh: Edinburgh
University Press, 2005), 1.

[5] E.A.R. Brown, 'The Tyranny of a Construct: Feudalism and the Historians of Medieval
Europe', *American Historical Review*, 79 (1974), 1063–88; Susan Reynolds, *Fiefs and
Vassals: The Medieval Evidence Reinterpreted* (Oxford: Oxford University Press, 1994).

'reification': do those of us who use the world feudal ... run the risk of turning feudalism, a classificatory construct by origin, into a thing which takes on its own explanatory and predictive power?[6]

Of these two issues—classification and reification—it is the latter that is clearly the more pernicious; and from both classification and reification springs a third issue, namely *contamination*—the importing into medieval history of post-medieval terms and their associated concepts that have a distorting effect on historical interpretations. Contamination formed at least part of the argument developed in 2002–2003 by R.R. Davies in his critical historiographical conspectus, 'The Medieval State: The Tyranny of a Concept?' In this essay, Davies noted mordantly that medieval historians appeared to be 'falling in love with the word "state"', a development he found worrying because (as he expressed it in an email to Susan Reynolds, published as part of the latter's rejoinder): '"a common vocabulary can lead to an unthinking assumption about concepts and phenomena" so that historians "unthinkingly equate the state with the modern state"'.[7] In Davies's view, a solution was to return to the language of the sources. The term that recommended itself to Davies because it was in contemporary usage was 'lordship' (L. *dominium*, F. *seigneurie*, G. *Herrschaft*): 'If there is a "master noun" in the medieval lexicon of power, it is surely this one', he wrote.[8]

The question mark included in Davies's title signalled his desire to query and to probe, rather than to legislate the medieval state out of existence. He was, above all, seeking to describe what he called the historian's 'recurrent dilemma' in choosing a vocabulary:

How can [the historian] write about a past society using its language and concepts without becoming incomprehensible to his [*sic*] current audience; but equally how can he employ current concepts and vocabulary, with all their attendant encrustations of meaning and their part in present-day conceptual schemes, without distorting and skewing the past?[9]

[6] Timothy Reuter, 'Medieval: Another Tyrannous Construct?', in Janet L. Nelson (ed.), *Medieval Polities and Modern Mentalities* (Cambridge: Cambridge University Press, 2006), 19–37, at 20.

[7] R.R. Davies, 'The State: The Tyranny of a Concept?', *Journal of Historical Sociology*, 15 (2002), 71–73, extended in R.R. Davies, 'The Medieval State: The Tyranny of a Concept?', *Journal of Historical Sociology*, 16 (2003), 280–300. See also M. Clanchy, 'Does Writing Construct the State?', *Journal of Historical Sociology*, 15 (2002), 68–70; J.P. Genet, *La genèse de l'État moderne: Culture et société politique en Angleterre* (Paris: Presses Universitaires de France, 2003), 13; S. Hindle, 'When and What was the State? Some Introductory Comments', *Journal of Historical Sociology*, 15 (2002), 63–65; S. Reynolds, 'The Historiography of the Medieval State', in M. Bentley (ed.), *Companion to Historiography* (London: Routledge, 1997), 117–38; S. Reynolds, 'There were States in Medieval Europe: A Response to Rees Davies', *Journal of Historical Sociology*, 16 (2003), 550–55.

[8] Davies, 'The Medieval State', 295.

[9] Davies, 'The Medieval State', 293.

Ultimately, as Davies readily acknowledged, terminological choices are in large part determined by a historian's nose—that is to say, by a mixture of personal preference and intuition informed by experience of the evidence. But these choices may prove to be significant outside of the original academic context in which they are deployed.

In this respect, it is not unfair to note that the term Davies elected to lead historians out of the conceptual quagmire—lordship—was not an altogether felicitous choice. Although *dominium* is a term with a sound medieval pedigree, it is not free from 'encrustations of meaning'. Not only is *dominium* one of the most frequently occurring and vexing terms in the medieval source material,[10] the term also has an extensive post-medieval history and carries differing valences within different scholarly traditions. This is perhaps most obvious in the sociology of Max Weber (d.1920), where *Herrschaft* serves as a structuring concept running through the argument of *Wirtschaft und Gesellschaft* ('Economy and Society') concerning the development of legitimate forms of authority in the context of the state. Weber's *Herrschaft* is a very different beast from the concept of *Herrschaft* ('lordship') as employed by, say, the medievalist Otto Brunner in his foundational interpretation of power in late-medieval Austria: *Land und Herrschaft* (partially translated as '*Land* and Lordship').[11] Indeed, the ideas underlying Weber's *Herrschaft* are, if anything, even more difficult to render in translation.[12] Among leading Weber scholars in the Anglophone world, Talcott Parsons (d.1979) favoured 'authority', while Reinhard Bendix (d.1991) was inclined to use 'domination'. Sam Whimster, the current editor of *Max Weber Studies* prefers 'rulership', especially in premodern contexts, because he believes that 'domination' reflects the exigencies

[10] J.H. Burns, *Lordship, Kingship, and Empire: The Idea of Monarchy, 1400–1525* (Oxford: Oxford University Press, 1992).

[11] Otto Brunner, '*Land*' *and Lordship: Structures of Governance in Medieval Austria*, trans. Howard Kaminsky and James van Horn Melton (Philadelphia: University of Pennsylvania Press, 1992); first published as *Land und Herrschaft: Grundfragen der territorialen Verfassungsgeschichte Südostdeutschlands im Mittelalter* (Baden bei Wien: Veröffentlichungen des Instituts für Geschichtsforschung und Archivwissenschaft in Wiem, 1939).

[12] For further reflections on the challenges of translation issues in conceptual history, see Martin J. Burke and Melvin Richter (eds), *Why Concepts Matter: Translating Social and Political Thought* (Leiden: Brill, 2012), esp. Melvin Richter, 'Introduction: Translation, the History of Concepts and the History of Political Thought', 1–40; Margrit Pernau and Dominic Sachsenmaier (eds), *Global Conceptual History: A Reader* (Bloomsbury: London, 2016), Part III ('Translations of concepts'), esp. Kari Palonen, 'Translation, Politics and Conceptual Change', 171–90; Willibald Steinmetz and Michael Freeden, Introduction. 'Conceptual History: Challenges, Conundrums, Complexities', in Willibald Steinmetz, Michael Freeden and Javier Fernández-Sebastián (eds), *Conceptual History in the European Space* (New York and Oxford: Berghahn, 2017), 1–46, at 16–17.

of power while 'authority' is best suited to legitimate power. The one translation no one has suggested as appropriate in this context is 'lordship'. And so we are brought full circle.[13]

LOOKING UNDER THE BONNET

The dilemma that Davies identified but did not resolve—the historian's need to choose between using potentially confusing medieval language and potentially contaminated modern conceptual terms—is precisely the one which we wish to explore. This is not a new endeavour. Conceptual history is a vibrant field of research being cultivated by at least two new online journals (*Political Concepts: A Critical Lexicon*; and *Contributions to the History of Concepts*), as well as a number of established organs of scholarship.[14] Within the historiography of what we call the late-medieval British–Irish isles, conceptual analysis of various kinds has long been central to research: witness the host of works on power, statehood, nationhood, ethnicity, race, identity, colonialism, imperialism, empire, gender, masculinity and so on. Some of the most methodologically sophisticated of such works, it is only fair to point out, have been written by contributors to this volume.[15]

---

[13] Melvin Richter, *The History of Political and Social Concepts: A Critical Introduction* (Oxford: Oxford University Press, 1995), ch. 3 ('The history of the concept of *Herrschaft* in the *Geschichtliche Grundbegriffe*'); Max Weber, *The Theory of Social and Economic Organization*, ed. and trans. A. M. Henderson and Talcott Parsons (1st edn., London: Hodge, 1947; 2nd edn., New York: Free Press of Glencoe, 1965); Max Weber, *Economy and Society: An Outline of Interpretative Sociology*, ed. and trans. Guenther Roth and Claus Wittich, 2 vols (Berkeley: University of California Press, 1978); Hans Henrik Bruun and Sam Whimster (eds), *Max Weber: Collected Methodological Writings* (London: Routledge, 2012), xii.

[14] http://www.politicalconcepts.org/; http://www.historyofconcepts.org/About.

[15] For example, Christine Carpenter, 'Introduction: Political Culture, Politics, and Cultural History', in C. Carpenter and L. Clark (eds), *Political Culture in Late Medieval Britain (The Fifteenth Century, IV)* (Woodbridge: The Boydell Press, 2004), 1–19; Christine Carpenter, 'Gentry and Community in Medieval England', *Journal of British Studies*, 33 (1994), 340–80; Jan Dunmolyn, 'Political Communication and Political Power in the Middle Ages: A Conceptual Journey', *Edad Media*, 13 (2012), 33–55; Christopher Fletcher, *Richard II: Manhood, Youth, and Politics, 1377–99* (Oxford: Oxford University Press, 2008); Ian Forrest, *Trustworthy Men: How Inequality and Faith Made the Medieval Church* (Princeton: Princeton University Press, 2018); W. Mark Ormrod, '"Common Profit" and "The Profit of the King and Kingdom": Parliament and the Development of Political Language in England, 1250–1450', *Viator*, 46 (2015); Andrea Ruddick, *English Identity and Political Culture in the Fourteenth Century* (Cambridge: Cambridge University Press, 2013); Simon Walker, *Political Culture in Later Medieval England*, ed. M.J. Braddick (Manchester: Manchester University Press, 2006); John Watts, '"Commonweal" and "Commonwealth": England's Monarchical Republic in the Making, c.1450–c.1530', in A. Gamberini, J.-P. Genet and A. Zorzi (eds), *The Languages of Political Society* (Rome: Viella, 2011), 147–63; and for the early modern period see Alison Cathcart, *Plantations by Land and Sea: North Channel Communities of the Atlantic Archipelago c.1550–1625* (Oxford: Peter Lang, 2021); Alexandra Walsham, 'The Dangers of Ritual', *Past & Present*, 180 (2003), 277–87.

For the most part, however, the methodological problems posed by conceptual history have remained hidden under the bonnet. Given how turgid and indigestible 'conceptual theory' can be in the hands of social scientists, this is hardly surprising.[16] But it is important to note that some of the most commonsensical advice on how to use concepts originated with the medievalist, Susan Reynolds, who exhorted scholars to distinguish carefully between words, concepts and phenomena—that is, the *words* we employ, the *concepts* or ideas that lie behind those words and the historical *phenomena* to which those words and concepts are taken to apply.[17]

For the purposes of this volume, it may be helpful to take another step at this point and to sub-divide the category of 'concepts' once more. This is intended to clarify the important distinction between terms and concepts that were in use *in* the past (that is, the terms and their underlying ideas as expressed in primary sources), and the terms and concepts that historians bring *to* the past as tools of analysis. For convenience we might describe this as a difference between *historical ideas* and *analytical categories*.[18] A particular concern of the present collection is to identify and consider the problems that arise when these two types of concepts become confused or conflated by historians. While the *analytical category* and *historical idea* are often related, they are not commensurate with each other. This approach gains theoretical ballast from the distinction made between *etics* and *emics* (or external or internal perspectives) in other disciplines that engage in cross-cultural analysis, notably linguistics and anthropology. The two approaches are complementary; neither can claim precedence over the other.[19]

For the study of *historical ideas*, there is already a range of sophisticated methodologies available. Perhaps the most rigorous and impressive such enterprise—or, at any rate, the most discussed—is the German approach to conceptual history (G. *Begriffsgeschichte*), mostly famously the *Geschichtliche Grundbegriffe* project associated with Otto Brunner and, above all, the early

---

[16] Birger Hjørland, 'Concept Theory', *Journal of the American Society for Information Science and Technology*, 60:8 (2009), 1519–36.

[17] Susan Reynolds, *Fiefs and Vassals: The Medieval Evidence Reinterpreted* (Oxford: Oxford University Press, 1994), esp. 12–13. Reynolds formulated her approach independently of the French school of semioticians, but it is compatible with the distinctions drawn by Saussure between the 'sign', the 'signifier' and the 'signified'.

[18] The phrase 'historical ideas' is used here to describe the language of the sources in preference to, say, 'historical terminology' because we are particularly interested in the concepts or ideas that *underlie* the words used in the primary sources—that is, the (often quite varied) *uses* to which particular terms are put by historical actors in particular contexts.

[19] For discussion, see J.W. Berry, 'Emics and Etics: A Symbiotic Conception', *Culture and Psychology*, 5:2 (1999), 165–71; Thomas N. Headland, Kenneth L. Pike and Marvin Harris, *Emics and Etics: The Insider/Outsider Debate* (London: Sage Publications, 1990). The value of the distinction is brought out by Sophie Page, Chapter 7 below.

modernist, Reinhard Koselleck.[20] Koselleck's particular concern was to map conceptual change and variation as a means of achieving a 'deeper understanding of the social world in its historical formation'.[21] In doing so, his editorial team alternated between 'semasiology' (the study of conceptual variation or differences in meaning for a given word); and 'onomasiology' (the study of all the names or terms in a given language for the same concept).[22] A separate historical enterprise, but one whose approach is in certain respects compatible with *Begriffsgeschichte*, was the approach to the history of ideas developed by the so-called Cambridge School of J.G.A. Pocock and Quentin Skinner.[23] Both these enterprises share the understanding that concepts acquire meanings from the *uses to which they are put*, and that a close contextualised reading is required in order to recover or understand the concepts as used in the past. In the case of the Cambridge school, this approach can be traced back to the linguistic philosophy of the later Wittgenstein. Wittgenstein insisted that (to quote from Skinner's formulation of his ideas) 'we ought not to think in isolation about "the meanings of words". We ought rather to focus on their use in specific language-games and, more generally, within particular forms of life'.[24]

Less celebrated and perhaps less rigorous, but in certain respects more stimulating in its approach, is the work of Raymond Williams (d. 1988) on *Keywords* (1976, 1983).[25] Williams sought to document the changes in meaning in a selection of certain 'strong, difficult and persuasive words in everyday usage' in English. His particular concern was not so much the 'original', 'true' or technical meaning of such words but with the fact that:

[20] O. Brunner, W. Conze and R. Koselleck (eds), *Geschichtliche Grundbegriffe* (Stuttgart: E. Klett, 1972–1989). On Koselleck's methodology, see Reinhard Koselleck, *Futures Past: On the Semantics of Historical Time*, trans. Keith Tribe (Columbia: Columbia University Press, 2004). For a discussion by a medieval intellectual historian of *Begriffsgeschichte* in practice, see Janet Coleman, 'The Practical Use of *Begriffsgeschichte* by an Historian of European Pre-modern Political Thought: Some Problems', *Finnish Yearbook of Political Thought*, 2 (1999), 28–40.

[21] Keith Tribe, 'The *Geschichtliche Grundbegriffe* Project: From History of Ideas to Conceptual History', *Comparative Studies in Society and History*, 31:1 (1989), 181.

[22] The most useful introduction is probably Richter, *History of Political and Social Concepts*, esp. 47–48. See also Martin J. Burke, 'Margins, methods and the historiography of concepts', in *Translatio Studiorum: Ancient, Medieval and Modern Bearers of Intellectual History*, ed. Marco Sgarbi (Leiden: Brill, 2012), 237–51.

[23] The methodological writings of both Skinner and Pocock are usefully collected in volumes published by Cambridge University Press: Skinner, *Visions of Politics I: Regarding Method* (Cambridge, 2002); Pocock, *Political Thought and History: Essays on Theory and Method* (Cambridge, 2009).

[24] Skinner, 'Interpretation and the Understanding of Speech Acts', *Visions of Politics I*, ch. 6 (quotation at 103).

[25] Raymond Williams, *Keywords: A Vocabulary of Culture and Society* (1976; 2nd ed., Fontana, 1983).

beginning in particular specialized contexts, [these keywords] have become quite common in descriptions of wider areas of thought and experience. This, significantly, is the vocabulary we share with others, often imperfectly, when we wish to discuss many of the central processes of our common life.[26]

The point about keywords is that they are as slippery in meaning as they are indispensable because of their general significance in contemporary culture and society. Historical, scholarly and popular usages endow such words with discrepant meanings that can make them difficult to employ as analytical categories. But keywords are too useful to be dispensed with because (to paraphrase Williams) the problem of their meanings is inextricably bound up with the problem that the words themselves are used to discuss.[27] Clearly, this is a form of conceptual history, which proves to be especially fruitful when concepts are understood as 'bundles of linked keywords'.[28] Despite its shortcomings, the open-endedness of Williams' approach—notably his concern to document meanings rather than to establish *the* meaning—attracts ongoing interest.[29]

A similar point has been made, much more recently, by Roberto Benigno in *Words in Time*, who argues that many of the concepts deployed by scholars in the social sciences and humanities overlap with everyday 'street talk'. Scholarly discourses have an influence in the public sphere whenever historians engage with the public, speak to the media or stand up in the lecture hall or classroom. Benigno calls for a 'reflexive and critical history [of concepts] which is able to take into account its own performative aspect, that is, the effects which its discourses have in the public sphere'.[30] In other words, thinking rigorously about our use of concepts in our own research will also spill over into wider

---

[26] Williams, *Keywords*, 2nd edn., 14.

[27] Ibid., esp. 15.

[28] For an exploration of 'keywords' and concepts in an early modern context, see Mark Knights, 'Towards a Social and Cultural History of Keywords and Concepts by the Early Modern Research Group', *History of Political Thought*, 31:3 (2010), 427–48 esp. 441–42.

[29] The continuing interest in Williams' approach is signalled by the recent appearance of *Keywords for Today: A 21st Century Vocabulary*, ed. Colin MacCabe and Holly Yanacek (Oxford: Oxford University Press, 2018). The original edition of *Keywords* (1976) was the subject of a critical essay by Quentin Skinner, now republished as Skinner, 'The Idea of a Cultural Lexicon', in *Visions of Politics*, I, (as cited above in note 23) ch. 9. Skinner makes a crucial distinction here between words and concepts, noting that an individual may possess a concept but have no single term in their lexicon to refer to that concept; and, indeed, a community of language users may all use a word and communicate successfully, even though 'there is no concept that answers to any of their agreed usages' (159–60). The debate is summarised in Fred Inglis, *Raymond Williams* (London: Routledge, 1995), 246–48.

[30] Benigno, *Words in Time*, 7, 13. This is a point picked up by Watkins in the present volume, citing Davies on the use of accessible language.

arenas of thought far from our control.[31] The simple problem of lexical selection—of choosing the right term—may be central to the role that historians, and their interpretations, play beyond the community of scholars. As Mieke Bal has put it in arguing for the 'centrality of conceptual reflection': 'Precisely because they travel between ordinary words and condensed theories, concepts can trigger and facilitate reflection and debate on all levels of methodology in the humanities'.[32]

A distinct but related set of problems confronts us when we employ terms and underlying concepts as *categories of analysis*. Such terms are brought *to* the past by historians accompanied by an extensive train of theoretical baggage from the social sciences. Here, again, it is useful to begin with a frank acknowledgement that the classical idea of a concept with a fixed definition is a will-o'-the-wisp.[33] Moreover, modern analytical categories themselves quickly become historical terms with a history of their own. Consequently, it is not necessarily helpful to provide an analytic definition of a given term, one that lays down the necessary and sufficient conditions for its application as a concept. Such prescriptivism is self-defeating because it forecloses on any real exchange of ideas. Instead, scholars end up in stand-offs over classification or in shoot-outs over definitions. On the other hand, the use of holistic concepts—terms to describe 'social wholes' or collective entities such as 'The British Empire' or 'The Renaissance'—has been staunchly defended by Robert C. Stalnaker, who argues that 'No effective precision is lost by this use of proper names, and a great deal of flexibility is gained'. Stalnaker does, however, offer one crucial caveat: 'What is illegitimate', he writes, 'and sometimes pernicious, are dummy terms which have infinite flexibility; they have no descriptive content or reference, are useless, even in heuristic terms, and function only as pseudo-explanations'.[34] What this suggests is that it is necessary to move beyond high-minded calls for 'all terms to be defined'. Clarity is of course crucial to conceptual analysis, but it is necessary to tread carefully between over-prescription and over-extension of concepts, especially if

---

[31] The intersection of academic and public perceptions of the Middle Ages is explored throughout the recent collection Andrew Albin, Marcy C. Erler, Thomas O'Donnell, Nicholas L. Paul and Nina Rowe (eds), *Whose Middle Ages? Teachable Moments for an Ill-Used Past* (New York: Fordham University Press, 2019), but see especially Part III, '#Hashtags'.

[32] Mieke Bal, *Travelling Concepts in the Humanities: A Rough Guide* (Toronto, Buffalo, London: University of Toronto Press, 2002), 28–29.

[33] Gregory L. Murphy, *The Big Book of Concepts* (Cambridge, MA; London: Massachusetts Institute of Technology Press, 2002), 2: 'The psychology of concepts is like other areas of psychology, in which a phenomenologically simple cognitive process ... turns out to be maddeningly complex'.

[34] Robert C. Stalnaker, 'Events, Periods, and Institutions in Historians' Language', *History and Theory*, 6:2 (1967), 159–79, at 179.

what we want is to compare cases successfully or engage with scholars in other disciplines.[35]

The challenge of making meaningful comparisons across time and space has become particularly acute with the 'global turn' in historiography. This has prompted scholars to think beyond conceptual history projects based on individual nations and languages, and to examine the transmission and translation (cultural and linguistic) of concepts in transnational and global contexts.[36] In an imperial context, this may involve paying particular attention to the 'mutuality of influence between colonial powers and their colonies'—as much with regard to concepts as to other aspects of cultural, political and economic exchange—as well as the unequal power hierarchies inherent in these interactions and flows.[37] One danger here is the danger that Western, Eurocentric terms and concepts are taken as normative or ideal by scholars seeking to make comparisons.[38] Moreover, when Western analytical categories have been exported to other parts of the world through what Steinmetz and Freeden call 'the anglicization and globalization of our contemporary conceptual space', they warn that 'superficial simultaneity of use may conceal a multiplicity of allusions to past experiences and future expectations'.[39] The same point could be made about historical terms commonly used across Latin Christendom during the Middle Ages. In both synchronic and diachronic contexts, practitioners of comparative conceptual history may be predisposed to emphasise convergence and similarity more than divergence.[40]

USING CONCEPTS: GOALS AND CHOICES

This volume addresses itself to this set of metahistorical and methodological questions concerning the use and abuse of concepts in medieval history. While the focus of our present effort is on the British–Irish insular world in the later Middle Ages, the methodological questions are not unique to historians of this

[35] For a helpful case study, see Rogers Brubaker and Frederick Cooper, 'Beyond "Identity"', *Theory and Society*, 29:1 (2000), 1–47, also discussed by Ruddick in the present volume.

[36] Margrit Pernau and Dominic Sachsenmaier, 'History of Concepts and Global History' in Pernau and Sachsenmaier (eds), *Global Conceptual History: A Reader* (London: Bloomsbury, 2016), 1–27.

[37] Pernau and Sachsenmaier, 'History of Concepts', 3 (for quote), 16–17. This dynamic may be a particularly interesting angle for historians of the medieval British–Irish isles to explore in the context of what Rees Davies dubbed 'the first English empire'.

[38] See also Willibald Steinmetz, 'Forty Years of Conceptual History: The State of the Art', in Pernau and Sachsenmaier (eds), *Global Conceptual History*, 339–66, esp. 341, 353–57; Steinmetz and Freeden, 'Introduction. Conceptual History: Challenges, Conundrums, Complexities', 17–24.

[39] Steinmetz and Freeden, 'Introduction. Conceptual History: Challenges, Conundrums, Complexities', 7.

[40] Steinmetz and Freeden, 'Introduction. Conceptual History: Challenges, Conundrums, Complexities', 21.

particular time and place; nor are the concepts, many of which will resonate with medievalists working on other parts of the medieval world and, indeed, historians of other periods. However, the genesis of this project lay in our growing, shared dissatisfaction with the conceptual toolkit currently employed by political-social historians of late-medieval Britain and Ireland—including ourselves. Active thinking about the repertoire of concepts commonly used in our field remains under-developed. As Sophie Page on 'Magic', Eliza Hartrich on 'Networks', and Carl Watkins on 'Crisis' demonstrate in what follows, medieval economic, social-economic and cultural historians have long led the way in giving nuanced and rigorous attention to problematic concepts, often leaving political historians behind on the starting blocks. But even so these chapters in particular show that this involves much more than the use of 'theory'. They reveal the difficulties arising as historians navigate between historical ideas and analytical categories in these sub-fields, and they propose ways to work constructively through those challenges. Overall, our goal is to encourage a more rigorous use of concepts in late medieval British-Irish historical research. We hope to prompt greater reflection on our shared use of concepts as 'tools of the trade' in this field, and on how conceptual alertness can enhance our work.

These essays are not an exercise in 'conceptual history'. We do, however, need to examine the careers of our chosen concepts because words carry with them 'the heritage of their past use'. Indeed there may be no such as thing as 'neutral' analytical language.[41] In part, our motivation in selecting some of these particular concepts is their potential to become 'tyrannous'— that is, to exert the same kind of distorting influence over historiography that Peggy Brown noted in respect of 'feudalism' back in 1974, as discussed above. Indeed, the more all-encompassing and ubiquitous a term, the more likely it is to exert a 'tyrannising' influence over the scholars who deploy it. But our primary interest is on how we can productively employ concepts of all kinds as medieval historians in our day-to-day research. The essays here seek to build a bridge between the work of formal 'conceptual historians' on the one hand and, on the other, historians who choose to draw concepts into their research agendas. The chapters provide a set of working examples of how particular concepts can be fruitfully put to work by medieval historians.

Of particular interest here is the relationship between categories of analysis and the terms found in medieval sources. The chapters explore the creative friction between historical ideas and analytical categories, and the potential for fresh and meaningful understandings to emerge from a dialogue fostered between the two planes of conceptualisation. Where the distinction between historical terms and analytical categories becomes fuzzy (and, therefore, particularly interesting), our work involves a dance between the two. Together we are asking if this creative friction helps us to think usefully about the concepts we apply. Can we construct workable modern categories of analysis from

[41] Pernau and Sachsenmaier, 'History of Concepts', 20.

the sources of the past? Can interrogating the concepts we use help us to think afresh about familiar historical problems and re-examine our assumptions about our field of study? Can an alertness to our conceptual toolkits make our work more accessible and available to others, locating a particular period or topic in a wider set of debates? Can this conceptual alertness suggest possible avenues of comparison, to link scholars from our immediate historiographical field to other medievalists, to early modernists, and modernists, and perhaps especially those working in non-anglophone historiographical contexts?[42] Our hope is that these questions may be answered affirmatively, in order to help provide better narratives of the past and better explanations of historical problems in medieval society.

More than this, we hope that scrutiny of these problems will have a broader application. Through the discussion of worked examples drawn from our respective areas of research on a specific time and place, our collective ambition is to generate a better understanding of how conceptual analysis can work in practice. This will, we hope, facilitate a more rigorous reflection on the problem of the use of concepts in history in general. We wish not only to explore the benefits that may arise from encouraging conceptual awareness and conceptual precision, but also to consider how medieval history can become a net exporter of conceptual ideas rather than a net importer from other historical fields and other disciplines.

'Don't think, but look!', runs Wittgenstein's aphorism in his discussion of 'family resemblance' concepts in *Philosophical Investigations*.[43] For our purposes, this is a rather high-minded way of answering the objection that conceptual work is 'theoretical' in the sense of being detached from the evidence base on which history must rest *in order to be* 'history'. Our intention is to examine the pitfalls and pay-offs of using concepts explicitly and rigorously. In this way we still recognise Brown's point, nearly five decades later, about concepts that feature in an 'unsatisfactory' way in historical work.[44] We would claim that conceptual work by historians must not become detached in this way, but remain firmly grounded in real examples if it is to be in any sense meaningful.

---

[42] A comparative agenda signalled by Brown, 'Tyranny of a Construct', 1087–88.

[43] The full quotation (from *Philosophical Investigations*, section 66) concerning the concept Wittgenstein chose as his exemplar ('games') runs as follows:

> Consider for example the proceedings that we call "games". I mean board-games, card-games, ball-games, Olympic games, and so on. What is common to them all?—Don't say: "There must be something common, or they would not be called 'games'"—but look and see whether there is anything common to all. For if you look at them you will not see something that is common to all, but similarities, relationships, and a whole series of them at that. To repeat: don't think, but look!

[44] Brown, 'Tyranny of a Construct', 1088.

CHAPTER 2

Feudalism: Reflections on a Tyrannical Construct's Fate

Elizabeth A. R. Brown

Forty-seven years have passed since the publication in 1974 of 'The Tyranny of a Construct: Feudalism and Historians of Medieval Europe'.[1] An impassioned denunciation of feudalism, the article was intended to accomplish the destruction of feudalism and all other feudal constructs, including feudal system, feudal society, and feudal monarchy. Because the constructs distort and oversimplify the complexities of any society or period to which they are applied—and particularly medieval Europe—I called for their abandonment. My article caused a stir, although the calculated dismissal it also encountered demonstrated feudalism's strength and staying power, and the devoted loyalty the feudal constructs engender.

[1] *American Historical Review*, 79:4 (1974), 1063–88. I am grateful for encouragement, suggestions, and corrections to Allan Appel, Suzanne Boorsch, Rowan Dorin, Theodore Evergates, Geoffrey Koziol, Susanne Roberts, M. Alison Stones, Thomas N. Tentler, and, particularly, Richard C. Famiglietti and Emily Zack Tabuteau. I am indebted as well for exchanges I have had over the years with Theodore Evergates, the late Susan Reynolds, and Stephen D. White, as well as Walter Goffart, the late Howard Kaminsky, and, particularly, the late Fredric L. Cheyette. Lucy L. Brown and Herbert H. Schaumberg have discussed and debated with me my ideas about the development of the physical and social sciences, and the relevance of experimental studies of human cognition to attitudes toward the feudal constructs. Jackson Armstrong, Peter Crooks, and Andrea Ruddick have been models of editorial patience and efficiency.

E. A. R. Brown (✉)
Professor of History Emerita, The City University of New York (Brooklyn College and The Graduate Center), New York, NY, USA

15
J. W. Armstrong, P. Crooks and A. Ruddick (eds), *Using Concepts in Medieval History*, https://doi.org/10.1007/978-3-030-77280-2_2

Here I will reflect on several of feudalism's many facets. First, I rehearse the reasons for and the timing of my assault on feudalism, and suggest that discontent with the constructs was far more widespread than I realized in the 1970s. After reviewing the arguments I advanced, I treat the feudal constructs' appeal and powers of endurance, and the cognitive roots of their users' and advocates' attachment to them. I then turn to the reactions to and the results of my attack, both short- and long-term, positive and negative, paying particular attention to Susan Reynolds's book, *Fiefs and Vassals*, published in 1994,[2] and examining the similarities and differences between our approaches to feudalism and to medieval society and politics. I then discuss the diminished fidelity that feudalism has commanded since 2000, and the progressive waning of the feudal constructs' influence on studies of medieval Europe, which focus increasingly on the complexities of its evolution. In conclusion I repeat the call I issued in 1974 to renounce the constructs and cautiously forecast their imminent demise, except as evidence of the styles of conceptualization that led their sixteenth- and seventeenth-century fabricators to invent them.

THE MOMENT

The campaign I launched in 1974 was motivated by personal feelings of inadequacy as well as professional frustration. The notion of 'feudalism' had filled me with trepidation since I first encountered the word in high school, and my misgivings intensified during my years in college and graduate school. Precisely what 'feudalism' was and why it commanded the attention it did, I did not comprehend. Always more interested in people than paradigms, a splitter rather than a lumper, more fox than hedgehog, I struggled to discern connections between such a neatly artificial monolith and what I had learned about the human beings who lived in medieval Europe.[3] Feudalism's relevance to the European middle ages, much less other times and cultures, escaped me, as did the reasons for its use as a standard for comparing eras. A teaching assistant and fledgling professor in the late 1950s and 1960s, I found the 'ism' impossible to teach. So I avoided it.

I had long taken comfort from the reservations Marc Bloch (1886–1944) expressed about *féodalité* in his post mortem masterpiece, *Le métier d'historien*,[4] which in my view trumped the generalizations he advanced in *La société*

---

[2] Susan Reynolds, *Fiefs and Vassals: The Medieval Evidence Reinterpreted* (Oxford: Oxford University Press, 1994).

[3] At Swarthmore College, Professor Mary Albertson introduced me to Eileen Powers' masterpiece, *Medieval People* (London: Methuen & Co., 1924), a seventh edition of which was published in 1939, and a tenth in 1963. In 1957, four years after its publication, when I was in my third year of graduate school, I acquired a now ragged copy of Isaiah Berlin, *The Hedgehog and the Fox*, which was based on an essay that appeared in 1951. See below, n. 37 and the accompanying text.

[4] M. Bloch, *Apologie pour l'histoire ou métier d'historien*, ed. Étienne Bloch (Paris: Armand Colin, 1993). I treasure the copy I bought in 1957 of *The Historian's Craft*,

féodale, first published in 1939 and 1940.[5] I was equally heartened by the studies, focussed on people and their actions, that Richard W. Southern and Georges Duby brought out in 1953.[6] Southern explored the 'making' of the middle ages by focussing on the region around Anjou; Duby examined eleventh- and twelfth-century society in and near Mâcon. Neither of them invoked feudalism. I was drawn as well to regional and technical investigations that revealed the complexities of medieval social and political life and to studies that elucidated the range and shifts in meaning of the words contemporaries used to describe those aspects of the world they inhabited.[7]

trans. Peter Putnam with an introduction by Joseph R. Strayer (Manchester: Manchester University Press, 1954).

[5] M. Bloch, *La société féodale. La formation des liens de dépendance* (L'Évolution de l'humanité, synthèse collective, 34:1; Paris: Albin Michel, 1939), and *La société féodale. Les classes et le gouvernement des hommes* (Paris: Albin Michel, 1940) (the second part of the volume in Henri Berr's series). In the English translation that appeared twenty years later the two divisions were rendered as 'The growth of ties of dependence', and 'Social classes and political organization': *Feudal Society*, trans. L.A. Manyon (London: Routledge & Kegan Paul; Chicago: University of Chicago Press, 1961). I discussed Bloch's mixed attitude toward the constructs in 'Tyranny', 1069–1070, and also in 'Reflections on Feudalism: Thomas Madox and the Origins of the Feudal System in England', in Belle S. Tuten and Tracey L. Billado (eds), *Feud, Violence and Practice: Essays in Medieval Studies in Honor of Stephen D. White* (Farnham: Ashgate, 2010), 135–55, at 136, 138–41.

[6] Richard W. Southern, *The Making of the Middle Ages* (New Haven: Yale University Press, 1953; cf. Brown, 'Tyranny', 1080–1; Georges Duby, *La société aux XIe et XIIe siècles dans la région mâconnaise* (Bibliothèque générale de l'École pratique des Hautes Études, 6e section; Paris: Armand Colin, 1953; reprinted, with different pagination, as Bibliothèque générale de l'École des Hautes Études en Sciences Sociales; Paris: S.E.V.P.E.N., 1971); see Brown, 'Tyranny', 1073–4, 1081–4. Fredric L. Cheyette commented on Southern and Duby, in 'George Duby's *Mâconnais* after Fifty Years: Reading It Then and Now', *Journal of Medieval History*, 28 (2002), 291–317, at 293.

[7] Notable among them are Jacques Flach (1846–1919), *Les origines de l'ancienne France*, 4 vols (Paris: L. Larose et al., 1886–1917), on whom see Alain Guerreau, *Le féodalisme: un horizon théorique* (Paris: Le Sycomore, 1980), 51–5; and Alain Guerreau, 'Fief, féodalité, féodalisme. Enjeux sociaux et réflexion historienne', *Annales: Économies – Sociétés – Civilisations*, 45:1 (1990), 137–66; Émile Lesne, 'Les diverses acceptations du terme "beneficium" du VIIIe au IXe siècle (Contribution à l'étude des origines du bénéfice ecclésiastique)', *Revue historique du droit français et étranger*, 4th ser., 3 (1924), 5–56; Charles Edwin Odegaard, *Vassi and Fideles in the Carolingian Empire* (Harvard Historical Monographs, 19; Cambridge MA: Harvard University Press, 1945); Léo Verriest, *Institutions médiévales. Introduction au Corpus des records de coutumes et des lois de chefs-lieux de l'ancien comté de Hainaut*, 2 vols (Société des bibliophiles belges séant à Mons, Publications, 41–42; Mons-Frameries: Union des imprimeries, 1946); Léo Verriest, *Questions d'histoire des institutions médiévales. Noblesse. Chevalerie. Lignages. Condition des biens et des personnes. Seigneurie. Ministérialité. Bourgeoisie. Échevinages* (Brussels: Chez l'Auteur, 1959/1960); Jan Dhondt, *Études sur la naissance des principautés territoriales en France (IXe–Xe siècle)* (Werken Uitgegeven door de Faculteit van de Wijsbegeerte en Letteren, Rijksuniversiteit te Gent, 102; Bruges: 'De Tempel', 1948); Yvonne Bongert, *Recherches sur les cours laiques du Xe au XIIe siècle* (Paris: A. & J. Picard, 1949); Jean-François Lemarignier, 'Les fidèles du roi de France', in *Recueil de travaux offert à M. Clovis Brunel* ..., 2 vols (Mémoires et documents publiés par la Société de l'École des chartes, 12; Paris:

At the time I did not fully realize how many other colleagues, living and dead, entertained doubts about feudalism that were virtually as severe as my own—in good measure because those who questioned feudalism's utility were reluctant to disown it entirely. Their hesitancy blunted the force of their criticisms.

In a review in *Speculum* in 1958, William Huse Dunham, Jr., suggested that disagreement about whether 'money-fiefs' and 'indentures' were or were not truly 'feudal' 'might be reduced if words like "feudalism", now less a term of convenience than a cover of ignorance, were expunged from the historical vocabulary'.[8] Clearly Dunham was no friend of feudalism. But he raised the point in a subordinate clause, and he did not insist on it. Like Marc Bloch, he was ambivalent. An old and familiar friend, the word certainly had flaws, but they were defects that Dunham was prepared to disregard. Thus, after advising historians to jettison the concept, Dunham proceeded to invoke feudalism's 'essence', and the possibility of its 'refinement', 'decline', and 'decay'.

Feudalism had long frustrated the most respected historians of the middle ages, even though they similarly balked at discarding the word. Although he regularly invoked feudalism and favoured the verb 'feudalize' and the adjective 'feudalized', as well as such expressions as 'feudal assemblies', 'feudal courts', and 'feudal law', Frederic William Maitland (1850–1906) denounced feudalism as excessively 'large and vague',[9] and called it 'unfortunate' because it draws 'our attention to but one element in a complex state of society and that element is not the most distinctive'.[10] When in 1929 Frank Murray

Société de l'École des chartes, 1955), II, 138–62. In his study *A Rural Society in Medieval France: The Gâtine of Poitou in the Eleventh and Twelfth Centuries* (Johns Hopkins University Press Studies in Historical and Political Science, ser. 82, 1; Baltimore: Johns Hopkins Press, 1964), 72, 94, 96, George Beech invoked 'feudalism' in studying the nobility and drew on Marc Bloch's *La société féodale* to flesh out 'the few scraps of information' that he had found, while cautioning that 'the lacunae of the documents ... cast a shadow of uncertainty on any assertion', and making clear 'that birth was a more important criterion for nobility than the ability to fight'.

[8] William Huse Dunham, Jr., review of Bryce D. Lyon, *From Fief to Indenture: The Transition from Feudal to Non-Feudal Contract in Western Europe* (Cambridge, MA: Harvard University Press, 1956), in *Speculum* 33:2 (1958), 300–4, at 304. Citing the *Oxford English Dictionary*, Dunham dated to 1776 the appearance of the term 'feudal System' and to 1839 the first use of 'feudalism', although in fact Thomas Madox (1666–1727) used the first expression, and in 1771 John Whitaker (1735–1808) employed the word 'feudalism' and introduced the notion of the feudal pyramid; see my article, 'Reflections on Feudalism', esp. 145n. 35, and 147–49, for the dates.

[9] F.W. Maitland, *The Constitutional History of England: A Course of Lectures*, ed. H A. L. Fisher (Cambridge: Cambridge University Press, 1st edn., 1908), 142–3; see also my essay, 'Reflections on Feudalism', 138–41.

[10] Frederick Pollock and Frederic William Maitland, *The History of English Law Before the Time of Edward I*, 2nd edn., 2 vols (first pub. 1898; ed. S. F. C. Milson; Cambridge: Cambridge University Press, 1968), I, 66, and see the following pages for Maitland's continued use of the term and his suggestion that the term 'feodo-vassalism' might be preferable to 'feudalism'. See also Maitland's *Domesday Book and Beyond: Three Essays in the Early History of England* (first pub. 1897; London: Collins, 1960), esp. part 8 of

Stenton delivered the Ford Lectures at Oxford on post-Conquest English governance, he was well aware of the problems posed by feudalism, which he declared 'only a term invented for the historian's convenience', and, anticipated Marc Bloch in cautioning that 'every historian inevitably uses it in accordance with his own interpretation'.[11] Still, he entitled the lectures and the resulting book *The First Century of English Feudalism*, and from the start his focus was on feudalism, of many sorts: Anglo-Norman, Norman, English, 'highly organized', 'an exotic institution in Brittany'. He applied the adjective feudal to an array of nouns, ranging from Europe, magnate, documents, and overlord to the more abstract anarchy, society, environment, and practice. Only at the end of the book's penultimate chapter, in a single long paragraph, did he voice his reservations about the terms. In 1966 Vivian Hunter Galbraith was similarly tentative in his disapproval of feudalism. Indecisively, he wondered if he was 'wrong in suggesting that Feudalism is a misleading, because imprecise, way of describing how men lived for many centuries', and gingerly raised the possibility 'that now research has taught us the too-wide context of this abstraction'. With evident hesitation, he finally submitted that perhaps 'the time has come to drop it'.[12] In 1970, H. A. Cronne acknowledged 'the confusion and the odium ['feudalism'] has caused'.. But in the end his awareness of the difficulty of '[avoiding] using it', led him to recommend that historians 'not be obsessed by it'.[13]

In 1965, my former graduate-school colleague Fredric L. Cheyette jumped into the simmering fray. Commenting on C. Warren Hollister's work on English military institutions and his article, 'The Irony of English Feudalism', Cheyette honed in on 'feudalism' and witheringly declared it 'not really "a

Essay I ('Domesday Book'), 189–212 ('The Feudal Superstructure'), at 211 (writing of 'feudalism' and 'vassalism').

[11] F. M. Stenton, *The First Century of English Feudalism 1066–1166. Being the Ford Lectures Delivered in the University of Oxford in Hilary Term 1929* (Oxford: Clarendon Press, 1932; 2nd edn. 1961), 214–15 (216–17 in the 2nd edn.). For the terms I mention, see ibid., (2nd edn., 1961), vii, ix, 8–9, 12–14, 16–17, 27, 33, 35–6, 145, and 223.

[12] V.H. Galbraith, *1066 and All That: Norman Conquest Commemoration Lecture Delivered to the Society on 14th October, 1966* (Leicester: The Leicestershire Archæological and Historical Society, 1967), 3, who remarked that in 1870 Freeman questioned 'Did the Feudal System ever exist anywhere?' (without, however, pursuing the implications of the question, I should note) and pointed out that Richard Southern avoided 'Feucalism, yet without affecting [his book's] popularity'. Like the others, Galbraith himself did not repudiate the feudal terms, declaring (ibid., 5) that in Domesday Book we find 'the introduction of the'Feudal System' into England'. See Edward Augustus Freeman, *The History of the Norman Conquest of England, its Causes and its Results*, 6 vols, 2nd edn. (Oxford: Clarendon Press, 1870), I, 90–92; the preface is dated 4 January 1867 (ibid., xii).

[13] Henry Alfred Cronne, *The Reign of Stephen 1135–54. Anarchy in England* (London: Weidenfeld and Nicolson, 1970), 4–8, where Cronne provided useful historiographical background and commentary. Cronne advised (ibid., 8), 'Let us rather study the characteristics of society as we find it revealed in the available sources of information, without bothering too much about the exact shade of meaning to be attached to the term "feudal" in relation to it'.

cover for ignorance" but simply an excuse for loose thinking', and 'nothing but a counter'.[14] Cheyette decried 'the arbitrary nature of any definition of "feudalism"', and enclosed the offending term in quotation marks to signal its questionable nature. Noting 'the danger of reification' associated with the word's continued use, he declared that all definitions of English 'feudalism' failed 'to distinguish between concepts and things'.[15] He proclaimed that using feudalism, however defined, as a means of evaluating evidence 'sends the historian off in the wrong direction from the beginning' in pursuit of a 'false problem [of] English historiography'. However, he was torn, since he believed that as 'a useful object of speech[,] it cannot simply be discarded—the verbal detours one would have to make to replace it would be strained as well as disingenuous'.[16] In the end, to justify its retention, he recommended adopting a broader, more general '[alternative] to a purely institutional definition of feudalism'. Taking as his point of departure Georges Duby's description of *féodalité* as 'une mentalité médiévale', Cheyette proposed that 'feudalism [be considered] a *technique,* rather than an *institution* (whatever that ambiguous word might mean)'.[17] He also suggested using the word in the plural to suggest the variety of institutions it represented: multiple feudalisms rather than just one or even two of them.[18] In the end, however, he reiterated his criticism of feudalism. In a gnomic and elliptical concluding paragraph, he disparaged as 'wordy and unresolvable debates about what this thing [the model] "really was"', and quoted Charles De Gaulle's remark 'Une constitution c'est un esprit. Des institutions ce sont des hommes', presumably to urge historians, however obliquely, to focus their attention not on models but rather on human beings.[19] Three years later, in 1968, Cheyette brought out *Lordship and Community in Medieval Europe,*[20] a collection of excerpts

---

[14] Fredric L. Cheyette, 'Some Notations on Mr. Hollister's "Irony"', *Journal of British Studies*, 5 (1965), 1–14 (at 2 and 4); and ibid., 2 (1963), 1–26, for Hollister's article. Cheyette commented on Hollister's other publications and the debates they stimulated in 'Some Notations', 1–2, esp. notes 1–4.

[15] Cheyette, 'Some Notations', 5. For Susan Reynolds's attention to the relationship among word, concept, and phenomenon, see below, n. 77.

[16] Cheyette, 'Some Notations', 2.

[17] Cheyette, 'Some Notations', 12.

[18] Cheyette, 'Some Notations', 13 ('in a sense, there was not one feudalism; there were a great many', suggesting in n. 33 that in 1962 Strayer perhaps '[did] not go far enough' in positing 'two feudalisms'); see below following n. 40, for the similar proposition that Thomas N. Bisson later made.

[19] Cheyette, 'Some Notations', 14.

[20] F. L. Cheyette, *Lordship and Community in Medieval Europe: Selected Readings* (New York: Holt, Rinehart, and Winston, 1968). In Susan Reynold's 'Fiefs and Vassals after Twelve Years', in Sverre Bagge, Michael H. Gelting and Thomas Lindkvist (eds), *Feudalism, New Landscapes of Debate* (The Medieval Countryside, 5; Turnhout: Brepols, 2011), 15–26, at 15, she wrongly wrote that Cheyette's book was published a year after my article (and thus in 1975), rather than six years before my essay, which both Cheyette and his anthology greatly influenced. Reynolds's essay and others in the volume were based

from both classic studies and recent works, some translated for the first time. The excerpts were chosen for the light they cast, first, on 'aristocratic society in northern Europe and in the crusader kingdom' and, second, on 'the continuing dialogue between concepts and empirical data' which informed research on the medieval nobility and communities. The title contains no reference to feudalism. Surprisingly, however, the concept features prominently in Cheyette's preface and introductory essay, where Cheyette invoked it to provide context and perspective for appreciating 'the dynamics of medieval society' revealed in the readings.[21]

Cheyette's introduction to the volume opens with the question 'What is feudalism?' and his essay surveys historians' different definitions of the word. Declaring the term a 'concept-theory', he acknowledged that it was particularly difficult to use, without specifying precisely what functions it might be expected to perform. Puzzlingly, three traditional appraisals of feudalism by Joseph R. Strayer, Otto Hintze, and Otto Brunner open the volume. These three sections contrast dramatically with the twenty-one selections that follow, which focus not on feudalism but on widely varied aspects of medieval social history, ranging from modes of association and representation to noble status and ideals, and civic spirit. In the other extracts feudal constructs, if not absent, play roles of minor importance.[22]

Despite his own focus on feudalism and his inclusion of conventional discussions of the term, Cheyette in the end insisted on the construct's deficiencies and the distorted view of the medieval past its dominance had produced, advocating different strategies for exploring medieval society. He declared:

> The task of the historian investigating institutions is not to define their essence, or to label one form as 'true' or 'classical' while shunting others into the shadows of 'proto-' or 'late,' but to describe the various shapes these habitual ways of acting took and to search out the strands connecting them to the culture in which they were embedded.[23]

Thus he argued against using a feudal standard to appraise institutions, and proposed instead an approach that would illuminate the workings of medieval society.

Cheyette's final statement goes far to explain his later claim (advanced in 2006 and published in 2010) that he had 'campaigned for much of [his] career to eliminate both word and concept from professional writing on the middle

---

on papers delivered at a conference on feudalism in Bergen in 2006, on which see below, at n. 108 and following.

[21] Cheyette, *Lordship and Community*, vii, 1–5.

[22] Exceptions are the essays by Édouard Perroy and William Huse Dunham, Jr., and one of the two essays contributed by Duby and one of Joshua Prawer's, whose authors use such terms as 'feudal régime', 'feudalism', and 'feudality': Cheyette, *Lordship and Community*, 137–79, 217–39.

[23] Cheyette, *Lordship and Community*, 10.

ages'.[24] Yet in the 1960s Cheyette's uneasiness with the feudal constructs, however deeply felt, was not expressed with the clarity and determination he later marshalled.

By the early 1970s the time was ripe for an unwavering, straightforward assault on feudalism. In *The New Yorker*, in 1969, James Stevenson's jocular lord raising a goblet and proclaiming 'Here's to feudalism and all the wonderful vassals that make it work', signalled that the moment for ending feudalism's sway was at hand.[25] The criticisms that feudalism and the feudal constructs provoked were becoming increasingly insistent and pointed, eerily echoing shifts in the physical sciences that accompanied the development of quantum mechanics.[26]

MY ARTICLE

In my denunciation of feudalism, forsaking the traditional 'noble style' of academic discourse, I spoke plainly. I did not mince words. "The Tyranny of a Construct: Feudalism and Historians of Medieval Europe"—the title of the article threw the gauntlet down.

I approached the topic obliquely, citing Thomas N. Bisson's work on medieval institutions of the peace as an example of the many important topics that historians' concentration on feudalism had led them to neglect.[27] Describing some historians' discomfiture with feudalism, I emphasized that the word and related terms like 'the feudal system' had been coined and became popular centuries after the period they were said to characterize.[28] In and of itself this did not compromise their potential value to historians, but, I contended, the circumstances of their genesis suggested the wisdom of treating them warily and circumspectly. After exploring the uses historians had

[24] Cheyette, '"Feudalism": A Memoir and an Assessment', in Tuten and Billado (eds), *Feud, Violence and Practice*, 119–33, at 120, where Cheyette singled out Stephen White as his 'welcome and learned companion', even though in my view White's commitment to the crusade against the constructs has been sporadic: Brown, 'Reflections on Feudalism', 135–8, and n. 121 below.

[25] Published in the 1 February 1969 issue of *The New Yorker* (on 26), the cartoon appeared on the cover of the issue of *The American Historical Review* in which my article was published. Cf. the cartoon that Jacob Adam Katzenstein contributed to *The New Yorker*, the issue dated 5 and 12 August 2019 (19), which shows a crowned princess and a jongleur companion walking hand-in-hand toward an imposing castle as she beseeches him, 'Try not to bring up feudalism with my dad tonight'.

[26] Thomas Kuhn, *The Structure of Scientific Revolutions* (Chicago: University of Chicago Press, 1962); 2nd edn. (International Encyclopedia of Unified Science, Foundations of the Unity of Science, 2, part 2; Chicago: University of Chicago Press, 1970); Michel Foucault, *Les mots et les choses* (Paris: Gallimard, 1966), translated with a special foreword as *The Order of Things: An Archaeology of the Human Sciences* (New York: Pantheon, 1971).

[27] Brown, 'Tyranny', 1063–4.

[28] Cf. the comments of Richard Abels, in 'The Historiography of a Construct: "Feudalism" and the Medieval Historian', *History Compass*, 73 (2009), 1008–31, at 1022–23.

made of the feudal constructs and the strikingly different definitions they had been given, I pounced, deriding the 'utility' and 'indispensability' ascribed to the terms as a simple means of introducing students to the medieval past and as a standard for evaluating different areas' deviation from or accordance with an ideal model.[29]

Lauding the descriptions of social and political life that Southern gave of eleventh- and twelfth-century Anjou in *The Making of the Middle Ages* and that Duby offered in his work on the Mâconnais',[30] I recommended discarding feudalism and the other feudal (and manorial) constructs. Rather than elaborating and refining models and using them to rank different societies, I argued, historians should follow Southern and Duby in studying the human beings who had lived in the past, and the bonds, rituals, and institutions that regulated their lives and ordered their existence—the actual functioning of society during the long centuries we call the middle ages. In another article, also published in 1974, I demonstrated the misunderstanding caused by the profligate use of the adjective 'feudal', and, in particular, its application to the financial aids tendered by subjects to their lords, whose incidence and rates were determined by custom and negotiation and which had no necessary connection with fief-holding.[31] Here my criticism of the construct was muted and oblique. By contrast, in 'Tyranny' I advocated uncompromisingly the complete and total abandonment of the feudal constructs and challenged historians to shift their focus from an arbitrarily defined concept to the actual contours of a diverse society and the intricate written and material traces that alone provide access to it.

When I showed a typescript of 'Tyranny' to Fredric Cheyette soon after I had finished it, his response was 'Peggy, don't publish this now. Wait for me to write my book describing how it really was'. At that point, in 1973, Cheyette had embarked on the research that culminated, twenty-eight years later, in his book, *Ermengard of Narbonne and the World of the Troubadours*.[32] As it

---

[29] Brown, 'Tyranny', 1066–80.

[30] See n. 6 above.

[31] E.A.R. Brown, 'Customary Aids and Royal Fiscal Policy under Philip VI of Valois', *Traditio*, 30 (1974),191–258, at 191n. 1, reprinted in my book, *Politics and Institutions in Capetian France* (Variorum Collected Studies Series, 350; Aldershot: Variorum, 1991), no. IX. I treated the issue at greater length in *Customary Aids and Royal Finances in Capetian France: The Marriage Aid of Philip the Fair* (Medieval Academy Books. 100; Cambridge, MA: Medieval Academy of America, 1992), 2–7. In a paper published four years earlier, I did not confront the issue directly but simply referred to 'aids' and, once, to 'customary aids'; I twice employed the adjective 'feudal', to describe the ties between the kings of France and England and issues arising from those bonds: 'Philip the Fair, *Plena Potestas*, and the *Aide pur fille marier*', in *Representative Institutions in Theory and Practice: Historical Papers Read at Bryn Mawr College, April 1968* (Studies Presented to the International Commission for Representative and Parliamentary Institutions, 39; Brussels: Éditions de la Librairie encyclopédique, 1970), 1–27, esp. 5.

[32] F.L. Cheyette, *Ermengard of Narbonne and the World of the Troubadours* (Ithaca NY: Cornell University Press, 2001). I prize my copy, in which, at my request, Fred wrote: 'OK,

was, Fred and I pursued our different paths, while working toward a common goal. Had I taken Fred's advice in 1974, the historiography of feudalism might well be different, although given the escalating dissatisfaction with the feudal constructs, someone else might well have launched the campaign I mounted.[33]

MY EXPECTATIONS AND FEUDALISM'S STRENGTHS

I hoped naively that a paradigm shift of seismic proportions would follow the appearance of my article. The heated debates that occurred, however, showed how deeply committed feudalism's supporters were to its defense.

I was not prepared for the resistance the article provoked. In 1974 I knew little about the creation of the feudal constructs and did not fully realize how many people, before me, had vainly decried the concepts and opposed their use, offering arguments similar to mine. Nor had I given serious thought to the reasons why the constructs possessed the appeal they did and why they continued to command the loyalty they had for centuries attracted. To be sure, in my article I repeatedly insisted on the allure of their simplicity, which contrasted with the complexities of human existence. Without pressing the point, I criticized them for 'pander[ing] to the human desire to grasp—or

Peggy, this is what it was really like'. For Cheyette's preliminary research and findings, see his essay 'The Castles of the Trencavels: A Preliminary Aerial Survey', in William C. Jordan, Bruce McNab and Teofilo F. Ruiz (eds), *Order and Innovation in the Medieval West: Essays in Honor of Joseph R. Strayer* (Princeton: Princeton University Press, 1976), 255–72, 498–99, for which Cheyette had not only acquired aerial photographs of the area but also visited the sites (ibid., 498n. 1). See also his articles 'The "Sale" of Carcassonne to the Counts of Barcelona (1067–1073) and the Rise of the Trencavels', *Speculum*, 63 (1988), 826–64; and 'Women, Poets, and Politics in Occitania', in Theodore Evergates (ed.), *Aristocratic Women in Medieval France* (The Middle Ages Series; Philadelphia: University of Pennsylvania Press, 1999), 138–233; as well as his review of Reynolds, *Fiefs and Vassals*, in *Speculum*, 71:4 (1996), 998–1006. Cheyette usefully discussed topics that still need study, in 'George Duby's *Mâconnais*', 317.

[33] In 'De feodale maatschappij der mideleeuwn', *Bijdragen en mededelingen betreffende de geschiedenis der Nederlanden*, 89 (1974), 193–211, which appeared in the same year as my article, Co Van de Kieft surveyed the many definitions of feudalism found in the work of Bloch, Duby, and others, without directly attacking the feudal constructs. In the article he emphasized as powerful determinants of medieval society the medieval economy's agrarian character, and the Church and Christian faith. In 1968, in contrast, Van de Kieft had written, 'La rencontre des structures économiques, sociales et politiques s'exprime avec tellement d'évidence dans les pouvoirs de l'aristocratie féodo-vassalique que l'on peut concevoir, à bon droit, une société féodale, une époque féodale dont l'histoire se déroulerait approximativement de 900 à 1200', in 'La périodisation de l'histoire au Moyen Âge', in Chaïm Perelman (ed.), *Les catégories en histoire* (Travaux du Centre national de recherches de logique; Brussels: Éditions de l'Institut de Sociologie, Université Libre de Bruxelles, 1969), 39–56, at 54–55. However, on the offprint of this piece that Van de Kieft sent me in 1982 he wrote beside this statement, 'I do not hold this opinion now'. In *Fiefs and Vassals*, 1, Susan Reynolds noted that Van de Kieft and I 'pointed out independently in 1974 [that] feudalism can mean a lot of different things'. I am grateful to Mayke de Jong, a student of Van de Kieft, for her counsel concerning his views. See n. 77 below.

to think one is grasping—a subject known or suspected to be complex by applying to it a simple label simplistically defined'.[34] However imprecisely, what I wrote witnessed my belief in a universal human desire to adopt simple, easy solutions even in the face of awareness, however vague, that they may be deceptive and misleading and that the truth is likely more complicated than they suggest. I was not aware that in these same years, in the early 1970s, scientists including Daniel Kahneman and Amos Tversky were investigating cognitive styles, processes, and biases in studies that supported my conviction.

Human beings, as cognitive scientists have shown, are intuitively inclined to accept simple, logical, widely endorsed propositions, to seek coherence and causal patterns, to avoid ambiguity, and to suppress doubt.[35] Such propensities, impulsive and automatic, produce feelings of cognitive ease. In contrast, questioning and scrutinizing readily grasped, uncomplicated solutions require attention and effort, and thus involve cognitive unease, if not pain. These inclinations are universal. The precise significance of their universality is, however, complicated by the fact that some human beings seem particularly attracted to simple solutions and particularly reluctant to reject them, whereas other human beings, differently inclined, have a propensity to question such easy solutions and find it far less difficult to discard them. The validity of the distinction seems clear, even if cognitive scientists have yet to scrutinize it, explore its nuances, and attempt to explain why it exists.[36] After all, some 2700 years ago Archilochus, impressed by the difference he perceived, dubbed hedgehogs those who knew 'one big thing', who were by nature theorists and simplifiers, whereas he labelled foxes those who were drawn to complexity, and knew 'many things'.[37] Archilochus surely did not intend to divide humanity into two diametrically opposed camps. Gradations evidently exist, and there

---

[34] Brown, 'Tyranny', 1065.

[35] Daniel Kahneman, *Thinking, Fast and Slow* (New York: Farrar, Straus and Giroux, 2011), esp. 19–70, 415; and, for 'cognitive ease' and 'cognitive strain', ibid., 59–70, 212. See also Gary Marcus and Annie Duke, 'The Problem with Believing What We're Told', *Wall Street Journal* (31 August–1 September 2019), C5. I explored remarks on this subject by Jeremy Bentham (1748–1832) and John Playfair (1748–1819) in '*Veritas* à la cour de Philippe le Bel de France: Pierre Dubois, Guillaume de Nogaret et Marguerite Porete', in Jean-Philippe Genet (ed.), *La vérité. Vérité et crédibilité: construire la vérité dans le système de communication de l'Occident (XIIIᵉ–XVIIᵉ siècle). Actes de la conférence organisée à Rome en 2012 par SAS en collaboration avec l'École française de Rome* (Collection de l'École française de Rome, 485/2; Histoire ancienne et médiévale, 128/2; Le pouvoir symbolique en Occident (1300–1640), 2; Paris/Rome; Publications de la Sorbonne/ École Française de Rome, 2015), 425–45, at 442–43; see also ibid., 433.

[36] Cf. Kahneman's comments on hedgehogs and foxes, in *Thinking, Fast and Slow*, 218–20, with reference to the findings of Philip E. Tetlock.

[37] Isaiah Berlin's book *The Hedgehog and the Fox*, has critically affected my thinking about concepts and theories, and a host of other topics. See my articles, 'Jürgen Habermas, Philippe le Bel, et l'espace public', in Patrick Boucheron and Nicolas Offenstadt (eds), *L'espace public au Moyen Âge. Débats autour de Jürgen Habermas* (Le Nœud Gordien; Paris: Presses universitaires de France, 2011),193–203, at 193–94; and 'The French Royal Funeral Ceremony and the King's Two Bodies: Ernst H. Kantorowicz, Ralph E. Giesey,

is no question that all human beings, even the foxiest, instinctively opt for simplicity. Still, people whose cognitive orientation inclines them toward complexity are far more likely than natural simplifiers to question and abandon simple solutions when confronted with persuasive contradictory evidence.

The general appeal of simple principles goes far to account for the endurance of the feudal constructs. They are easy to understand and remember. They are untaxing. They are manipulable. Their use and endorsement by generations of distinguished thinkers endow them with respectability and authority. Since the sixteenth century they have been linked with the quest for patterns of human development, holistic models, and structures of social activity, an enterprise that has always been privileged over the pursuit of *realia*.[38] In themselves they are not demonstrably false, even though they fall short of reflecting or expressing the tangled reality of lived existence. Despite their shortcomings, increasingly evident, thinkers and writers who are by nature averse to complexity remain devoted to the constructs, which makes feudalism particularly difficult to unseat. Such thinkers' predilection for the constructs inclines them not only to disregard logical arguments against the concepts but also to overlook or dismiss evidence of diversity and complexity that undermines their validity—just as their proponents' fidelity fortifies the general human tendency to favour simplicity and thus to cling unquestioningly to feudalism and the feudal constructs.

REACTIONS, 1974–1994

My crusade against feudalism elicited a range of responses, positive and negative. The division of opinion was clearly manifested one evening in Baltimore, shortly after my article appeared. There Joseph R. Strayer, one of feudalism's most stalwart propagators and supporters, chivalrously supported me when, with John W. Baldwin and Gabrielle M. Spiegel, talk turned to feudalism. John and Gaby raised the subject, advancing vehement objections to my views. Entering the discussion, Joe declared 'But of course she is right'— and proceeded, area by area, to describe the myriad tenurial and political regimes that characterized different areas of medieval France in the eleventh and early twelfth centuries, regimes that no single concept could adequately represent. I was gratified, although not for long. Gaby's and John's disapproval represented the tip of an iceberg.

Adversaries and nay-sayers abounded. My most dedicated and eloquent antagonist, Thomas Bisson, was wedded to the construct. In 1978 he declared

---

and the Construction of a Paradigm', *Micrologus*, 22 (Le Corps du Prince) (2014), 105–37, at 108–9.

[38] See, e.g., Guerreau, 'Fief, féodalité, féodalisme', 152–53; and Peter Coss, 'From Feudalism to Bastard Feudalism', in Natalie Fryde, Pierre Monnet, and Otto Gerhard Oexle (eds), *Die Gegenwart des Feudalismus; Présence du féodalisme et présent de la féodalité; The Presence of Feudalism* (Veröffentlichungen des Max-Planck-Instituts für Geschichte, 173; Göttingen: Vandenhoeck & Ruprecht, 2002), 79–108, at 79.

feudalism a 'congenial tyrant', maintaining that even if the word has many definitions, historians 'do not ordinarily make the mistake of relying on such definitions in their research'. He argued that historians 'have no disagreement over the elemental subject matter of feudalism—namely, vassals, lords of vassals, and fiefs', which he considered a 'very practical' if 'not very illuminating definition'. 'The historian's task', he concluded, 'is to describe the function of lordship, vassalage, and the fief as so many changing and measurable variables in a total historical experience in which they were more or less, but always differently, important'.[39] From Bisson's perspective, then, historians were bound to focus on the role feudalism and its components played in medieval society, not medieval society in its totality.

Tom Bisson and I debated feudalism more than once. In 1979, rising to defend the term, Bisson feigned weakness before proclaiming that feudalism could not be abandoned. Describing himself as 'limping out on to this battlefield on my wretched little nag, already maimed by Maitland and battered by Bloch, facing a proud and victorious charger draped elegantly in Brown, cheered on, I fear, by a tumultuous court of stony-hearted knights and ladies who had been deceived by this villain too often to have any sympathy for it now',[40] Bisson argued that multiple 'feudalisms' should be substituted for a single model. Although his reference to plural 'feudalisms' suggested that he recognized the importance of different modes of organizing and regulating medieval European society, he added:

> There are certain uniformities of structure and nomenclature widely evident in medieval Europe which ... are usually so peculiarly integrated in local or regional circumstances ... as to defy our efforts to abstract them usefully. Therefore we are bound to admit that feudalism in medieval European history, if it is to mean anything, must be a phenomenon of societies, local and regional; to put it in a formula, feudalism is vassalage and the lordship of vassals, the fief, and their appurtenant incidents and ceremonial, as these function in a specific society or culture.[41]

He ended, paraphrasing Stevenson, 'So here's to feudalisms, and to all the wonderful historians who make them work'.[42] Thus Bisson continued to

[39] T. Bisson, 'The Problem of Feudal Monarchy: Aragon, Catalonia, and France', *Speculum*, 533 (1978), 460–78, at 461.

[40] T. Bisson, '*Pro feodalitatibus*', a paper presented at the Fourteenth International Congress on Medieval Studies at Western Michigan University on 4 May 1979.

[41] Bisson, '*Pro feodalitatibus*'; for a variety of feudalisms, see above at n. 18.

[42] Bisson, '*Pro feodalitatibus*'.

assume the primary importance of the feudal components as keys to understanding the different social settings in which they could be found. In his eyes what was feudal was determinative, other phenomena ancillary.[43]

It is worth, however, reflecting on his remark, 'if it—feudalism—is to mean anything'. Bisson himself assumed that feudalism meant something, and that it could indeed have multiple senses, signified by the plural 'feudalisms' he recommended pursuing. Indeed he was so convinced of the concept's authenticity as to bet me a case of champagne that he would find the noun *feodalitas* used in a genuine medieval text to designate phenomena like those the construct feudalism encompasses (which has not yet happened). Still, his comment in 1979 'if it is to mean anything', clearly acknowledged the possibility that it—feudalism—might indeed mean nothing at all.[44]

Reactions to the article in France were curious. Reminiscing in 2013,[45] Philippe Contamine declared that my essay had caused a stir in Paris when it appeared—which surprised me greatly. In 1974 and subsequent years, none of my French colleagues mentioned the article to me, nor was I ever invited to lecture on or discuss my ideas on *féodalité* or *féodalisme*. Indeed, the international conference on 'Feudal Structures and Feudalism in the Mediterranean West between the Tenth and Thirteenth Centuries', held at the École française in Rome in October 1978, demonstrated how little attention was paid to my attack—or to other scholars' objections to the construct.[46] The passage of time altered nothing.[47] When in 1986 I raised with French colleagues the

[43] In Brown, 'Reflections on Feudalism', 137n. 7, I quoted excerpts from Bisson's description of the National Endowment for the Humanities summer seminar, 'Medieval European Feudalism', given at the University of California at Berkeley, June 23–August 15, 1986; I am grateful to him for sending me a copy of the description, in which he proposed that the concept filled 'a need particularly associated with explanatory generalizing and teaching'—while not being 'a requirement for research'. In a letter dated 24 March 1986 he commented, 'I no longer believe the conceptual problem worth discussing until people like you and me work directly with the sources for vassalage and laws of fiefs'.

[44] Cf. Stenton's comment (*First Century,* 2nd ed., 216), 'But unless the term [feudalism] is to lose all significance, it should at least be reserved for some definite form of social order'.

[45] Remarks made by Philippe Contamine at the inauguration of the Journée d'étude 'Kings like semi-gods: Autour des travaux d'Elizabeth A.R. Brown', at Université de Paris—La Sorbonne, Centre Roland-Mousnier, 15 June 2013.

[46] The papers were published in *Structures féodales et féodalisme dans l'Occident méditerranéen (X^e–XIIIe siècles). Bilan et perspectives de recherches. Colloque international organisé par le Centre National de la Recherche Scientifique et l'École française de Rome (Rome, 10–13 octobre 1978)* (Collection de l'École française de Rome, 44; Rome: École française de Rome, 1980), a volume of 800 pages.

[47] Long after the article was published it was sometimes mentioned in connection with Reynolds's book *Fiefs and Vassals;* see Élisabeth Magnou-Nortier, 'La féodalité en crise. Propos sur "Fiefs and Vassals" de Susan Reynolds', *Revue historique,* 2962 (600) (1996), 253–348, at 254–55; and also Eric Bournazel and Jean-Pierre Poly, 'Introduction générale', in Eric Bournazel and Jean-Pierre Poly (eds), *Les féodalités* (Histoire générale des systèmes politiques; Paris: Presses universitaires de France, 1998), 3–12, at 6. A translation

possibility of presenting in Paris a talk on the origins of the constructs, they were not interested, saying that the terms *féodalité* and *féodalisme* were falling out of favour and coming to be considered *passé*, and that they were never used by thoughtful scholars, who employed in their stead the more general term *société*. This was not the case. My attack was simply being disregarded.

Georges Duby and many others continued to invoke the constructs and to use the adjective feudal lavishly, applying it to things as disparate as society, imagination, and revolution. In 1976, in his *Crise du féodalisme*, Guy Bois shifted the feudal focus from fief to field, and from Ganshof to Marx.[48] Two years later Duby's *Les trois ordres et l'imaginaire du féodalisme* featured both *féodalisme* and *féodalité*, even though Duby expressed hesitations about the precise meaning of the terms.[49] In the book, to provide social and political context for the trifunctional ideas expressed by Gerard of Cambrai and Adalbero of Laon in the eleventh century, Duby invoked *la révolution féodale* that he believed contemporary charters and notices disclosed. Still, as he had in the past, Duby occasionally referred (certainly when I was present) to 'la société que nous *appellons* féodale [my italics]'.[50] Nonetheless, his deep and lasting devotion to the constructs were witnessed by the title given to the collection of his works that Gallimard published in the year of his death, 1996: *Féodalité*.[51]

of my article by Réjean Girard, 'La tyrannie d'un *construct:* la féodalité et les historiens de l'Europe médiévale', will appear in a collection of essays edited by Richard M. Pollard. In the introduction to his translation, which he prepared in consultation with Professor Pollard at the Université de Québec à Montréal, M. Girard noted the absence of references to the article in popular French manuals on medieval history, 'bien que les problèmes reliés à la définition et à la généralisation du concept y soient évoqués'.

[48] G. Bois, *Crise du féodalisme: économie rurale et démographie en Normandie orientale du début du 14ᵉ siècle au milieu du 16ᵉ siècle* (Cahiers de la Fondation nationale des sciences politiques, 202; Presses de la Fondation nationale des sciences politiques/Éditions de l'École des Hautes Études en Sciences Sociales, 1976), with a 2nd edn. in 1981; translated into English in 1984 as *The Crisis of Feudalism: Economy and Society in Eastern Normandy c. 1300–1550* (Past and Present Publications; Cambridge: Cambridge University Press; and Paris: Éditions de la Maison des Sciences de l'Homme, 1984).

[49] G. Duby, *Les trois ordres ou l'imaginaire du féodalisme* (Bibliothèque des histoires; Paris: Gallimard, 1978); translated by Arthur Goldhammer as *The Three Orders: Feudal Society Imagined* (Chicago: University of Chicago Press, 1980), esp. 183–205 (section III, 'La révolution féodale'); see the translation, *The Three Orders*, 147–66. In this section, Duby declared of the new mode of production whose appearance he hypothesized (ibid., 189; trans. 153), 'Mieux vaut ne pas l'appeler féodal—le fief n'a rien a voir ici—mais seigneurial', thus indicating the preferability of 'lordship' to 'feudalism' to characterize the essence of eleventh-century society.

[50] Georges Duby, 'Vers la féodalité en Aquitaine au onzième siècle', a lecture presented at Columbia University on 15 April 1986, and a seminar on Andreas Capellanus given at New York University on 18 April 1986. See Elizabeth A. R. Brown, 'Georges Duby and the Three Orders', *Viator*, 17 (1986), 51–62, esp. n. 3; and Brown, 'Tyranny', 1073–74.

[51] Published by Gallimard in Paris in 1996 in the series Quarto, with an introduction by Jacques Delarun; Gallimard republished the volume in 1999, in the series Le Grand Livre du Mois. In 2002 another compendium of Duby's writings entitled *Qu'est-ce que la société féodale?* was published by Flammarion in Paris, in the series Mille & Une Pages, with

French allegiance to the feudal constructs was (and has remained) strong. Inspired by Duby, in 1980 Jean-Pierre Poly and Éric Bournazel published *La mutation féodale*, the label they fashioned as a rival to Duby's *révolution féodale* to characterize the development of European society in the tenth through the twelfth centuries.[52] Two years later, in 1982, in an article entitled 'L'Europe de l'An mille' that Poly contributed to a three-volume history of the Middle Ages directed by Robert Fossier, devotion to the feudal constructs led Poly to contrast the free communities found in the Midi with 'le "féodalisme" rampant du Nord'[53]—an area from which it would be difficult to exclude Picardy, Fossier's own region of expertise, where Fossier had demonstrated the importance of rural communities and communes, courts of free men, and allodial, free property.[54] Dominique Barthélemy's attachment to the constructs may have led him to minimize the differences among allods, fiefs, and manse when discussing the lands of the lords of Coucy. It may also have led him to assume that in the courts of the *châtelains*, concerning which little documentation survives, 'se débatt[ai]ent les questions féodo-vassaliques [et] s'élabor[ai]ent le vocabulaire et les règles de la "féodalité" classique'.[55] On the other hand, like Fossier's, other French studies provided grist for the mills of those concerned with the precise meanings of terms and the phenomena they represented. In an article published in 1982, 'Faut-il traduire vassal par vassal? (Quelques réflexions sur la lexicologie du français médiéval)', Theo Venckeleer showed that in the medieval romances he had studied vassal meant simply 'man' (*vir*), or, perhaps, *vrai homme*—nothing more.[56] In 1988, contesting the conclusions

introductions by Dominique Iogna-Prat and Mirna Velcic-Canivez. See Theodore Evergates, 'The Feudal Imaginary of Georges Duby', *Journal of Medieval and Early Modern Studies*, 27 (1997), 641–60, at 653.

[52] J.-P. Poly and É. Bournazel, *La mutation féodale. X^e–XIIe siècle* (Nouvelle Clio, 16; Paris, Presses universitaires de France, 1980, and 2nd ed., 1991). On Poly's work on Provence, see n. 57 below. Duby wrote the preface to Guy Bois's book, *La mutation de l'an mil: Lournand, village mâconnais, de l'Antiquité au féodalisme* (Nouvelles études historiques; Paris: Fayard, 1989).

[53] In R. Fossier (ed.), *Le Moyen Age*, 3 vols (Paris: Armand Colin, 1982–3), II (*L'éveil de l'Europe, 950–1250*, 1982), 19–78, esp. 30, 38, 54–57, 60.

[54] R. Fossier (ed.), *Histoire de la Picardie* (Toulouse: Privat, 1974), esp. R. Fossier, 'La société picarde au Moyen Age', ibid., 135–76, at 159–67. See R. Fossier, *La terre et les hommes en Picardie jusqu'à la fin du XIIIe siècle*, 2 vols (Publications de la Faculté des lettres et sciences humaines de Paris, série Recherches, 48–49; Paris and Louvain: B. Nauwelaerts, 1968); a new edition was published in 1987 in Amiens (Centre régional de documentation pédagogique).

[55] D. Barthélemy, *Les deux âges de la seigneurie banale. Pouvoir et société dans la terre des Sires de Coucy (milieu XIe–milieu XIIIe siècle)* (Publications de la Sorbonne, Université de Paris IV, Série Histoire ancienne et médiévale, 12; Paris, 1984), 13–16, 34–42 (sources), 108–9, 117 ('hiérarchie féodale'), 157 (courts), 158 (esp. n. 63) (allod, fief, and manse); cf. ibid., 374–75 (on arbitration), and 492 (the dangers of projecting onto the past 'l'image d'une féodalité "classique"').

[56] T. Venckeleer's article appeared in Quirinus Ignatius Maria Mok, Ina Spiele, Paul E.R. Verhuyck (eds), *Mélanges de linguistique, de littérature et de philologie médiévales, offerts*

of Jean-Pierre Poly,[57] Gérard Giordanengo questioned the importance of fiefs and vassalage in eleventh-century Provence and Dauphiné, and argued that the use thirteenth- and fourteenth-century rulers made of these mechanisms to increase their authority was just one of the many devices they employed.[58] The research that Hélène Débax was doing during these years, beginning in 1984, would soon culminate in publications that, while rendering nominal and titular homage to feudal and structural constructs, illuminate the complexities of the lives lived, the lands possessed, and the rituals performed in southern France in the eleventh and twelfth century.[59]

Closer to home, the work of Theodore Evergates and Emily Zack Tabuteau demonstrated the dispensability of the feudal constructs and provided positive support for my campaign. In a study focussed on Champagne published in 1975, Evergates spelled out in detail the diverse social and tenurial configurations in twelfth- and thirteenth-century France revealed by recent studies.[60] As Strayer had done in Baltimore, Evergates moved systematically from region to region, demonstrating the critical significance of birth, wealth, allodial holdings, and positions of power in determining the characteristics of the aristocracy in different regions. Seconding my stand, Evergates concluded 'that the previous exclusive concentration on the peculiarities of tenure and personal relationships distorts the image of medieval society'.[61] In a review published in 1979 he stressed that 'detailed local and regional studies' (like those he

---

à J. R. Smeets (Leiden: Comité de rédaction, 1982), 303–16; Susan Reynolds referred to it in 'Fiefs and Vassals after Twelve Years', 20n. 8, and later publications. Felice Lifshitz proposed that in Dudo of Saint-Quentin's Gesta Normannorum, the word vassalus, used once, means 'fighter' and has no other, more technical, connotations: 'Translating "Feudal" Vocabulary: Dudo of St. Quentin', first published in The Haskins Society Journal: Studies in Medieval History, 9 (2001), 39–56, reprinted in her Writing Normandy: Stories of Saints and Rulers (Variorum Collected Studies, 1095; London and New York: Routledge, 2021), 206–24, at 213; on Dudo (fl. late tenth century), see ibid., 188 (a notice Lifshitz first published in 1998).

[57] J.-P. Poly, La société féodale en Provence du Xe au XIIe siècle (Paris: Hachette, 1973). Three years later Poly brought out La Provence et la société féodale (879–1155). Contribution à l'étude des structures dites féodales dans le Midi (Collection 'Études'; Paris: Bordas, 1976), but his approach was fundamentally similar despite his introduction of the modifier 'dites' into the phrase 'structures féodales'.

[58] G. Giordanengo, Le droit féodal dans les pays de droit écrit: l'exemple de la Provence et du Dauphiné, XIIe-début XIVe siècle (Bibliothèques des Ecoles françaises d'Athènes et de Rome, 1ère sér., 266; Rome: École française de Rome, 1988).

[59] Hélène Débax received her doctorate in 1997 for a thesis entitled Structures féodales dans le Languedoc des Trencavel (XIe-XIIe s.), for which see H. Débax (ed.), Les sociétés méridionales à l'âge féodal (Espagne, Italie et sud de la France, Xe-XIIIe s.). Hommage à Pierre Bonnassie (Collection "Méridiennes"; Toulouse: CNRS, Université de Toulouse-Le Mirail, 1999), 441.

[60] Theodore Evergates, Feudal Society in the Bailliage of Troyes under the Counts of Champagne, 1152–1284 (Baltimore: The Johns Hopkins University Press, 1975), esp. 136–53.

[61] Evergates, Feudal Society, 153, 251 n.49.

had surveyed in 1975) 'no longer permit the construction of vast syntheses or comparative models in the tradition of earlier general works on feudalism', and he declared that 'to characterize [medieval Europe] as a feudal society … is to misrepresent its complexity and evolution', pointing to the fundamental changes that occurred between the ninth and the thirteenth centuries.[62]

As concerns the components of the feudal constructs, Emily Tabuteau's meticulous studies of eleventh-century Normandy, published in 1977, 1981, and 1988, made clear their relative insignificance in eleventh-century Normandy. There, as she showed, numerous sorts of property and property transfers existed, including sales, exchanges, tenures in alms, conditional gifts, rentals, life estates, mortgages—as well as fiefs.[63] Eschewing reliance on later documentation (or models) that might lead her to 'find what one seeks even though it is not there', Tabuteau declared it preferable 'to tolerate gaps in our knowledge than to read back into the eleventh-century conditions that did not exist until the twelfth'. Tabuteau concluded that 'even in the late eleventh century Normans did not live in a predominantly "feudal world", either tenurially or mentally'. 'Although Normandy was undoubtedly predominantly tenurial by the late eleventh century', she declared, 'it was by no means predominantly feudal, unless "tenurial" and "feudal" are taken as synonyms, which they should not be'.[64]

The intricate and convoluted Norman property-holding arrangements described by Tabuteau implied that definition and rationalization occurred in England after 1066, a consequence of the Normans' victory over the English—even as the complexities her charter-based evidence disclosed suggested that the twelfth-century Norman and English tenurial landscape might be more elaborate than has been recognized.[65] As Thomas Bisson declared, Tabuteau's analysis of Norman charters '[laid] firmly to rest the

[62] T. Evergates, review of John Critchley, *Feudalism* (Boston: George Allen and Unwin, 1978), in *American Historical Review*, 84:2 (1979), 418. Ending his review, Evergates declared 'It is not clear what is achieved by cramming bits and pieces of information on hundreds of societies widely scattered in time and place into the worn mold of feudalism'.

[63] E.Z. Tabuteau, 'Ownership and Tenure in Eleventh-Century Normandy', *American Journal of Legal History*, 21:2 (1977), 97–124; E.Z. Tabuteau, 'Definitions of Feudal Military Obligations in Eleventh-Century Normandy', in Morris S. Arnold, Sally A. Scully, and Stephen D. White (eds), *On the Laws and Customs of England: Essays in Honor of Samuel E. Thorne* (Chapel Hill: University of North Carolina Press in Association with the American Society for Legal History, 1981), 18–59, at 19; E.Z. Tabuteau, *Transfers of Property in Eleventh-Century Norman Law* (Chapel Hill; University of North Carolina Press, 1988), 3; see also the review of the volume by R.C. van Caenegem, in *American Journal of Legal History*, 26 (1982), 391–93, at 392.

[64] Tabuteau, *Transfers of Property*, 2–3 and passim; Tabuteau, 'Definitions of Feudal Military Obligations', 59.

[65] Tabuteau, *Transfers of Property*, 4–6; Tabuteau, 'Definitions of Feudal Military Obligations', 41, 59; see also van Caenegem's review, 392, and above, at n. 11, for Frank Murray Stenton's work.

famous thesis of Charles Homer Haskins that "systematic feudalism" existed in Normandy before the Conquest'.[66]

Tabuteau's findings subverted not only widely accepted notions about pre-Conquest Normandy, but also called into question the model of the 'truly seignorial (or feudal) world' that S. F. C. Milsom (in 1976) and Robert C. Palmer (beginning in 1981) posited for England before Henry II introduced common law actions.[67] So too, as concerns judicial action and the settlement of disputes over land, did findings that Stephen D. White published in 1987.[68] Although Milsom and Palmer believed with many others that disputes over land would necessarily have been tried in 'the court of the lord in whose fief, honor, or *casamentum* the disputed property lay', White showed that between 1050 and 1150 in Touraine, a region whose customs resembled those of England, the lord's court 'was not the only forum or even the principal forum in which disputes that raised issues about inheritances were heard and dealt with'.[69] Compromise and mediation were markedly preferred to judicial decision, and when judgments were made they were often rendered by ecclesiastical courts or impromptu gatherings of prominent laymen and clerics.[70]

During these years I continued my attack on feudalism in articles in the *Oxford Dictionary of the Middle Ages*, the *Encyclopædia Britannica*, and Norman F. Cantor's *The Encyclopedia of the Middle Ages*.[71] Having begun investigating the origin and development of the feudal constructs and having been increasingly impressed by their novelty, artificiality, and excessive simplicity, as well as the vocal opposition they encountered from the beginning, I brought a fuller historiographical perspective to my discussion of the

---

[66] T. Bisson, review of Tabuteau, *Transfers of Property*, *Speculum*, 66:3 (1991), 698–700, at 699.

[67] S.F.C. Milsom, *Historical Foundations of the Common Law* (London: Butterworths, 1969); S.F.C. Milsom, *The Legal Framework of English Feudalism. The Maitland Lectures Given in 1972* (Cambridge Studies in English Legal History; Cambridge: Cambridge University Press, 1976). See Robert C. Palmer's review of Milsom's *Legal Framework*, 'The Feudal Framework of English Law', *Michigan Law Review*, 79:5 (1981), 1130–64. For additional bibliography, see Stephen D. White, 'Inheritances and Legal Arguments in Western France, 1050–1150', *Traditio*, 43 (1987), 55–103, at 57n. 8.

[68] White, 'Inheritances', 96.

[69] White, 'Inheritances', 96–103, esp. 96.

[70] White, 'Inheritances', passim, esp. 64–70. In another study of the same region White showed the importance of ecclesiastical mediation in resolving feuds and demonstrated that the absence of established governmental institutions did not result in unbridled violence, although warfare made peasants 'more and more vulnerable to pressure exerted by lords': Stephen D. White, 'Feuding and Peace-Making in the Touraine around the Year 1100', *Traditio*, 42 (1986), 195–263, esp. 261 and n. 256.

[71] The volume edited by Cantor was published by Viking in New York in 1999. Although an earlier article on 'feudalism' in Wikipedia gave the classic definitions of the term while referring readers for further information to the articles I wrote for these reference works, the version posted on 26 December 2020 featured my article and Susan Reynolds's book and cited my entry in the *Encyclopædia Britannica Online*.

concepts. Thus my essays began by emphasizing feudalism's relatively recent genesis and the impossibly sweeping role it had been created to fulfil:

> Since the eighteenth century, 'feudalism' (or 'feudality'; in French, *féodalité*) has been employed as a shorthand term to characterize the social, economic, and political conditions in western Europe during much of what is termed the Middle Ages, the long stretch of centuries between the fifth and fifteenth, C.E.

I bided my time and continued to hope, although how difficult the battle would be was becoming increasingly clear. After all, despite Emily Tabuteau's explicit disclaimers, David Corner declared that her book raised vital questions 'about the growth of feudalism',[72] whereas Charles Donahue, Jr. described her work as 'the first major study of a "truly feudal" world to appear since Milsom's study'.[73] Thanks to the dogged loyalty of the feudal constructs' champions and their widespread cognitive appeal, feudalism's powers of endurance were just beginning to be scathed.

SUSAN REYNOLDS, *FIEFS AND VASSALS*, AND THE AFTERMATH

Susan Reynolds's interest in medieval society—in English towns and in medieval kingdoms and communities[74]—, as well as her penchant for controversial causes, led her to become a staunch ally in my campaign against feudalism.[75] Soon after we met, not long after 1974, she and I considered writing a book together in hopes of laying the feudal constructs to permanent rest.[76] I was eager to investigate the actual nature and functioning of property-holding and politics in different times and places during the Middle Ages.

---

[72] D. Corner, review in *American Journal of Legal History*, 34 (1990), 98–99.

[73] From the endorsement that Donahue wrote, which appeared on the cover of Tabuteau's book.

[74] S. Reynolds, *An Introduction to the History of English Medieval Towns* (Oxford: Clarendon Press, 1977, with a corrected edn., 1982); S. Reynolds, *Kingdoms and Communities in Western Europe, 900–1300* (Oxford: Clarendon Press, 1984, with a 2nd edn. in 1997).

[75] In precisely what sense(s) I was Reynolds's 'forerunner' is an involved question. See Philippe Buc, 'What Is Order? In the Aftermath of the "Feudal Transformation" Debates', *Francia*, 46 (2019), 281–300, at 282. In 'Historiography of a Construct', 1021, Abels described Reynolds as 'further developing' my criticisms of the feudal constructs. In 'Feudalism', *International Encyclopedia of the Social and Behavioral Sciences*, 2nd edn., ed. James D. Wright, vol. 9 (Oxford: Elsevier, 2015), 111–16, at 114, Levi Roach described me as opposing all models of feudalism (and particularly its use 'as a socioeconomic model') and Reynolds as combatting the 'legal-tenurial' model. He distinguished Reynolds's attack as 'more fundamental' than mine, and he credited her with presenting 'feudalism *tout court* [as] an Early Modern invention'; cf. Brown, 'Tyranny', 1063–65, and also Brown, 'Reflections on Feudalism', 138–47.

[76] In 'Fiefs and Vassals after Twelve Years', 15, Reynolds wrote that we planned a book 'about the problem of feudalism' and that I was interested in taking 'a wide look at the ideas behind the word *feudalism*', whereas I recollect wanting to collaborate on a series of essays featuring sources related to the development of property-holding and their proper

I also wanted to scrutinize the full range of words the relevant contemporary sources used to describe property-holding and clientage and associational relationships, and try to establish the things the terms represented in their textual, social, political, and economic contexts—in which, I thought, words like *feudum, beneficium,* and *vassus* might designate different phenomena and evoke different concepts from those with which they are linked as components of the feudal constructs.[77] Impressed by the differences in the evolution of social and political institutions within disparate regions of what is now France, I wished to examine a few areas of medieval Europe, carefully selected, to assess the diversity of their social and political institutions.

Reynolds, by contrast, was eager to focus on the construct's two principal constituents—fiefs and vassals—in order to determine whether the sources support the early prominence and the meaning and significance that feudalism's champions accord to them—and particularly to fiefs, on which she focussed her energy.[78] For my part, I was reluctant to pay more attention than they had already received to such treacherous protagonists as 'fiefs' and 'vassals', particularly in the guises bestowed on them by the construct's inventors. These, after all, were the villains I blamed for blocking progress toward more accurate and credible representations of the medieval past.[79]

interpretation, and the ways in which different regions evolved from the tenth century onwards. Thus, I did not favour placing particular emphasis on 'fiefs' and 'vassals' but thought that words like *feodum* and *vassus* should be examined with other similar terms in the specific documentary contexts in which they appeared.

[77] Like Cheyette, Reynolds has insisted that words, concepts, and phenomena must be meticulously distinguished: see Cheyette, 'Some Notations', 5, and Reynolds, *Fiefs and Vassals*, 12–14, esp. n. 33, where she confessed to 'painstakingly reinvent[ing] the wheel', citing John Lyons, *Semantics*, 2 vols (Cambridge: Cambridge University Press, 1977). In 2009 she presented and analyzed the diagram of Charles K. Ogden and Ivor A. Richards illustrating the relationship of word to concept (or notion), and phenomenon, which Lyons treated in *Semantics*, I, 96–98: Reynolds, 'The Use of Feudalism in Comparative History', first published in Benjamin Z. Kedar (ed.), *Explorations in Comparative History* (Publication of the Institute for Advanced Studies, The Hebrew University of Jerusalem; Jerusalem: Hebrew University Magnes Press, 2009), 191–207, at 194–97, reprinted in S. Reynolds, *The Middle Ages without Feudalism. Essays in Criticism and Comparison on the Medieval West* (Variorum Collected Studies Series, 1019; Farnham: Ashgate, 2012), no. VI. In 2011 she also focussed on this issue, in 'Fiefs and Vassals after Twelve Years', 17–18 (first delivered in 2006). In 'Use of Feudalism', 192, she again compared my work to that of Co Van de Kieft (see n. 33 above).

[78] Reynolds, *Fiefs and Vassals*, 14, but cf. 17–47, esp. 47 ('having concluded that vassalage is too vacuous a concept to be useful, I shall concentrate my attention primarily on fiefs, which raise much more substantial issues'). Geoffrey Koziol emphasized to me on 28 December 2020 the abundant references to oaths and acts of commendation and alliance in early acts, which merit study and analysis.

[79] In his introduction to *Lordship and Community*, 5, Cheyette noted that fiefs and vassalage had 'been associated with the term "feudalism"' since the construct's invention, and he warned that 'if a historian approaches medieval society primarily in terms of fief and vassalage … [he] must assume, explicitly or implicitly, that fief-holding and vassalage were in fact of primary importance in medieval society, indeed, that they determined its nature'. Cheyette himself compellingly questioned whether 'lordship and vassalage did

Susan Reynolds was, however, resolved. Intent on demonstrating the distortions caused by viewing the past through the 'feudal' spectacles of the construct's defenders,[80] she decided to confront head on their conceptions of 'fiefs' and 'vassals'—as well as the construct itself. In her book *Fiefs and Vassals: The Medieval Evidence Reinterpreted*, published in 1994, she presented her findings in sections delimited by modern rather than medieval political and geographical boundaries, surveying the regions that now constitute France (which she treated at greatest length), Italy, England, and Germany.[81]

form the primary social tie among the class of rulers of late eleventh-century England' (cf. ibid., 9). In contrast, as has been seen, in 'Problem of Feudal Monarchy', 461, Bisson argued the central importance for medieval historians of lordship, vassalage, and the fief. Reynolds, in 'Fiefs and Vassals after Twelve Years', 15, expressed her debt to Cheyette for 'the idea of approaching the subject [of feudalism] … through an investigation of the medieval evidence about fiefs and vassalage, which medievalists have long taken as key institutions of what most of them characterize as feudalism'. She herself indeed believed that '[n]either the great extension of knowledge nor the elaboration of interpretations in the past two centuries seem to have led to serious questioning of the fundamental importance of fief-holding and vassalage' (ibid., 16). More recently, in 2018, Reynolds herself wrote that the 'focus on relations between lords and those whom historians call their vassals has distracted attention from so much else in medieval societies': S. Reynolds, 'Still Fussing about Feudalism', in Ross Balzaretti, Julia Barrow, and Patricia Skinner (eds), *Italy and Early Medieval Europe: Papers for Chris Wickham* (The *Past & Present* Book Series; Oxford: Oxford University Press, 2018), 87–94, at 94.

[80] See, e.g., Reynolds, *Fiefs and Vassals*, 322. The 'feudal' perspective vitiated her attempts to establish the precise nature and function of the so-called *fiefs de reprise* recorded in the French Midi by leading her to assume that they were equivalent to what Italian historians term *feudi oblati* (in German *Lehnsauftragung*), all of which she presented as allodial lands definitively 'converted' into fiefs, as later legal scholars described them: ibid., the various pages referred to in her index, s.v., *fiefs de reprise, feudi oblati, Lehnsauftragung,* and especially 50, 230, 233, 390. In 1687, at the University of Leipzig, Johann Friedrich Egger defined the *feudum oblatum* as 'feudum, quo dominus de re antea ipsi a vasallo sub conditione investiendi tradita, vasallum investit': *De feudis oblatis, Von Aufgetragenen Lehen* … (Leipzig: Andr. Mart. Schedius, 1715), nos. 46–47. Charles-Edmond Perrin gave examples of twelfth-century acts that distinguished German from Italian and French customs governing such fiefs: 111 (*mos theutonicus, Karlenses custume, ius et consuetudo teutonice [romanie] terre*): *La société féodale allemande et ses institutions du Xe au XIIe siècles*, 4 parts (Les cours de Sorbonne, Histoire du Moyen Âge; Paris: Centre de documentation universitaire, 1956–7), II, 111. Cheyette commented on *fiefs de reprise* in his review of Reynolds's book, in *Speculum*, 71:4, 1003–4 ('she does not herself escape the analytical categories of rights and obligations associated with property' in considering 'documents from Montpellier' which reveal 'that scribal words do not always correspond one-to-one with social processes'). Cheyette elaborated on these land transfers and their ceremonial function in twelfth-century Occitania, first (in 1999) in 'On the *fief de reprise*', in *Les sociétés méridionales à l'âge féodal*, 319–24 (at 324, 'a ritual of succession … fix[ing] in the landscape the paired and inseparable values of fidelity and good lordship'), and then (in 2001) in *Ermengard*, 220–32.

[81] Reynolds, *Fiefs and Vassals*, 75–180, 258–322 (France, 168 pp.), 181–257 (Italy, 76 pp.), 323–95 (England, 72 pp.), 396–474 (Germany, 78 pp.). As to Spain, the Spanish Jesuit Luís de Molina (1535–1600) declared 'quamuis frequens sit vsus feudorum in Germania, in Gallia, & in Italia, nullus, aut ferè nullus, est vsus eorum in Hispaniis', although he believed 'Apud Iaponenses nil videri esse frequentiùs, quàm feuda': *De iustitia, Tomus secundus, De contractibus* (Mainz: Balthasar Lippius, sumptibus Arnoldi

Within each area she assessed the relevance of the feudal model to modes of property-holding and dependence during the early and later Middle Ages, and concluded that before the mid-eleventh century what she termed 'classic feudalism' did not exist in any of them.[82] Later, she argued, in the twelfth and thirteenth centuries, 'fiefs' and 'vassals' came to possess something approaching the meaning and significance they possess in the traditional feudal model. This occurred, she contended, through the intervention and actions of two groups of individuals: professional lawyers (some commenting on or inspired by the Lombard *Libri Feudorum*), and officials serving rulers who used grants of land, ties of fidelity, and enforcement of the obligations entailed by these bonds to extend and consolidate their power.[83]

Mylii, 1602), 1055 (disp. 485). See, however, Bisson, 'The Problem of Feudal Monarchy', 463–70. In 'Feudalism in Twelfth-Century Catalonia', in the special issue on 'Structures féodales et féodalisme', *Publications de l'École Française de Rome*, 44 (1980), 173–92, Bisson concluded that Catalonia 'could be called a "feudal monarchy" ... only in a severely qualified sense', involving 'diffusion and diversity', and that it was characterized 'by a feudalism distinctively her own'. The paper was reprinted in Bisson, *Medieval France and her Pyrenean Neighbors: Studies in Early Institutional History* (Studies Presented to the International Commission for the History of Representative and Parliamentary Institutions, 70; London: Hambledon Press, 1989), 153–78, no. 7. For Spain, see below, at and following n. 110; see also the comments of Steffen Patzold, *Das Lehnswesen* (Beck-'sche Reihe, Wissen; Munich: C. H. Beck, 2012), 58–63. Fuller consideration of the Latin kingdom of Jerusalem and Cyprus might have affected Reynolds's conclusions: Abels, 'Historiography of a Construct', 1023–4, 1028n. 52, giving bibliography. Peter W. Edbury has cautioned that 'the absence of evidence ... is not evidence that ... features did not exist' although he has also emphasized that 'Frankish society in the twelfth century was not tidy; nor was it schematized', and, citing Joshua Prawer, has stressed that 'the Frankish conquest of the Holy Land at the start of the twelfth century did not entail the importation of a fully-fledged "feudal system" from the West'. See Peter W. Edbury, 'Fiefs, vassaux et service militaire dans le royaume latin de Jérusalem', in Michel Balard and Alain Ducellier (eds), *Le partage du monde. Échanges et colonisation dans la Méditerranée médiévale* (Paris: Publications de la Sorbonne, 1998), 141–50, at 142–5, reprinted in Edbury, *Law and History in the Latin East* (Variorum Collected Studies Series, 1048; Aldershot: Ashgate, 2014), no. I; and 'Fiefs and Vassals in the Kingdom of Jerusalem, from the Twelfth Century to the Thirteenth', *Crusades*, 1 (Aldershot: Ashgate, for the Society for the Study of the Crusades and the Latin East, 2002), 49–62, at 50, 52–53, reprinted in his *Law and History in the Latin East*, no. II.

[82] In *Fiefs and Vassals*, 115–23, Reynolds enumerated problems she confronted in developing her hypotheses: the hazard of 'generalization about property rights' when there was 'probably ... a great deal of local variation'; the 'danger of teleology'; the difficulty of establishing the meaning(s) of words used to designate property holdings, including the 'uncertain' relationship between words and phenomena. For her ideas and methodology, see particularly ibid., 166, 179–80, 259.

[83] Reynolds, *Fiefs and Vassals*, 256–59, 270–8, 288, 320. In her conclusion, as earlier in her book, Reynolds privileged governmental over legal activity to explain systematization of property holding: *Fiefs and Vassals*, 74, 478–79 ('increasingly bureaucratic government and expert law'), 482 ('the development of the new sort of government and law'); see, however, 180, 257, 278, and also 235–40 and 257 (Frederick Barbarossa's 'rather patchy' development of feudal administrative and governmental devices). In 2012 she laid greater emphasis on the role of 'academic lawyers': see the 'Introduction' to *The Middle Ages without Feudalism*, ix–xv, at xiii. See too her earlier discussion of professional law and

This conclusion echoes the position of Charles-Edmond Petit-Dutaillis and subsequent historians of 'feudal monarchy', who have depicted rulers (and particularly Philip Augustus of France) as acquiring and solidifying power by enlisting administrators and jurists to fashion a systematic feudal régime with the ruler at its summit,[84] which in 1978 Thomas Bisson characterized as the 'feudalizing of royal power'.[85] Such a notion, yet another construct, risks obscuring the nature and number of strategies rulers used to increase their authority, whereas characterizing as feudal the administrative records compiled by rulers prejudges the possibly—indeed likely—diverse reasons for their appearance and the varied uses to which rulers put them.[86] Recognizing

lawyers in 'Afterthoughts on *Fiefs and Vassals*', first published in *Haskins Society Journal*, 9 (2001, for 1997), 1–15, at 13–14, reprinted in *The Middle Ages without Feudalism*, no. I.

[84] C.-E. Petit-Dutaillis, *La monarchie féodale en France et en Angleterre, X^e–XIIIe siècle* (L'Évolution de l'Humanité, Synthèse collective, 41; 2ème Section [*La reconstitution du pouvoir monarchique*]; Paris, La renaissance du livre, 1933), where, at 2–3, he underscored the role of 'the jurists', whom he presented as 'co-ordinat[ing] and systematis[ing] the practices of the administration'; see also ibid., 223, 246–47, 336–47 ('Le roi seigneur supérieur'), and the conclusion, 424–27, which stressed the importance of Roman law in promoting the growth of monarchical power without insisting on 'feudal' elements; tr. as *The Feudal Monarchy in France and England from the Tenth to the Thirteenth Century*, trans. E. D. Hunt (London: Kegan Paul, Trench, Trubner & Co., 1936), 2, 200, 220, 301–10, and 376–9. In relation to Philip Augustus, and royal and comital administrative record-keeping, see: Josette Metman, 'Les inféodations royales d'après le "Recueil des actes de Philippe Auguste"', in Robert-Henri Bautier (ed.), *La France de Philippe Auguste: le temps des mutations. Actes du Colloque international organisé par le C.N.R.S. (Paris, 29 septembre–4 octobre 1980)* (Colloques internationaux du CNRS, 602; Paris, Éditions du Centre National de la Recherche Scientifique, 1982), 503–17, at 517; John F. Benton, 'Written Records and the Development of Systematic Feudal Relations', in John F. Benton, *Culture, Power and Personality in Medieval France*, ed. Thomas N. Bisson (London: Hambledon Press, 1991), 275–90 (a paper presented at a conference at the Centre for Medieval Studies in Toronto, 6–7 November 1981); Bisson, 'Problem of Feudal Monarchy', 474, and also 461; John W. Baldwin and C. Warren Hollister, 'The Rise of Administrative Kingship: Henry I and Philip Augustus', *American Historical Review*, 83:4 (October 1978), 867–905, at 881, 895–96, 901, 903–4; John W. Baldwin, *Knights, Lords, and Ladies: In Search of Aristocrats in the Paris Region, 1180–1220* (The Middle Ages Series: Philadelphia: University of Pennsylvania Press: 2019), 121, the conclusion of a chapter examining royal registers and surveys (ibid., 101–21).

[85] Bisson, 'Problem of Feudal Monarchy', 477, who also wrote of the 'feudalizing' of rural settlements, the 'de-feudalizing of royal administration', and the 'very retarded [feudalizing]' in Picardy (commenting on the work of Robert Fossier) (ibid., 466, 474). Bisson offered useful comments on the historiography of the notion and the phrase, ibid., 461–62.

[86] In 'The Chancery Archives of the Counts of Champagne: Codicology and History of the Cartulary-Registers', *Viator*, 16 (1985), 159–79, Theodore Evergates argued (ibid., 178) that the volumes 'were primarily memorial books produced during moments of institutional insecurity', rather than volumes compiled for administrative purposes. See also Evergates's introduction to his edition, Littere Baronum: *The Earliest Cartulary of the Counts of Champagne* (Medieval Academy Books, 107; Toronto: University of Toronto Press, 2003), 3–22. See also Constance Brittain Bouchard, *Sword, Miter, and Cloister: Nobility and the Church in Burgundy, 980–1198* (Ithaca NY: Cornell University Press,

these difficulties, Reynolds acknowledged them. While she did not describe the precise strategies pursued by these lawyers and administrators, the exact definitions and conceptions of 'fiefs' and 'vassals' that resulted from their activity, the ways in which their work affected actual practice, the nature of the systematization to which they contributed, or its relative importance among the many means of expanding power and authority that rulers pursued, she made clear that these topics, with others, 'deserve much closer study'.[87]

In addition to stressing the need for further inquiry into the development of centralized governance, since 1994 Reynolds has continued to press for progress in revisiting the evidence without the misleading presuppositions the feudal constructs encourage.[88] In 2012 she advocated exploring 'collective values and activities in medieval government and law', including 'government by consultation and consensus', 'collective judgements, and the belief in natural, given units of society and politics bound together by descent, law, and custom'.[89] Surveying the field in 2018, in what she declared was her swan-song to feudalism, she noted that there was 'still a great deal to investigate, including rights of property and collective bonds and conflicts'.[90]

Thus, in the end, Reynolds's ultimate objective has been the same as mine: to persuade historians to reevaluate the surviving testimony concerning medieval Europe with open minds and full awareness of the problems caused by reliance on feudal models. But in 1994 this larger goal was eclipsed by Reynolds's proximate goal of proving the irrelevance of fiefs and vassals to early medieval society and the systematization of the institutions of fiefs and

1987), 37–43; and the introduction and conclusion by Patrick Geary and Michel Parisse to Olivier Guyotjeannin, Laurent Morelle, and Michel Parisse (eds), *Les cartulaires. Actes de la Table ronde organisée par l'École nationale des chartes et le G.D.R. 121 du C.N.R.S. (Paris, 5–7 décembre 1991)* (Mémoires et documents de l'École des chartes, 39; Paris: École des chartes, 1993), 13–24 (Geary, 'Entre gestion et *gesta*'), 503–11 (Parisse, 'Conclusion'). Also important are essays in Jean-François Nieus (ed.), *Le vassal, le fief et l'écrit: pratiques d'écriture et enjeux documentaires dans le champ de la féodalité (XIᵉ–XVᵉ s.). Actes de la journée d'étude organisée à Louvain-la-Neuve le 15 avril 2005* (Textes, Études, Congrès, 23; Louvain-la-Neuve: Université catholique de Louvain, 2007), especially those by Nieus, Dirk Heirbaut (esp. at 98), and Karl-Heinz Spiess (esp. at 160 and 167).

[87] Reynolds, *Fiefs and Vassals*, 215–31, where she presented a number of hypotheses; see particularly 225. The work of Gérard Giordanengo on the feudists of the twelfth through the sixteenth centuries casts considerable doubt on the general (and practical) importance of their writings and debates, and on the influence they may have exercised (directly or indirectly) on rulers and their officials: Gérard Giordanengo, 'La littérature juridique féodale', in Nieus (ed.), *Le vassal, le fief et l'écrit*, 11–34. See as well the chapter 'Les féodalités italiennes', which Giordanengo contributed to Bournazel and Poly (eds), *Les féodalites*, 211–62, where, adopting a feudal perspective in deference to the book's orientation, he demonstrated the diversity of institutions in Italy and the differences among Italian feudists.

[88] Reynolds, 'Fiefs and Vassals after Twelve Years', 25–26.

[89] Reynolds, 'Introduction', *The Middle Ages Without Feudalism*, ix–xv, at xiv.

[90] Reynolds, 'Still Fussing about Feudalism', 94.

vassalage by centralized powers from the late twelfth century onwards.[91] Her concentration on fiefs and vassals permitted and, in some measure, encouraged scholars sympathetic to feudalism to focus as before on its traditional components and the development of feudal monarchy.[92]

'HOW IT REALLY WAS': THE PROSPECTS FOR THE FUTURE

In 1998, twenty-four years after I launched my attack, Constance Brittain Bouchard endorsed my challenge to reject the feudal constructs, which she declared 'an eminently sensible suggestion that has regrettably not yet been fully adopted'. Noting that '[m]any medievalists, especially in the United States, have dropped the term entirely',[93] she suggested, encouragingly, that the cause would one day be triumphant. Some progress had evidently been made since 1981, when John F. Benton declared that my article 'should have led historians to think at least twice before using the term "feudalism" and yet has had strikingly little effect'.[94] Nonetheless, there was (and is) a long way to go before the constructs are vanquished. Little wonder that in 2003 Fredric Cheyette called impatiently on his colleagues to stop 'bother[ing] with

[91] In 'Fiefs and Vassals after Twelve Years', 15–16, Reynolds acknowledged that the book 'had a relatively narrow scope' and 'became increasingly negative, as, to my increasing surprise, I gradually found how scarce was the medieval evidence, especially before the thirteenth century, for the concepts or phenomena that modern medievalists characterize as noble fief-holding and vassalage'.

[92] In her review of Reynolds's book, almost a hundred pages long, Magnou-Nortier, 'La féodalité en crise. Propos sur "Fiefs and Vassals" de Susan Reynolds', focussed on the meanings of specific Latin and vernacular terms. In 1998, Jim Bradbury cited Reynolds's book in concluding that 'at about the time of Philip Augustus something akin to feudalism was becoming visible' and that 'Philip and his government [probably] contributed to this development': *Philip Augustus, King of France 1180–1223* (London: Longman, 1998), 227–30 (esp. 228 and 229n. 30, referring to Reynolds's book), 234. Reynolds's arguments persuaded Dirk Heirbaut of the necessity of continuing to study 'feudalism' in order to produce different and better constructs to replace those she attacked: Heirbaut, 'Dispute Resolution. Feudalism', available on Heirbaut's website, with a translation into German forthcoming (in D. von Mayenburg et al. (eds), *Geschichte der Konfliktlösung in Europa. Ein Handbuch*); and Dirk Heirbaut, 'The Quest for the Sources of a Non-Bureaucratic Feudalism: Flemish Feudalism during the High Middle Ages (1000–1300)', in Nieus (ed.), *Le vassal, le fief et l'écrit*, 97–122, at 122. In his own work Heirbaut distinguishes between 'real' and 'personal' feudalism; see Heirbaut, 'Flanders: A Pioneer of State-Oriented Feudalism? Feudalism as an Instrument of Comital Power in Flanders during the High Middle Ages (1000–1300)', in Anthony Musson (ed.), *Expectations of the Law in the Middle Ages* (Woodbridge and Rochester: Boydell & Brewer, 2001), 23–34, at 24.

[93] C.M. Bouchard, *"Strong of Body, Brave and Noble": Chivalry and Society in Medieval France* (Ithaca: Cornell University Press, 1998), 35–46, esp. 35, 37.

[94] Benton, 'Written Records and the Development of Systematic Feudal Relations', 275n. 1.

"feudalism", the *mutation féodale* [and] "feudal revolution"', and 'abandon [them] and all their works and blandishments'.[95]

Predictably, the feudal constructs have retained much of their allure. Their general popular appeal as simple keys to the past explains why journalists still use them as they do, with abandon and remarkable imprecision.[96] So too do scholars and researchers writing textbooks and works directed at a wide and general readership. Let me give two examples.

In the survey of French history through 1799 that James B. Collins wrote in 2002 for the Thomson Learning Academic Resource Center,[97] 'feudal monarchy' is the second of four periods into which he divided French history through 1799.[98] A chapter on 'State and Society in Medieval France' focuses on 'feudalism', said to have been 'born' between the late tenth- and early twelfth-century, and to have 'created a synthesis of the rural institutions and the central state'.[99] Collins wrestled with the construct, whose relevance to 'the reality of political life' he questioned.[100] Still, in his view, it was feudalism, defined as 'the integrated hierarchy of a pyramid of homages', that advanced

---

[95] F.L. Cheyette, 'Some Reflections on Violence, Reconciliation, and the Feudal Revolution', in Warren Brown and Piotr Górecki (eds), *Conflict in Medieval Europe. Changing Perspectives on Society and Culture* (Aldershot, Hants., and Burlington VT: Ashgate, 2003), 243–64, at 245–46 and 258. Cheyette noted that proponents of the mutational, transformational approaches had difficulty 'accommodat[ing] the discoveries of detailed research in the sources' (ibid., 247). In Cheyette, 'George Duby's *Mâconnais*', 303, he declared himself unable to discern traces of a 'crisis of the year 1000' or a 'feudal revolution' in documents from the Midi. Warren Brown and Piotr Górecki provide a useful survey of the debates over feudal revolution and mutation, in their essay, 'What Conflict Means: The Making of Medieval Conflict Studies in the United States, 1970–2000', in Brown and Górecki (eds), *Conflict in Medieval Europe*, 1–35, at 27–33; see also Stephen D. White, 'Tenth-Century Courts at Mâcon and the Perils of Structuralist History: Re-reading Burgundian Judicial Institutions', in ibid., 37–68, at 37–38nn. 2 and 3; Patrick Boucheron, 'An mil et féodalisme', in Christian Delacroix, François Dosse, Patrick Garcia, and Nicolas Offenstadt (eds), *Historiographies. Concepts et débats*, 2 vols (Folio Histoire; Paris: Gallimard, 2010), 952–66, on which see Buc, 'What is Order? In the Aftermath of the "Feudal Transformation" Debates', 289–94.

[96] See, e.g., Miriam Pawel, 'California Calls It "Feudalism"', *New York Times* (14 September 2019), A27; and David Brooks, 'The Case for New Optimism', *New York Times* (22 January 2021), A23.

[97] J.B. Collins, *From Tribes to Nation: The Making of France 500–1799* (Toronto: Wadsworth: 2002), iii.

[98] *From Tribes to Nation*, v; see also J.B. Collins, *The State in Early Modern France* (New Approaches to European History; Cambridge: Cambridge University Press, 1995), 1–6.

[99] Collins, *From Tribes to Nation*, 35–85, esp. 35, 52–53 ('The Birth of Feudalism'); the next chapter 'The Origins of France and of Western Civilization, 1095–1270', ibid., 87–135, features the Church, towns, and culture (ibid., 35).

[100] Collins, *From Tribes to Nation*, 56–57. Collins wrestled elsewhere with the problems associated with the construct: ibid., 36, 40–43, 57. In his introduction (ibid., vi) he stressed his desire 'to inquire about lived life', and 'to offer readers a small taste of human life in France'.

the development 'of a more cohesive kingdom', until, in the sixteenth century, the king 'assert[ed] his absolute right to make law'.[101]

In books combining history and travel, published in 1994 and 2011, Ina Caro repeatedly invoked the feudal constructs, attesting to their popularity and marketability. In *The Road from the Past: Traveling through History in France*,[102] she suggested visiting the 'feudal fortress' of Cinq-Mars-la-Pile in the Loire valley because it '[fit] to perfection the type of building fashionable in 1050, when feudalism was the rage'.[103] She recommended visits to castles in the Dordogne valley for the spring, 'which was', she wrote, 'the height of the feudal social season'.[104] In a second book, insisting on 'the chaos of the feudal world', Caro declared that '[i]n many ways, the feudal system [was not] terribly good for business'.[105]

Some scholarly publications and conferences demonstrated the constructs' vigour, despite indications that fidelity to them was weakening. In 1995 a collaborative historical dictionary on medieval France contained numerous articles written from the classic 'feudal' perspective by a number of colleagues who had (and have) supported my crusade—and who cited my work in their entries. Dedicated to 'feudalism', 'fief/*feudum*', 'fief holding', and '*fief-rente*', and to 'aids', 'feudal aids', and 'feudal incidents',[106] the entries, by John Bell Henneman, Theodore Evergates, Constance B. Bouchard, and Stephen Morillo, raise some doubts about the appropriateness of the feudal constructs and their appendages. Still, the presence of the terms, traditionally defined, in a dictionary compiled as a general reference work suggests the endorsement and approval of the dictionary's editors (and doubtless publisher).

In 1998, with the collaboration of nine colleagues, Eric Bournazel and Jean-Pierre Poly presented *Les féodalités* as one of the world's chief political systems, in a volume more than 800 pages long. In the first portion, the histories of the various countries that once constituted medieval Europe were viewed from a feudal perspective with emphasis on elements deemed

[101] Collins, *From Tribes to Nation*, 53–59.

[102] Ina Caro, *The Road from the Past: Traveling through History in France* (A Harvest Book; Harcourt Brace, 1994); in an endorsement on the cover Arthur Schlesinger, Jr., praised the book as '[t]horoughly delightful, the essential traveling companion'.

[103] Caro, *Road from the Past*, 5.

[104] Caro, *Road from the Past*, 117.

[105] Ina Caro, *Paris to the Past. Traveling through French History by Train* (New York: W. W. Norton, 2011), 30, 34.

[106] William W. Kibler and Grover A. Zinn (eds), *Medieval France: An Encyclopedia* (New York and London: Garland, 1995). I contributed articles on Philip IV the Fair and his sons Louis X and Philip V. See also Steffen Patzold, *Das Lehnswesen* (Munich: C.H. Beck, 2012), comments at 121, and notably the succinct definition of the feudal 'model' he gives at 9–12, and the simplified graphic representation he presented on the book's final page at 129. With Reynolds, Patzold figures prominently in the nine essays, all focussed on the concept of feudalism rather than medieval society and politics, in Simon Growth (ed.), *Der geschichtliche Ort der historischen Forschung. Das 20. Jahrhundert, das Lehnswesen und der Feudalismus* (Normative Orders, 28; Frankfurt/New York: Campus Verlag, 2020).

feudal, and, in the second, shorter, part, the universality of the concept was tested in segments examining the traces of 'feudal' elements discernible in the ancient near East, the Hellenistic world, China, southeast Asia, and Japan. The contributors demonstrated the pliability and adaptability of the constructs and sometimes questioned their relevance, and in the end Bournazel and Poly proclaimed that no true 'feudal system' could be found except in the west and in Japan. There, they contended, 'ties of dependence, which contained and structured the violence of warfare, impregnated all of society [my translation]',[107] whereas elsewhere other relationships, particularly familial, were more prominent. The vagueness of this definition and the hesitations expressed in some of the articles were heartening.

At least two important conferences focussed directly and explicitly on feudalism, thus, like Bournazel's and Poly's emphasis on *féodalités*, witnessing the significance and importance attributed to the construct—even though the speakers took a variety of different positions.

A conference held in Bergen, Norway, in September 2006, aimed to disclose 'new landscapes of debate' about feudalism. The papers, published in 2011, revealed a range of attitudes to the term.[108] The newness of the landscape lay not so much in the views that were expressed, but in the overall lack of enthusiasm for feudalism. To be sure, some speakers supported and used the construct. Others, however, disregarded it. Still, others denied its usefulness and denounced it as a hindrance to productive research. In the end, the conveners of the conference (who edited the resulting volume) sided with the constructs, although they acknowledged that the issues were far from simple. While cautioning that 'Feudalism in practice differs considerably from Ganshof's neat picture—in itself not intended as a complete picture of practice over the whole feudal area', they concluded that 'it seems premature to pronounce its death at the present moment'.[109] Clearly, their faith in feudalism was not complete, and the fact that they mentioned the possibility of its death was encouraging. But support it they did, even if most of the participants did not.

At the conference in Bergen, Adam J. Kosto, a devotee of feudalism, regretted Spain's absence from volumes and conferences focussed on

[107] Poly and Bournazel, 'Conclusion générale', in Poly and Bournazel (eds), *Les féodalités*, 751–74, at 753–54.

[108] See n. 20 above. Sverre Bagge, Michael H. Gelting, and Thomas Lindkvist, the editors of the conference volume, analyzed the standpoints of the different contributors, in their 'Introduction', *Feudalism, New Landscapes of Debate*, 1–13; see also my review of the book, available online in *The Medieval Review* '12.06.10, Bagge, Feudalism'. For the essay that Fredric Cheyette wrote for the conference but published apart, in 2010, see n. 24 above.

[109] 'Introduction' to Bagge, Gelting, and Lindkvist (eds), *Feudalism, New Landscapes of Debate*, 5, 13.

feudalism, and called for 'a place at the table' for Iberia and 'Iberian feudalism'.[110] His wish was answered in 2019, when in September, at the University of Salamanca, an international conference focussed on 'Los procesos de formación del feudalismo. La Península Ibérica en el contexto europeo', celebrating and assessing a book published in 1978 by Abilio Barbero and Marcelo Vigil, *La formación del feudalismo en la Peninsula Ibérica*.[111] The conference papers have not yet been published, but attitudes toward the benefit of applying the constructs to the history of Iberia were mixed. In his paper, entitled 'Feudalism and Social Reordering in Eleventh-Century Francia', Charles West straddled the fence, declaring that 'feudalism can be a helpful heuristic device for some historians', particularly those interested in structure and 'explicitly systematic social theory', while focussing his own attention on the Peace of God and the 'gigantic aristocratic kinship network' created by noble marriage alliances.[112]

As the division of opinions at these conferences show, since the turn of the century inroads have been made into feudalism's authority. It is encouraging to find Barbara Rosenwein acknowledging in her textbook, *A Short History of the Middle Ages,* that the term 'feudalism' has been attacked for the 'many different and contradictory ways' it has been used and defined. Even more cheering is her declaration that that the term can 'ordinarily' be dispensed with—although students may be confused by her endorsement of it as a 'fuzzy category' useful for contrasting ancient and medieval society.[113] Still, her statement is a step in the right direction.

However slowly, textbooks and conferences will eventually respond to shifts in scholarship.[114] The fuller and more varied views of medieval social and political life that research unencumbered by feudalism has produced in the past

---

[110] A.J. Kosto, 'What about Spain? Iberia in the Historiography of Medieval European Feudalism', in Bagge, Gelting, and Lindkvist (eds), *Feudalism, New Landscapes of Debate,* 135–58, at 157.

[111] Abilio Barbero and Marcelo Vigil, *La formación del feudalismo en la Peninsula Ibérica* (Crítica /Historia, 4; Barcelona: Editorial Crítica, 1978).

[112] I am grateful to Charles West for sharing his paper with me in advance of publication.

[113] B. Rosenwein, *A Short History of the Middle Ages* (Toronto: University of Toronto Press, 4th edn., 2014), 131. In 1998, Barbara Rosenwein and Lester K. Little edited *Debating the Middle Ages: Issues and Readings* (Malden: Blackwell, 1998). In a section entitled "Feudalism and its Alternatives" (ibid., 105–210), they included my article together with selections from descriptive and analytical works by a number of authors including Dominique Barthélemy and Fredric Cheyette.

[114] Christoph Bramann, *Das 'Lehnswesen' im Geschichtsschulbuch. Bindungsadministrative und fachwissenschaftliche Einflussfaktoren auf die Darstellungen zum Lehnswesen in hessischen Geschichtsschubüchern für das Gymnasium zwischen 1945 und 2014* (Georg Eckert Institut: Beiträge 2017, urn:nbn:de.0220-2017-0228), https://repository.gei.de/handle/11428/271 [1 February 2021], demonstrates how little effect scholarly debate about and research on feudalism has had on medieval history textbooks in Hesse. I thank Dr. Bramann for sharing with me his ideas about his research.

decades give reason to hope for more radical change and the final rejection of the constructs in the not-too-distant future.[115]

Historians who have plumbed the sources with humanistic, geographical, and anthropological rather than feudal lenses have described social and political mechanisms and institutions striking for their diversity and their testimony to the human ability to adapt to variable circumstances. Finer and more probing accounts of medieval property-holding, dispute resolution, and manipulations of authority have been written, and the persistence of feudal and seignorial customs and payments after 1500 has attracted notice.[116] Let me give a few examples.

Fredric Cheyette's book on Ermengard of Narbonne, published in 2001, dramatically demonstrated the dispensability of feudalism, and the solid advantages that accrue from its absence.[117] Focussing on Ermengard and her associates, the power she exercised and the means she used to enforce her authority, the social conditions of her subjects, and the ties of fidelity that informed relationships, Cheyette demonstrated the intricate complexities of lordship and life in Ermengard's Occitania.

Hélène Débax has shown that the society of the region Cheyette investigated conformed to none of the feudal models.[118] Although she often uses feudal vocabulary, her work reveals the same diversity that Cheyette described.[119] Demonstrating her investment in and commitment to the sources, an extensive collection of acts documenting variations among tenurial

[115] See the work surveyed by Buc, 'What is Order? In the Aftermath of the "Feudal Transformation" Debates', esp., 281–82, 286–88, 291–92, 296.

[116] See my essay, 'On 1500', in Peter Linehan and Janet L. Nelson (eds), *The Medieval World* (London: Routledge, 2001), 691–710, at 694–98; in the 2nd edn., ed. Peter Linehan, Janet L. Nelson, and Marios Costambeys (London: Routledge, 2018), 811–30, at 814–18. For evidence supporting my hypotheses, see Giordanengo, 'La littérature juridique féodale', 26–27; and also Antheun Janse, 'Feudal Registration and the Study of Nobility: The Burgundian Registers of 1475', in Nieus (ed.), *Le vassal, le fief et l'écrit*, 173–87; Henri Sée, 'La portée du régime seigneurial au XVIIIᵉ siècle', *Revue d'histoire médiévale et contemporaine*, 103 (1908), 173–91; Albert Soboul, 'La Révolution française et la "féodalité". Notes sur le prélèvement féodal', *Revue historique*, 2401 (1968), 33–56; and James Lowth Goldsmith, *Les Salers et les d'Escorailles, seigneurs de Haute Auvergne, 1500–1789*, trans. Jacques Buttin (Publications de l'Institut d'Études du Massif Central, 25; Faculté des lettres et sciences humaines, Université de Clermont-Ferrand II; Clermont-Ferrand: Institut d'Études du Massif Central, 1984), esp. 218.

[117] Cheyette, *Ermengard of Narbonne and the World of the Troubadours*. See above, notes 32 and 80.

[118] H. Débax, 'L'aristocratie languedocienne et la société féodale: le témoignage des sources (Midi de la France: XIᵉ et XIIᵉ siècles)', in Bagge, Gelting, and Lindkvist (eds), *Feudalism, New Landscapes of Debate*, 77–100, at 78 ('une société qui n'est conforme ni au modèle de Ganshof, ni au modèle des feudistes').

[119] H. Débax, *La féodalité languedocienne. XIᵉ–XIIᵉ siècles. Serments, hommages et fiefs dans le Languedoc des Trencavel* (Tempus; Toulouse: Presses universitaires du Mirail 2003), in which the last chapter demonstrates in detail the striking assortment of mechanisms the Trencavel lords used to secure their power (ibid., 269–325).

arrangements accompanies her 2012 study of collective lordship of castles in northern and southern medieval France.[120]

In another domain Felice Lifshitz has demonstrated the liberating effects of discarding assumptions anchored in and fostered by the feudal model in analyzing such texts as the *Gesta Normannorum* of Dudo of Saint-Quentin.[121] Setting aside traditionally conceived notions of 'feudo-vassalic relations', aiming to grasp 'the contextualized usage of language', she attends to the 'multi-faceted' range of words and phrases that designate landed holdings, grants, gifts, and personal relationships, which she characterizes as 'sociopolitical vocabulary'.[122] Such an approach rejects the over-simplifications associated with the feudal model and reveals not only the richly diverse fabric of the societies in which the words were used but also the reasons why the texts have been misconstrued when viewed from feudalism's perspective.

Fuller understanding of the invention of the constructs has also made even clearer their irrelevance to medieval society. Fashioned in the late sixteenth and early seventeenth centuries by lawyers and philosophers seeking to provide a simple and easily comprehensible explanation of current institutions and practices, they reflect the influence of the styles of scientific and philosophical

---

[120] H. Débax, *La seigneurie collective. Pairs, pariers, paratge: les coseigneurs du XIe au XIIIe siècle* (Collection 'Histoire': Rennes: Presses universitaires de Rennes, 2012), esp. 343–429; see the review by Theodore Evergates, in *American Historical Review* 118:5 (2013), 1581.

[121] F. Lifshitz, 'Translating "Feudal" Vocabulary', in Lifshitz, *Writing Normandy*, 206–24, esp. 206–7, 210–11, 213, 217 ('feudo-vassalic relations, as traditionally conceived, fail to help us understand Dudo's sociopolitical vocabulary'); see also F. Lifshitz, 'Viking Normandy: Dudo of St. Quentin's *Gesta Normannorum*' (her introduction to her online translation of the *Gesta Normannorum*, written in 1996 and revised in 2008), in Lifshitz, *Writing Normandy*, 181–87, at 186–87; and F. Lifshitz, 'Still Useless After All These Years: The Concept of "Hagiography" in the Twenty-First Century', in Lifshitz, *Writing Normandy*, 26–45, at 29n. 10. On 19 July 2019, Stephen D. White promised in an email to tell me when next 'we have a chance to talk about it face to face' his reasons for featuring the 'fief' in the title of a paper on *Raoul de Cambrai* despite the fact that the word does not appear in the poem itself, where 'terre' is often found. See White, 'The Discourse of Inheritance in Twelfth-Century France: Alternative Models of the Fief in "Raoul de Cambrai"', in George Garnett and John G. Hudson (eds), *Law and Government in Medieval England and Normandy: Essays in Honour of Sir James Holt* (Cambridge: Cambridge University Press, 1994), 173–97, reprinted in White, *Re-Thinking Kinship and Feudalism in Early Medieval Europe* (Variorum Collected Studies, 823; Aldershot and Burlington VT: Ashgate Variorum, 2005), no. V; Buc discussed White's ideas in 'What is Order? In the Aftermath of the "Feudal Transformation" Debates', 293–94. Patrick Wormald described the poem as 'the most eloquent testimonial to the passions aroused by lords and their patronage', as he called on historians to focus on 'lordship'—rather than the 'fief'—in investigating eleventh- and twelfth-century Europe. See Wormald's review of Reynolds, *Fiefs and Vassals*, in *Times Literary Supplement* (10 March 1995), 12.

[122] Lifshitz, 'Translating "Feudal" Vocabulary', in Lifshitz, *Writing Normandy*, 207, 211, 217, 222; see also her references to 'sociopolitical discourse', ibid., 207, 209–10, 212–13.

thinking and conceptualization associated with Nicolaus Copernicus (1473–1543), Galileo Galilei (1564–1642), and Isaac Newton (1642–1727).[123] In 1608 *feudalité* appeared in the work of Charles Loyseau (1566–1627), and a century later Henri, count of Boulainvilliers (1658–1722), attributed to Charlemagne the introduction of 'la police des Fiefs', whereas Nicolas Brussel (†1750) sought the 'essence primodiale' of the fief and wrote that between the eleventh and the thirteenth centuries 'tout en France étoit en fief, ou apartenance de fief'. In England Henry Spelman (†1641) pursued the fief to Roman times and declared the 'feudal law' 'the Law of Nations ... in our Western Orb', whereas Thomas Madox (1666–1727) devised 'the feudal system' and introduced it to England, half a century before the word feudalism and the notion of the feudal pyramid were launched.[124] The opposition to the oversimplification and distortion this systematization entailed was from the start eloquent, articulate, but ineffective in the face of feudalism's popularity. Finally the balance seems to be shifting.

CONCLUSION

Feudalism and such kindred abstractions as the feudal system, feudal society, feudal monarchy are powerful enemies because of their simplicity, familiarity, versatility, and the endorsement respected scholars and teachers have, over the centuries, given them. These qualities, however, are no substitute for truth and accuracy, which the feudal constructs demonstrably lack. Invented centuries after the period they purport to describe, the concepts deform, distort, and caricature medieval society by oversimplifying the complex reality they are said to represent. As Louis Chantereau Le Febvre (1588–1658)[125] and many others have insisted, the constructs are and always have been misleading and

[123] Brown, 'Reflections on Feudalism', 140–54. Cf. the thumbnail sketches given by Reynolds and Cheyette, with both of whom I shared my findings about the creation of the constructs. See Reynolds, *Fiefs and Vassals*, 3–14 (referring to my work on 3n. 4); Reynolds, 'Still Fussing about Feudalism', 87, 91–94; and Reynolds, 'The Historiography of Feudalism in France', Osamu Kano and Jean-Loup Lemaître (eds), with Takashi Adachi, Yoshiya Nishimura, and Michel Sot, *Entre texte et histoire. Études d'histoire médiévale offertes au professeur Shoichi Sato* (De l'archéologie à l'histoire; Paris: Éditions de Boccard, 2015), 293–308, at 293 (esp. n. 1), 295, 303–4. See Cheyette, 'Some Notations', 6–7; Cheyette, *Lordship and Community*, 5; Cheyette, 'Some Reflections on Violence', 244–45; and Cheyette, '"Feudalism": A Memoir', 119–30. In 2005 Cheyette prepared a short article on 'Feudalism' for the *Dictionary of the History of Ideas* that was never published but that can be consulted (as 'Feudalism. Preprint for the *Dictionary of the History of Ideas*') on the site devoted to Cheyette's publications at Amherst College https://amherst.academia.edu/FredricCheyette/Papers [1 February 2021].

[124] Brown, 'Reflections on Feudalism', 140–54, and see n. 8 above.

[125] See particularly Louis Chantereau Le Febvre, *Traité des fiefs, et de leur origine. Avec les preuves tirées de divers autheurs anciens et modernes ...* (Paris: Louis Billaine, 1662), esp. 2 and 4. Following the *Traité* are two hundred pages of texts (including much of Henry Spelman's *Archæologus ...* [London: John Beale, 1626]) and three hundred pages of collected documents (separately paginated), which range in date from 1091 to 1279.

treacherous decoys obstructing not only understanding of the medieval past but also the search for valid paradigms and models.

Almost half a century after I first denounced them, I am delighted that my call to arms has gained as many adherents as it has.[126] Belief in the constructs' validity and their relevance to an earlier time and society, and conviction that they accurately describe medieval European society have waned in the face of increasingly numerous studies of its complexity, the result of patient, meticulous, and rigorous probing of a multitude of sources, written and material. In the face of such studies, even those who are by nature hedgehogs rather than foxes, who are devoted to theories, principles, and simplicity, have acknowledged the constructs' deficiencies and sometime absurdities, and have begun avoiding their use. In 2021 it is high time for feudalism and the concepts it has spawned to be discarded entirely, except for the light they shed on the thought processes of those who, long ago, invented them and those who, today, stubbornly refuse to jettison them. Historians concerned with regularities will devise models that advance recognition of patterns of human behaviour, rejecting notions fashioned hundreds of years ago by thinkers impressed by scientific systematizers and familiar with but a fraction of the sources now available to shed light on the intricate workings of medieval society. Investigating medieval society and government undistracted by the feudal prism,[127] historians will frame ever more nuanced and sensitive—and truer—accounts of the human beings whose thoughts and actions we seek to comprehend and illuminate.[128]

---

[126] I have been particularly heartened by a paper David Snyder presented in January 2014, 'The Construct of Feudalism: A War with the "Tyrant"', (available on https://www.academia.edu), and his subsequent description to me (on 15 December 2020) of the resistance he has subsequently mounted to charges that his view of history is 'parochial' because it does not 'give primacy to theoretical debates'.

[127] In a paper entitled 'The Feudal Prism', delivered in October 1989 at the Seventh Colloquium of Soviet and American Historians in Moscow, I argued that the feudal constructs had vitiated understanding of medieval 'lordships, communities, and kingdoms', the topic of the session.

[128] In order to expose the feudal constructs' absurdity (and also, I admit, test the limits of scholarly credulity), in 2004 I wrote a paper concerning my discovery of a *proto-collum feodale* that I claimed to have found among the muniments of Saint-Denis. The *protocollum*, which I attributed to Charlemagne's brother Carloman, features the noun *feodalitas*, the phrases *pyramis feodalis* and *systema feodalis*, and ends 'Vivat feodalitas, vivantque vassalli admirabiles, operatores sui'. The inspiration for the lark was an invitation to present a short paper at Giles Constable's 75th birthday party, where it was taken by some to be a serious report, as it was ten years later at a seminar at the Centre for Medieval Studies at the University of York. To prevent further misunderstanding, I refrain from publishing it here but will gladly make it available to anyone who is interested—on condition that its fictional nature and the circumstances of its creation be fully recognized in any reference to it.

Part II

Concepts in Use

CHAPTER 3

Colony

Peter Crooks

I begin not at the beginning, but with the word: *colony*. Having returned England after sixteen years, disgruntled, disillusioned, a recluse, unable to abide his wife's company except from the far end of a long dining table, a famous traveller reflected upon the one objection that could be raised against him as a discoverer of the remote nations of the world. He had omitted to claim in the name of his Sovereign the countries he had encountered—the lands of the diminutive Lilliputians, of the giants of Brobdingnag, and of the Houyhnhnms, a race of rational horses with whom Lemuel Gulliver (for that was our traveller's name) had come to identify until they expelled him as a base Yahoo who might pollute the ranks of their society. Gulliver explains that it would have been imprudent to conquer such a 'magnanimous nation' as the Houyhnhnms, who should rather be invited to send some of their kind to civilize Europe. But he follows this with 'another Reason which made me less forward to enlarge his Majesty's Dominions by my Discoveries':

> To say the Truth, I had conceived a few Scruples with relation to the distributive Justice of Princes upon those Occasions. … Here commences a new Dominion acquired with a Title by *Divine Right*. Ships are sent with the first Opportunity; the Natives are driven out or destroyed, their Princes tortured to discover their Gold; a free Licence given to all Acts of Inhumanity and Lust; the earth reeking with the Blood of its Inhabitants: And this execrable Crew of Butchers employed in so pious an Expedition, is a *modern Colony* sent to convert and civilize an idolatrous and barbarous People. (*Gulliver's Travels*, IV.12)

P. Crooks (✉)
Department of History, Trinity College, Dublin, Ireland

© The Author(s), under exclusive license to Springer Nature
Switzerland AG 2022
J. W. Armstrong, P. Crooks and A. Ruddick (eds), *Using Concepts in Medieval History*, https://doi.org/10.1007/978-3-030-77280-2_3

This colony of Jonathan Swift's imagination is 'modern' in the sense of not being 'ancient', whereas my concern in this chapter is primarily with what happened in the middle. But I open with *Gulliver's Travels* in order to register at the outset some problems presented by the word 'colony'—problems of *meaning* (that is, of sense and range and reference) and problems of *appraisal* (that is, of moral evaluation or attitude).[1] For all that has been written about colonial and postcolonial mentalities—about Orientalism and colonial discourse, about imperial imaginaries and regimes of racial representation, about colonial knowledge and epistemic violence—the basic term 'colony' has been neglected. We do not have a detailed diachronic study of its lexical semantics or its conceptual history. 'Colony' and 'colonialism' are not among Raymond Williams' *Keywords*. Nor is 'Kolonialismus' a *Begriff* in the *Geschichtliche Grundbegriffe* of Reinhart Koselleck and his collaborators. As Ann Laura Stoler has noted: 'Today, "What is a colony?" barely merits an analytical pause; it remains undisturbed, a quiescent non-question'.[2]

Colonial studies emerged as a serious academic pursuit at precisely the time colonial empires of the modern world ceased to exist in the era of decolonization. As a result, the terms of analysis could not escape their past conceptual histories. The core challenge became, in Frederick Cooper's formulation, how to 'study colonial societies, keeping in mind—but not being paralyzed by—the fact that the tools of analysis we use emerged from the history we are trying to examine?'[3] For medievalists, the danger of analytical paralysis may feel acute. Our terminological challenge is to find an appropriate means of denoting and describing a medieval *phenomenon* in the absence of a contemporary term: this is a problem of categories of analysis. And if the phenomenon exists, how are we to access and retrieve the conceptual world in the absence of the lexical point of entry—the word 'colony'. Recent work on the construction of race and racialized thought in the Middle Ages has faced precisely this problem of bridging the gap between analytical categories and historical ideas. 'Race' is a post-medieval word: but both Steven Epstein and, more recently, Geraldine Heng have argued that notwithstanding absence of the word it is possible to detect 'a way of thinking that closely resembled modern forms of racism, in a vocabulary suited to the times'.[4] The argument here turns on the distinction

[1] Swift's complicated position as an 'anti-colonial colonialist who attacked the oppression which he himself advocated and from which he profited' is examined in Wolfgang Zach, 'Jonathan Swift and Colonialism', *The Canadian Journal of Irish Studies*, 26 (2000), 36–46, at 41.

[2] Ann Laura Stoler, 'Colony', in J.M. Bernstein, Adi Ophir and Ann Laura Stoler (eds), *Political Concepts: A Critical Lexicon* (Fordham University Press: New York, 2018), 45–58, at 46.

[3] Frederick Cooper, *Colonialism in Question: Theory, Knowledge, History* (Berkeley: University of California Press, 2005), 4.

[4] Geraldine Heng, *The Invention of Race in the European Middle Ages* (Cambridge: Cambridge University Press, 2018), 26; Steven Epstein, *Purity Lost: Transgressing Boundaries in the Eastern Mediterranean, 1000–1400* (Baltimore: Johns Hopkins University Press, 2007), 201.

between the linguistic resources available to past actors—the vocabulary of the sources—and the concepts they possessed.

'Colony' is a much older word than 'race'. It derives from a Latin root, *colonia*, whose etymology takes us back to *colonus*, a farmer or tiller of the soil. *Colonus* itself is derived from the verb 'to till'—*colo, colere*—whose fourth principal part *cultus* gives us 'cultivate' and by extension 'culture'. Empire, so we have been told, has always been a 'language of power'.[5] I hope to show by analogy that, even in the Middle Ages, 'colony' masked its raw power in a language of cultivation, in the two primary senses of that word: cultivation as tillage; cultivation as civility.

COLONY AND ITS COGNATES: A LEXICAL CAREER

The lexical, conceptual and definitional neglect of 'colony' is surprising given the remarkable career of *colonia*, and its various cognate forms, from their emergence in English in the mid-sixteenth century. By the time of Gulliver's *Travels into Several Remote Nations of the World* (1726), 'colony' had acquired at least two additional forms: a verb, *to colonize* (1622); and the noun, *colonist* (1701). The great ramification of the term came in the following century, which saw *colonization* (1770), *colonial* (adjective, 1776), a *colonial* (noun, meaning someone from the colonies, 1865), a *colonialism* (noun, meaning a turn of phrase from the colonies, equivalent to a 'provincialism'), *coloniality* (1867), *colonialist* (*adj.* 1867), and, finally, *colonialism* (1886).[6] Swift's vocabulary was simpler, consisting of 'colony' (singular) and 'colonies' (plural), but even this limited lexicon allowed for shades of meaning which reflect two of the principal Classical usages.

The Latin *colonia* originally served as a collective noun for a group of settlers, often veteran soldiers who were sent out to settle at a designated place. The word is encountered in this sense in Classical texts in the idiom *coloniam deducere*, which humanist writers in the sixteenth century picked up and variously rendered as 'deducing colonies', 'translating of colonies', or 'conducting and establishing colonies'.[7] When Swift speaks of 'colonies' plural, he seems to have in mind an animate group of settlers, as when he states that because countries he described 'do not appear to have any desire of being conquered and enslaved, murdered or driven out by colonies', they were 'by no means proper objects of our zeal, our valour, or our interest' (*Gulliver's Travels*, IV.12). Likewise, he can refer to *planting colonies*, as with

---

[5] David Armitage, *The Ideological Origins of the British Empire* (Cambridge: Cambridge University Press, 2000), 29.

[6] These dated citations are drawn from the *Oxford English Dictionary*.

[7] Clare Carroll and Vincent Carey (eds), *Solon His Follie, or, A Politique Discourse Touching the Reformation of Common-Weales Conquered, Declined or Corrupted* (Binghamton, New York: Medieval & Renaissance Texts & Studies, 1996); William Herbert, Arthur Keaveney, and John A. Madden (eds), *Croftus, sive, de Hibernia Liber* (Dublin: Irish Manuscripts Commission, 1992).

his sardonic protest that his description of the modern colony as a site of conquest and massacre 'doth by no means affect the *British* Nation, who may be an Example to the whole World for the Wisdom, Care, and Justice in planting Colonies' (*Gulliver's Travels*, iv.12).[8] A secondary Classical sense of *coloniae*, which came to displace the original collective noun, referred not to animate settlers but to the inanimate place they settled. Roman *coloniae* were military establishments, the newly established and garrisoned settlements which served as the bulwarks of the *imperium Romanum*. Consequently, the Latin idiom became *in coloniam deducere*.[9] When Swift refers to his 'modern colony' in the singular, he does not mean a group of settlers but rather a civil establishment, a new society formed overseas. More importantly, what 'colony' here refers to, its referent, is the outcome of a whole process of discovery, conquest, enslavement, and plantation—a process we might now be content to call 'colonialism'.

I have so far considered the range of meanings that 'colony' can hold; but I also want to consider *reference* and *attitude*. 'Colony' is not a neutral noun. It is a strong 'appraisive' or evaluative word.[10] It appears to have been through the influence of the *studia humanitatis* that the classical term *colonia* was revived among English authors in the sixteenth century to describe the positive social effect of establishing an overseas settlement in vacant or unexploited land overseas. Sir Thomas More's *Utopia* (1516) may have been the first work of English humanism to use the Latin term to describe the positive social effect of establishing an overseas settlement in vacant or unexploited land overseas:

> Wherever the natives have much unoccupied and uncultivated land, they found a colony under their own laws (L. *coloniam suis ipsorum legibus propagant*) … The inhabitants who refuse to live according to their laws, they drive from the territory which they carve out for themselves. … They consider it a most just cause for war when a people that does not use its soil but keeps it idle and waste nevertheless forbids the use and possession of it to others who by the rule of nature ought to be maintained by it.[11]

Thomas More's case that a refusal to allow 'waste' ground to be settled and cultivated might provide a just cause for war and dispossession was taken up in

---

[8] 'Planting colonies' appears in 1584 in Hakluyt's *Discourse on Western Planting*, which refers to 'planting one or two colonies of our nation' in the New World.

[9] R.A. Van Royen, 'Some Observations on the Latin Concept of "Colonia"', *Proceedings of the Dutch Archaeological and Historical Society*, 6 (1975), 30–36, esp. 34.

[10] 'Appraisive' is the word used by Quentin Skinner for terms of this kind: Quentin Skinner,. 'The Idea of a Cultural Lexicon', in *Visions of Politics I: Regarding Method* (Cambridge, Cambridge University Press, 2002).

[11] George M. Logan and Robert M. Adams (eds), *More: Utopia* (Cambridge: Cambridge University Press, 2002), 136–37. For comment: David Armitage, 'Literature and Empire', in *The Oxford History of the British Empire*, i: *The Origins of Empire* (Oxford: Oxford University Press, 1998), 108.

the latter half of the sixteenth century by English authors writing in the vernacular advocating specifically for colonization ventures. Swift was writing within, while also reacting through satire against, a utopian tradition. In describing a 'modern colony' as an 'execrable Crew of Butchers', Swift upends the appraisal. He unmasks 'colony' as a term whose moral significance is to be weighed and contested.

In so doing, Swift foreshadows the definitive change in attitude in the final decades of the nineteenth century. For much of its intellectual history in the Anglophone world—stretching from Sir Thomas More in the sixteenth century to John Stuart Mill in the nineteenth, and well beyond—*colony*'s evaluative force, its moral charge, its intended effect, was positive.[12] At precisely the time that *colonialism* emerged as a term to describe a system of domination—first attested in 1886, the year of the Berlin Conference—*colony* underwent a significant change. In the context of the British empire of the Victorians, the 'colonial empire' referred to the white settler dominions. Now it came to embrace also the non-settler dependencies, above all India under the *Raj*.[13] From referring to the colonizers, *colony* and *colonial* now came to refer to the colonized populations in the era of Europe's 'new imperialism'. A related shift was one of attitude or moral evaluation. 'Colonialism' became a term of attack used to describe a form of power deemed to be illegitimate, first by polemicists and then, after the Second World War, by a self-consciously inter-*national* community. By 1960, the United Nations General Assembly could declare that an 'end must be put to colonialism', which it defined as the 'subjection of peoples to alien subjugation, domination and exploitation'.[14]

Colony, then, experienced a double-layered semantic shift from the late nineteenth century—a movement in reference *away* from the colonists to the colonized, and a change in attitude *away* from the positive to the negative. This had a profound effect on the academic study of colonialism, most fundamentally blurring the issue what constituted the proper objects of analysis. As early as 1870, the French political economist Paul Leroy-Beaulieu (d. 1916) proposed a taxonomy of modern colonies including *colonies de peuplement, colonies d'exploitation, colonies de plantation*.[15] In an effort to sharpen their conceptual tool-kits, twentieth-century scholars elaborated the typologies and specialist usages creating a confusion of compounds—'saltwater colonialism', 'internal colonialism', 'settler colonialism', 'hyper-colonialism'—and

---

[12] Duncan Bell, 'John Stuart Mill on Colonies', in *Reordering the World: Essays on Liberalism and Empire* (Princeton: Princeton University Press, 2016).

[13] D. K. Fieldhouse, *Colonialism, 1870–1945: An Introduction* (London: Weidenfeld and Nicolson, 1981), 6. See also Barbara Cassin et al. (eds), *Dictionary of Untranslatables: A Philosophical Lexicon* (Princeton: Princeton University Press, 2014), 1056–57.

[14] Declaration on the Granting of Independence to Colonial Countries and Peoples. United Nations General Assembly Resolution 1514 (XV), 14 December 1960.

[15] M. Paul Leroy-Beaulieu, *De la colonisation chez les peuples modernes* (Paris: Guillaumin, 1874).

a proliferation of process-driven agglutinations: *decolonization, recoloniza-tion, anticolonialism, neocolonialism, post-colonialism* (with a hyphen) and the ubiquitous *postcolonialism* (without one).[16] In a recent contribution, twelve distinct forms of colonialism are articulated 'distinguished by colonizers' moti-vations'.[17] The semantic movement across these terms is considerable. At first, and maybe second, glance 'internal colonialism' looks like an oxymoron, while 'settler colonialism' is surely a tautology. 'Settler' and 'colonist' were origi-nally so close in meaning as to be used as effective synonyms. But according to Lorenzo Veracini: 'Colonialism and settler colonialism are not merely different, they are in some ways antithetical formations'.[18] That perceived antithesis in meaning is a measure of how far the term had trailed away from its original root.

Then there is the question of periodization. *Colonia* may be a classical term, but a resilient orthodoxy holds that 'colonialism' is peculiar to the modern world—that, indeed, 'it' may be one of modernity's defining features. Two of the best single-volume overviews of *Colonialism* both originally published in German with the single-word title, *Kolonialismus*—by Jürgen Osterhammel (1995) and Wolfgang Reinhard (2011)—begin *c.*1500, with barely a back-wards glance to the Portuguese expansion of the fifteenth century as a prelude to colonialism proper.[19] On the other hand, there is a universalist posi-tion which argues that: 'Colonialism is present throughout history, virtually from the times of the Uruk, so it is not a phenomenon that is exclusive to modern societies. It is a universal position that goes back to the first complex societies'.[20] By encompassing everything, colonialism may explain nothing.

[16] Michael Hechter, *Internal Colonialism: The Celtic Fringe in British National Devel-opment* (University of California Press, 1975); Lorenzo Veracini, '"Settler Colonialism": Career of a Concept', *The Journal of Imperial and Commonwealth History* 41:2 (2013), 313–33; Stuart Ward, 'The European provenance of decolonization', *Past and Present*, no. 230 (2016), 227–60.

[17] Nancy Shoemaker, 'A Typology of Colonialism'. Perspectives on History, October 2015: https://www.historians.org/publications-and-directories/perspectives-on-history/october-2015/a-typology-of-colonialism. The typology enumerates the following types of colonialism developed from North American and Pacific examples: Settler, Planter, Extractive, Trade, Transport, Imperial Power, Not-in-My Backyard, Legal, Rogue, Missionary, Romantic, and Postcolonial Colonialism.

[18] Lorenzo Veracini, 'Introducing: Settler Colonial Studies', *Settler Colonial Studies*, 1:1 (2011), 1–12.

[19] The English-language editions are Jürgen Osterhammel, *Colonialism: A Theoretical Overview* (Princeton: Princeton University Press, 1997); Wolfgang Reinhard, *A Short History of Colonialism* (Manchester: Manchester University Press, 2011).

[20] Maria Eugenia Aubet, *Commerce and Colonization in the Ancient Near East* (Cambridge: Cambridge University Press, 2013), 42–43.

ANOTHER TYRANNOUS CONSTRUCT?

Historians of the Middle Ages who employ the language of 'colony' can hardly ignore the term's semantic range and conceptual instability. The cacophony of discrepant meanings provoked the ancient historian Sir Moses Finley to insist on treating 'colony' as a term of art:

> When I now suggest the need for converting "colony" into a technical term, I am not embarking on the absurd enterprise of trying to change the world's speech habits, or even my own ... I do not mind such metaphors as the 'English colony in Florence' ... any more than I mind 'a nudist colony' or a 'colony of bees'.[21]

Sir Moses may not have objected to 'nudist colony', but his technical definition had the effect of ruling most of the Middle Ages out of colonial history. Little wonder, then, that Marjorie Chibnall cited approvingly the comment of the archaeologist Brad Bartel that 'there are so many definitions of colonialism and imperialism as to make the terms almost useless'.[22]

The utility of a concept depends, however, on the analytical task it is asked to perform. By contrast with the heavily freighted *colonialism* ('a set of political systems involving conquest and rule by a state over other, previously independent and usually distant territories'),[23] *colonization* has travelled light among medievalists—at least, 'colonization' in the weaker sense of migration and settlement that has been current among medievalists since the writings of Richard Koebner (d.1958) and Charles Verlinden (d.1996).[24] 'Colonization' appears to have been particularly popular in the 1990s, an interest perhaps

[21] M.I. Finley, 'Colonies: An Attempt at a Typology', *Transactions of the Royal Historical Society*, 26 (1976), 167–88, at 109. For his comments on the Middle Ages, see esp. ibid., 172–77.

[22] B. Bartel, 'Comparative Historical Archaeology and Anthropological Theory', in Stephen L. Dyson (ed.), *Comparative Studies in the Archaeology of Colonialism* (Oxford: British Archaeological Reports, 1985), 8–37, cited in Brian Golding, *Conquest and Colonisation: the Normans in Britain, 1066–1100*, 2nd ed. (Basingstoke: Palgrave Macmillan, 2013), 167; Francis James West, 'The Colonial History of the Norman Conquest?', *History: Journal of the Historical Association*, 84 (1999), 219–36 (at 224); Marjorie Chibnall, *The Debate on the Norman Conquest* (Manchester: Manchester University Press, 1999), 121.

[23] The definition of colonialism is in Stephen Howe, *Ireland and Empire: Colonial Legacies in Irish History and Culture*, 2nd ed. (Oxford: Oxford University Press, 2002), 12. Howe's definition of *colonization* involves more than merely migration and settlement; he uses the term to denote 'population movements in which the migrants retain strong links with their or their ancestors' state of former residence, and by this gain significant privileges over other inhabitants of the new territory, either wholly dispossessing them or instating legal and other structures that systematically disadvantage those earlier inhabitants' (ibid.).

[24] Richard Koebner, 'The Settlement and Colonization of Europe', in M.M. Postan (ed.), *The Cambridge Economic History of Europe from the Decline of the Roman Empire: Volume 1: Agrarian Life of the Middle Ages*, 1:1–91 (Cambridge: Cambridge University

encouraged by the 400th anniversary of Columbus' crossing of the Atlantic which brought European colonization and its medieval precursors renewed attention. Angeliki Laiou delivered a paper at the Harvard Dunbarton Oaks symposium marking the Columbian quincentennial examining the interaction of peoples in the medieval Mediterranean: its title was 'The Many Faces of Medieval Colonization'.[25] Colonization, and not colonialism, was second in the trio of keywords that formed the subtitle of Robert Bartlett's *The Making of Europe: Conquest, Colonization and Cultural Change* (1993).[26] When, on the other hand, R.R. Davies uses the phrase 'Colonial Wales' to denote the structure of domination that emerged after the Edwardian conquest of 1284, he was using the adjective *colonial* in a stronger sense. The term refers not merely to the process of migration and settlement, but to a durable (though not necessarily stable) political relationship in which one people or territory was subordinated to the authority of another—in short 'colonialism'.[27] There is a quite a lot at stake in the choice of the term, not least its rebuke to the modernist position that colonialism is quintessentially a feature of the post-medieval world.

Other medievalists find such flirtations with modern categories deeply problematic, perhaps even pernicious. '"Colony" and "colonialism" are two of the most dangerous concepts in historical writing': such was the view of crusades historian John Pryor, expressed at a symposium in Jerusalem in 1984. It was not just that the terms were conceptually diffuse. They combined to create another tyrannous construct. The analogy between 'colonialism' and E.A.R. Brown's original tyrannous construct (Chapter 2, above) was explicitly drawn—though, intriguingly, the symposium hoped that 'feudalism' would survive to be found once more on the pages of *Traditio*. 'Colony' and 'colonialism' were, by contrast, ruled out by Pryor and others:

> [Colony] is ... a word which cannot be divorced from the history of the concept, from the writings of Adam Smith and Marx all the way to the present time. ... In other words, not only is the word [colony] not neutral but it also serves to cloud and distort communication between scholars. When we transpose a concept like this from a modern experience to the Middle Ages, we implicitly and unavoidably drag with it a ragbag of associations.

Press, 1966); Charles Verlinden, *The Beginnings of Modern Colonization: Eleven Essays* (Ithaca, NY: Cornell University Press, 1970).

[25] Angeliki E. Laiou, 'The Many Faces of Medieval Colonization', in Elizabeth Hill Boone and Tom Cummins (eds), *Native Traditions in the Postconquest World* (Washington, 1998); see also Michel Balard and Alain Ducellier (eds), *Coloniser au Moyen Âge* (Paris: Armand Colin, 1995). For an important conceptual discussion concerning the case of medieval Ireland, see Brendan Smith, *Colonisation and Conquest in Medieval Ireland: The English in Louth, 1170–1330* (Cambridge: Cambridge University Press, 1999), 1–9.

[26] Robert Bartlett, *The Making of Europe Conquest, Colonization and Cultural Change, 950–1350* (London: Allen Lane, 1993).

[27] R.R. Davies, 'Colonial Wales', *Past & Present*, 65 (1974), 3–23.

Giles Constable, who moderated the proceedings, recommended that his colleagues should move on from semantic arguments. 'There has been a great deal of confusion about the term "colony"', he observed: 'I think we shall substantially advance the field, however, if we stick to what the actual circumstances were, rather than spending too much time on definitions'.[28]

The Jerusalem symposium had the virtue of drawing out one of the principal anxieties bound up with the application of the word 'colony' to the Middle Ages: that of intruding an alien concept into an antecedent era where it has little, if any, explanatory power.[29] 'Colonialism', it has been remarked, 'is one of the great mirrors of our time: all those who look into the mirror tend to see the reflection of their own preoccupations and views of the world'.[30] Perhaps a 'hall of mirrors' is a better metaphor, with its concave and convex reflections pulling our collective memories of the Middle Ages into grotesque distortions of past reality. The categories and attitudes espoused by modern European colonial empires—a cocktail of paternalistic claim-making, benevolent distain, Orientalist allure, and imperial apologetics—shaped many of the priorities and themes of medieval historiography from the late nineteenth century. Prior to World War I, French historians such as Emmanuel-Guillaume Rey (d. 1916) and René Grousset (d. 1952) advanced a benevolent interpretation of the Frankish expansion into the Holy Land in the era of the crusades. They developed these 'colonialist' models precisely in the era of French occupation of Middle East.[31] Similarly, the doyen of historians of the 'Norman' invasion of Ireland, Goddard Henry Orpen, published his magnum opus, *Ireland under the Normans,* in two instalments (1911, 1920) during the Irish 'Revolutionary Decade', which saw Britain's rule in Ireland constitutionally tested and militarily contested. Orpen's mastery of the historical sources and archaeological evidence was remarkable, and in many respects his narrative of 'Norman' expansion in thirteenth-century Ireland remains unsurpassed

[28] Giles Constable and John H. Pryor, 'The Crusading Kingdom of Jerusalem—The First European Colonial Society? A Symposium', in B.Z. Kedar (ed.), *The Horns of Ḥaṭṭīn* (Jerusalem, 1992), at 342, 357.

[29] A similar anxiety is expressed by Joel Rosenthal about what he describes provocatively as the 'postcolonial assault' of Jeffrey Jerome Cohen (ed.), *The Postcolonial Middle Ages* (New York: Palgrave, 2001). 'Postcolonial explorations of medieval European society ... rest on the idea that ideologies and analytical methods that have been fruitful for twentieth century ... criticism can be applied to this earlier world' (Joel T. Rosenthal, 'Review of *Review of The Postcolonial Middle Ages*, by Jeffrey Jerome Cohen', *The History Teacher* 35:4 (2002), 534–36).

[30] Chris Gosden, *Archaeology and Colonialism: Cultural Contact from 5000 BC to the Present* (Cambridge: Cambridge University Press, 2004), 7.

[31] The late nineteenth-century interpretations advanced by historians from France and Britain are examined in Alan V. Murray, 'Franks and Indigenous Communities in Palestine and Syria (1099–1187): A Hierarchical Model of Social Interaction in the Principalities of Outremer', in Albrecht Classen (ed.), *East Meets West in the Middle Ages and Early Modern Times: Transcultural Experiences in the Premodern World* (Berlin: De Gruyter, 2013), ch. 4, esp. 292–3.

as a single coherent historical interpretation. It was also, quite unapologet-
ically, an exercise in imperial apologetics, one which sought to establish on
secure scholarly foundations the benefits that 'Norman' rule brought to 'anar-
chic Ireland'.[32] Such academic contributions were not mere backdrop; they
formed part of wider instrumentalization of medieval evidence. This pursuit
of the Middle Ages within the public sphere has often served dark political
or polemical ends, justifying territorial claim-making and military aggression.
Notable here is the *Ostsiedlung* interpretation of medieval Germanic settlement of the 'empty spaces' of barbaric Eastern Europe.[33] Equally sinister is
the occlusion from collective memory of unfavoured 'out-groups' such as the
Arab populations in Palestine. As Christopher Tyerman has observed: 'Such
things are ... potentially just as corrosive as the most rancid application of
colonialism'.[34]

However superficially plausible, the very idea that we can eschew abstractions and understand past societies solely on their own terms seems likely to
encourage an unfortunate state of theoretical or conceptual innocence. The
argument of Joe Cleary about the appropriateness of the theoretical framework of 'colonialism' to the study of modern Ireland is, in this context, quite
germane:

> The fact that peasants in medieval Europe did not consciously think of them-
> selves as living in a feudal system does nothing to diminish the theoretical value
> of the term "feudalism". Similarly, the theoretical value of the term "colonial-
> ism", which historically emerges as a conceptual rationalization of European
> overseas rule and only later as part of a wider oppositional critique of that
> enterprise, can never be made to rest simply on the subjective consciousness of
> the colonized.[35]

Anyone familiar with E.A.R. Brown's 'crusade against feudalism' will greet
Cleary's choice of comparator with a wry smile—even when 'feudalism' is
used, as it is here, in its Marxian sense. But the point remains that the validity
of 'colonialism' as an analytical category does not depend on whether the
objects of analysis would have recognized or understood the terms of the

[32] Goddard Henry Orpen, *Ireland under the Normans, 1169–1333* (Dublin: Four Courts, 2005).

[33] For the 'instrumentalization' of the Middle Ages in modern nation- and state-building enterprises, see the case studies in R.J.W. Evans and Guy P. Marchal (eds), *The Uses of the Middle Ages in Modern European States: History, Nationhood and the Search for Origins* (Basingstoke: Palgrave Macmillan, 2011); and for the *Ostsiedlung* specifically, see Jan M. Piskorski, 'The Medieval Colonization of Central Europe as a Problem of World History and Historiography', *German History*, 22:3 (2004), 323–43.

[34] Christopher Tyerman, *The Debate on the Crusades* (Manchester: Manchester Univer-sity Press, 2011), 176.

[35] Joe Cleary, 'Misplaced Ideas? Locating and Dislocating Ireland in Colonial and Post-colonial Studies', in Crystal Bartolovich and Neil Lazarus (eds), *Marxism, Modernity and Postcolonial Studies* (Cambridge: Cambridge University Press, 2002), 108.

debate. Clearly, then, methodological concerns of this kind are not a special affliction of medievalists. Even when no one disputes the applicability of colonial terminology, historians have to assert their disciplinary credentials to tame over-mighty concepts and demystify the high-priests of theory. Nicholas Thomas opens his book *Colonialism's Culture* with the paradox that while 'colonialism' requires close study, 'the discussion may be obstructed if we assume that the word relates to any meaningful category or totality'. 'Much writing in the field', he continues:

> seems less inclined to localize or historicize analysis, than [to] put Fanon and Lacan (or Derrida) into a blender and take the result to be equally appetizing for premodern and modern; for Asian, African and American; for metropolitan, settler indigenous and diasporic subjects.[36]

Historical explanation needs to be source-driven, lest interpretative interest is leached away by an agentless abstraction. The historian's attitude was pithily signalled by Frederick Cooper when he up-ended Gayatri Chakravorty Spivak's famous rhetorical question, 'Can the subaltern speak?' with a question of his own: 'Can the theorist listen?'[37] In the context of the present collection, we might change the question again: 'can the medievalist listen?'.

THE VOCABULARY OF COLONY: THE CASE OF MEDIEVAL IRELAND

In an influential paper published in 1984, R.R. Davies offered a re-appraisal of two master nouns in medieval Irish historiography: 'lordship' and 'colony'. Raising issues of conceptualization that he would later develop in his work on the 'medieval state' (and discussed in Chapter 1, above), Davies encouraged a joint meeting of the British Academy and Royal Irish Academy to examine 'the largely unquestioned assumptions upon which our scholarly edifices are built—to examine, for example, how far the character and presuppositions of our documentation colour and even impede our understanding of the past and to examine, likewise, how far our vocabulary, categories and metaphors serve to determine the way we order our thoughts about the past'. The two keywords around which his essay pivoted were both concepts, but of different kinds and qualities. Although, Davies did not describe his methodology using the language of emic/etic viewpoints, the distinction is helpful. 'Lordship' (L. *dominium*) he described from an 'emic' perspective, exploring the connotations of the term in medieval society; *colony* by contrast was 'etic' category, brought by historians to their sources to sharpen the analysis. While noting

---

[36] Nicholas Thomas, *Colonialism's Culture: Anthropology, Travel and Government* (Cambridge: Polity Press, 1994), ix.

[37] Frederick Cooper, 'Conflict and Connection: Rethinking Colonial African History', *American Historical Review*, 99:5 (1994), 1516–45, at 1528.

that the two terms had quite distinct careers, Davies was nonetheless able to assert that in the century after the English conquest of Ireland in the late twelfth century: 'A momentous change, more in perceptions than in institutions, had taken place. The language of lordship has been overlaid by the vocabulary of colony'.[38]

What was this 'vocabulary of colony'? Davies did not mean to suggest that the term *colonia* itself was a significant feature of this perceptual or institutional landscape. True, the term was not unknown. The account of the first crusade by Guibert of Nogent (d.1124), for instance, flashes its classical erudition when it imagines the pristine crusader kingdom of Jerusalem as a 'new colony of Holy Christendom' (L. *sanctae Christianitatis novae coloniae*).[39] Gerald of Wales describes how the king of England should turn Wales into a colony by expelling its inhabitants to other kingdoms (L. *Unde et expulso prosus veteri colono, aliaque ad regna translato, de Cambria coloniam princeps efficere praevalebit*).[40] The phrase appears in Gerald's *Descriptio Cambriae* ('Description of Wales'), but only in one manuscript witness, and Gerald appears to have excised it from later recensions. *Colonia* appears, then, to have been a rare, even rarefied, term used by classicizing authors to ornament their Latin prose. What Davies intended to expose for discussion were aspects of English lordship in Ireland whose character could be categorized analytically as 'colonial': military intervention by an external power, the bureaucratic routinization of metropolitan authority, and a racialized construction of difference. But can we press this further? If, following Davies and many others, we accept the category of 'colony' as valid in the case of late-medieval Ireland, how should the medievalist listen for the 'colonial' in the sources? Ireland was not labelled a *colonia* in the Middle Ages, so seeking a vocabulary of colony may seem a curious, if not quixotic, quest. Here the approach of the French philosophers Deleuze and Guattari may be useful. Rather than isolating concepts singly, they describe each concept as a combination (*chiffre*) or a multiplicity. 'Concepts are centers of vibrations, each in itself and every one in relation to all the others. This is why they all resonate rather than cohere or correspond with

[38] R.R. Davies, 'Lordship or Colony?', in James Lydon (ed.), *The English in Medieval Ireland: Proceedings of the First Joint Meeting of the Royal Irish Academy and the British Academy, Dublin, 1982* (Dublin: Royal Irish Academy, 1984), 142–60, at 157.

[39] Robert Levine (ed.), *The Deeds of God Through the Franks: A Translation of Guibert de Nogent's Gesta Dei Per Francos* (Woodbridge: Boydell & Brewer, 1997), 149. The Latin text is R.B.C. Huygens (ed.), *Dei Gesta per Francos et Cinq Autres Textes. Corpus Christianorum, Continuatio Mediaevalis* (Turnholt: Brepols, 1996), at 127: 'Baluinum ex Edessa transferunt et sanctae Christianitatis novae coloniae regnare constituent'.

[40] Giraldus Cambrensis, *Descriptio Cambrie*, in *Giraldi Cambrensis opera*, ed. J.S. Brewer, J.F. Dimock and G.F. Warner, 8 vols (London: Rolls Series, 1861–91), vi (London, 1868), 225 n. 4. The passage is discussed most recently in Michael A. Faletra, *Wales and the Medieval Colonial Imagination: The Matter of Britain in the Twelfth Century* (New York: Palgrave Macmillan, 2014), 158; and A. Joseph McMullen and Georgia Henley (eds), *Gerald of Wales: New Perspectives on a Medieval Writer and Critic* (University of Wales Press, 2018).

each other'.[41] Concepts are not, then, reducible to any single term within the lexicon (such as *colonia*), nor does a conceptual field need to be fully coherent. Rather we should listen for conceptual resonances and sympathetic vibrations within the language of our source material.

Waste and inhabitation, uprooting and enrooting, planting, cultivating, edifying, civilizing: I want to suggest that this suite of keywords resonated together to form a 'vocabulary of colony' in late-medieval Ireland. The written sources for both the English royal government in Ireland, and the major lordships, are, of course, quite patchy for the century after the English invasion of Ireland, which commenced in the late 1160s. The scale of colonization has typically been inferred from the changing morphology of physical settlement and by reading backwards from the evidence of manorial records which post-date the first English incursions into Ireland by up to a century.[42] There are, however, enough fragments of evidence to suggest that a language of 'inhabitation' was current in the earliest Latin sources—both record sources and narratives—to describe the twelfth-century conquest and colonization of Ireland.[43] In 1171–1172, during his expedition to Ireland, Henry II famously granted the city of Dublin—which had been abandoned by its Ostmen rulers and taken into Henry's possession on the submission of Strongbow—to the men of Bristol for the purpose of inhabiting it (L. *civitatem meam de Duvelina ad inhabitandam*). The charter continues with an injunction re-stating the king's wish and command that the Bristollians should inhabit the city of Dublin (L. *ut ipsi eam inhabitent*) and hold it of the king forever.[44] The most recent and penetrating analysis of rather fragmentary record evidence for the century after the conquest has argued that English royal government pursued an active policy of pushing back the Irish frontier and promoting English settlement.[45] A writ from 1219, during the minority of King Henry III, is of particular interest because it uses the language of inhabitation unmistakably in the sense of promoting colonization. Written in the name of the boy-king, the writ orders Thomas fitz Anthony (d. *c.*1227), a major English baron in southern Leinster, not to impede the bishop of Waterford from receiving

[41] Gilles Deleuze and Félix Guattari, *What Is Philosophy?* Translated by Hugh Tomlinson and Graham Burchell (Columbia University Press, 1994), 23.

[42] For a critical historiographical review, see John Gillingham, 'A Second Tidal Wave? The Historiography of English Colonization of Ireland, Scotland and Wales in the Twelfth and Thirteenth Centuries', in Jan M. Piskorski (ed.), *Historiographical Approaches to Medieval Colonization of East Central Europe: A Comparative Analysis Against the Background of Other European Inter-Ethnic Colonization Processes in the Middle Ages* (1st ed., Boulder, 2002).

[43] For Angevin propaganda concerning Ireland, see Colin Veach, 'Henry II and the Ideological Foundations of Angevin Rule in Ireland', *Irish Historical Studies*, 72:161 (2018), 1–25.

[44] Dublin City Library and Archives, Royal Charter no. 1.

[45] Eoghan Keane, 'Managing a Medieval Frontier: Government Policy Towards the Irish Marches and the Lands Beyond Them, c.1200–c.1318' (University of Dublin, PhD, 2020).

'English' upon his land for the purpose of inhabiting it (L. *in eadem Anglicos receptare ad eam inhabitand'*). 'Inhabiting' here holds a stronger sense than merely occupying, or dwelling upon, the land. The bishop of Waterford's intention appears to have been to populate or settle his land with English cultivators; in other words, to colonize it.[46]

The process of aristocratic settlement in Ireland is nowhere more vividly captured than in the metrical French history of the conquest, *La geste des Engleis en Yrlande* (better known by the title attributed to it by Orpen, 'The Song of Dermot and the Earl').[47] The author describes how one of the first *conquistadores* in Ireland, Hugh I de Lacy (d.1186) set out for his lordship of Meath in order to occupy the land.[48] The verb that is used to describe this process is *herberger,* which the poem's nineteenth-century editor, Goddard Henry Orpen, translated as 'to plant'. In fact, the versifier uses *herberger* in more senses than one. The first sense is occupation: 'Hugh de Lacy, who was so bold', the *Geste* tells us, set out for Meath in order to plant or occupy his lands (F. *Pur sa terre herberger*). Having been apportioned among his brave vassals, the land then planted in the sense of 'built upon' with castles and cities (F. *en tel manere | Esteit herbergé la tere | E de chastels e de cités'*). In the next line, the metaphor switches with the introduction of the verb *araciner,* 'to take root':

> *Ki ben est[eint] aracinez*   (Thus well rooted were
> *Les gentils vassalsa alosés.* The noble renowned vassals.)[49]

The settlement of Meath is here described as an act of occupation, edification, and putting down roots. Similar language of planting and enrooting is found in the other principal narrative of the twelfth-century conquest of Ireland, Gerald of Wales's *Expugnatio Hibernica*. In the scene describing the siege of Wexford, Gerald puts a speech into the mouth of one of the invaders, Robert FitzStephen, in which he declares his noble motives in coming to Ireland. Referring to Diarmait Mac Murchadha, the Irish king of Leinster who sought their military assistance and so initiated the sequence of events that led to the invasion, FitzStephen declares: 'This man loves our people; he is encouraging our people to come here, and has decided to plant and enroot

---

[46] *Rotuli litterarum clasuarum in turri Londinensi asservati, 1204–24,* ed. T.D. Hardy (2 vols, London, 1833–44), i, 394; summary translation in English available in *Calendar of Documents Relating to Ireland, 1171–1307,* ed. H.S. Sweetman and G.F. Handcock, 5 vols (Public Record Office: London, 1875–86), i, no. 132.

[47] The literature on the *Geste* is reviewed in Keith Busby, *French in Medieval Ireland, Ireland in Medieval French: The Paradox of Two Worlds* (Turnhout, 2017), 77–107.

[48] For de Lacy, see Colin Veach, *Lordship in Four Realms: The Lacy Family, 1166–1241* (Manchester: Manchester University Press, 2014).

[49] G.H. Orpen (ed.), *The Song of Dermot and the Earl* (Oxford, 1892), lines 2940–43, 3201–9. The Orpen translation of this passage is followed in Evelyn Mullally (ed.), *The Deeds of the Normans in Ireland. La geste des Engleis en Yrlande* (Dublin: Four Courts Press, 2002).

them permanently (L. *plantare et immobiliter radicare proposuit*)' here in this island.[50]

The *Expugnatio* served as a foundation story for the English colony in Ireland throughout the Middle Ages. By the early fifteenth century, it had been rendered into English as 'The Conquest of Ireland' in a dialect that makes the Irish provenance of the translation certain.[51] The anonymous translator rendered the key Latin phrase as 'owr lond folke wyll setten & planten stydfastly yn thys lond, nowe & euer'. The second in this brace of verbs—*setten & planten*—provides one the earliest occurrences in English of the verb 'to plant' used to refer to the creation of a permanent human settlement overseas—in short, to a plantation. It was the work of sixteenth-century authors to couple the verb *plant* with the new-fangled *colony* to create the compound phrase, 'to plant colonies'. Less immediately striking, perhaps, but in its way just as important, is *setten,* literally 'to sit' upon or settle the land. F.W. Maitland long ago pointed out the etymological connection between the common-or-garden word 'sitting' and the technical term *seisin* in English common law. Seisin referred to possession in the sense of a physical entry upon the land.[52] It is surely striking, then, that the translator of the 'Conquest of Ireland' should reach for the word *setten*, with its immanent sense of possession. The text was completed around the second decade of the fifteenth century at a time when petitions to the English crown warned that the lordship of Ireland was on the point of being utterly destroyed. The phrase 'our people will sit ... in this land, now and forever' surely resonated with its readers, conveying the message that the English settlement of Ireland would endure.

The elements in this vocabulary served a larger ideational purpose of claim-making by implication. The process of clearing the woods, and then cultivating and edifying the cleared land, established effective occupation and possession. Long before the English came to Ireland, this was how Brutus of Troy was imagined to have acquired possession of the island of Albion. According to Geoffrey of Monmouth, when Brutus first landed, he found Albion uninhabited except for a few giants. Having driven these giants off into mountain caves, Brutus apportioned out the land and the settlers 'began to till the fields and build homes (L. *agros incipiunt colere, domos aedificare*). Within a short space of time, the country appeared to have been occupied for many years'.[53]

---

[50] Giraldus Cambrensis, *Expugnatio Hibernica: The Conquest of Ireland*, ed. and trans. A.B. Scott and F.X. Martin (Royal Irish Academy: Dublin, 1978), 1.9, 48 (L. *Gentem hic nostram diligit, gentem hic nostram attrahit, gentem hic nostram in insula plantare et immobiliter radicare proposuit*).

[51] Caoimhe Whelan, 'The Transmission of the *Expugnatio Hibernica*', in Henley and MacMullen (ed.), *Gerald of Wales: New Perspectives*.

[52] F.W. Maitland, *The History of English Law before the Time of Edward I* (2 vols, 1895), ii.4 'Ownership and Possession'.

[53] Geoffrey of Monmouth, *The History of the Kings of Britain: An Edition and Translation of the 'De gestis Britonum' [Historia Regum Britanniae]*, ed. Michael D. Reeve, trans. Neil Wright (Woodbridge: Boydell, 2007), book 1, pp. 27, 29.

Alongside this Galfridian narrative of the first inhabitants of Britain, we may set the Giraldian account in the *Topographia Hibernie* of the first inhabitants of Ireland beginning with the granddaughter of Noah, who fled to the west hoping to escape the flood. For his cyclical narrative of five waves of legendary ante- and post-diluvian invaders, Gerald of Wales depended closely upon the *Lebor Gabála Érenn* ('Book of the Taking of Ireland'), an influential work of synthetic pseudo-history in Middle Irish which had been composed in its original form in the mid-eleventh century. Gerald follows the *Lebor Gabála* in recounting how each wave of new arrivals found the island deserted and then gradually they made the physical imprint of human habitation felt through cultivation. After the arrival of 'Bartholanus', in the second wave, four huge forests were cut away at the very roots in the interests of agriculture. The next wave witnessed the arrival of the Nemedus with his four sons on the shore of an abandoned land, and 'many woods and groves were changed to fields and plains'; their progeny multiplied so that 'they filled the whole island with more inhabitants than it ever had' until warfare and plague reduced their numbers and the island was abandoned and left vacant for two hundred years. Gerald continues the tale down as far as the fifth wave of invaders under 'Milesius' (that is, Míl Espáine). At this point, Gerald takes a sharp argumentative detour. Abandoning the Irish origin tale, Gerald drew instead on what he called 'the British History' (that is, the fictional narrative of Geoffrey of Monmouth), which recounts how one Gurguintius, king of the Britons, was in the Orkney Islands when he received an embassy from a fleet of Basques (*Basclenses*). The Basque fleet informed the king that the reason for their coming was that they might settle in a country of the west (L. *ut aliquam scilicet terram in occidentis partibus inhabitarent*), and they urgently requested of the king that he should grant them some land to inhabit (L. *ut aliquam terram eis inhabitandam concederet*). At length the king granted the island of Ireland to be settled by them (L. *eis inhabitandam concessit*) and gave them pilots to speed them on their journey. Gerald notes that the island was 'then either entirely uninhabited or had been settled by him'.[54] He thereby sets up one of the ancient claims of the kings of England to rule Ireland.

The argument only became more vehement with the passage of time. John Trevisa (d.1402) completed a Middle English version of the story over two centuries later in 1387 by translating the Latin universal history of Ranulph Higden (d.1364)—who had himself leaned heavily on Gerald's narratives in constructing the *Polychronicon*. Trevisa's translation of the *Polychronicon*, which was widely disseminated, describes Ireland not merely as uninhabited or empty (L. *vacuam*) at the time of the Basque settlement, as Higden put it, but as 'void and waste' (*the kyng sent hem to Irlond tat was too voyde and wast*).[55] As this imagined geography developed over time, it was almost as though

---

[54] *Giraldi Cambrensis opera*, v, 141.

[55] Higden's Latin is given with facing translation by Trevisa in *Polychronicon Ranulphi Higden monachi Cestrensis: Together with the English translations of John Trevisa and of an*

Ireland's original uninhabited state became progressively more pristine. By the late 1470s, when William Worcestre (d. c.1482) compiled a geographical note on Ireland, he recorded that the island of Ireland was not populated (L. *non populata*) when it was peopled by 'Gombatruz, king of England', who gave the fleet of Spanish exiles the island of Ireland to inhabit. He adds that 'Ireland was then wild and empty (L. *siluestrem et vacuam*)', introducing the sense of an untamed wilderness into the tale.[56] It was not merely that Ireland lay waste and unoccupied when it was first claimed, but also its current population was imagined as primitives unable to properly cultivate the land. It was Gerald of Wales who, in his first book on Ireland, the *Topographia Hibernie*, did most to generate the canonical the image of the Irish as pastoralists who had not proceeded to the higher stages of civilised life. The idea proved durable. In its entry for 1316, the *Vita Edwardi Secundi* describes the Irish as a wild people dwelling in the mountains and forests: 'They do not cultivate the land (L. *terras non colunt*), but live instead on their livestock and the dairy produce from them; and if from time to time they need bread, they come down to the English towns on the coast; they sell livestock and buy grain'.[57] It hardly needs emphasis that these ideas were central to the Tudor representations of barbarity, a central component in the Tudor 'ideology of colonization' in Ireland and the Americas.[58]

We have seen that the 'vocabulary of colony' was not merely descriptive; it was explicitly argumentative. But how far did this translate into anything significant in terms of policy? In the later Middle Ages, the English lordship of Ireland suffered in effect from depopulation. Thomas Walsingham, the St Albans chronicler, reported at the time of King Richard II's first expedition to Ireland (1394–1395) that so many people born in Ireland had come to England in search of profit 'that Ireland was almost bereft of men to cultivate that land and to defend it' (L. *ut illa terra et cultoribus et defensoribus pene uacuaretur*). In consequence, Walsingham goes on, 'the mere Irish, enemies of the English, had almost wasted that part of the island which was obedient to the king of England, and subjected to their evil rule'.[59] Walsingham's report

Unknown Writer of the Fifteenth Century, ed. J.R. Lumby (London, 1879), 345–46 (book 1, chapter XXXIII).

[56] John Harvey (ed.), *William Worcester: Itineraries* (Oxford: Clarendon Press, 1969).

[57] Wendy R. Childs (ed.), *Vita Edwardi Secundi* (Oxford Medieval Texts. Oxford: Oxford University Press, 2005), *s.a.* 1316.

[58] David B. Quinn, *The Elizabethans and the Irish* (Cornell University Press, 1966); Nicholas P. Canny, 'The Ideology of English Colonization: From Ireland to America', *The William and Mary Quarterly*, 30:4 (1973), 575–98; Andrew Hadfield, 'Briton and Scythian: Tudor Representations of Irish Origins', *Irish Historical Studies*, 28:112 (1993), 390–408; Jane H. Ohlmeyer, 'A Laboratory for Empire?: Early Modern Ireland and English Imperialism', in Kevin Kenny (ed.), *Ireland and the British Empire* (Oxford: Oxford University Press, 2004), 26–60.

[59] John Taylor, Wendy R. Childs and Leslie Watkiss (eds), *The St Albans Chronicle: The Chronica Maiora of Thomas Walsingham, Vol. 1: 1376–1394* (Oxford: Oxford University Press, 2003), *s.a.* 1394.

occurs in the context of the order, issued at the time of Richard II's expedition, for the return to Ireland of all those in England who were born in Ireland. Four years later in 1398, the duke of Surrey, on his appointment to the lieutenancy of Ireland, demanded that from each parish of England, or every second parish, a man or his wife should be sent at the King's costs to Ireland to inhabit that land (F. *pur la dite terre enhabiter*), especially in the waste lands upon the marches, for the king's profit.[60] It was, in effect, a call for the recolonization of the country.[61] The terms would become influential. In 1474, reconquest and inhabitation are unmistakably linked in the 'articles of instruction' issued to Sir Gilbert Debenham as chief governor of Ireland. This text proposes that persons of Irish birth dwelling in England should be ordered to return to Ireland, not simply to take up residence wherever they originated but 'to enhabit such countries as shall [be?] conquered'.[62] A renewed conquest of Ireland was, in other words, to be made effectual by 'inhabiting' the land. In 1515, a treatise on the 'State of Ireland and Plan for its Reformation' was presented at the court of Henry VIII. In developing its ideas, the 'State of Ireland' relied heavily on existing texts, in particular the mysterious author 'Pandarus' whose work, *Salus Populi* (Health of the People), survives only in fragmentary form.[63] The 'State of Ireland' echoes the 1398 call of Surrey in asking the king to send one man from each parish in England, Cornwall, and Wales to Ireland in order 'to inhabyte' lands in the earldom of Ulster (which since 1461 had come to the English Crown) and south of Dublin. The tract further emphasizes that these new settlers should be 'acquainted with tilling of the land' so that within a few years the earldom of Ulster would return to its former profitability. The author set his text in a long historical context of the first English conquest of Ireland: here the vocabulary explicitly links the first conquest and 'inhabitation' of the land in the sense of colonization. Referring to the famous twelfth-century conqueror, Strongbow, the author records: 'He dyd conquyre all the lande, unto lytell, and dyd inhabyte the same with Englyshe folk, subget to his lawes, after the manner of Ingland'. It may seem far-fetched to link this image of Strongbow as conqueror with Spanish conquistadores of the New World. But the 'State of Ireland' text of 1515 is almost contemporaneous with a moral play (*c*.1519)

[60] J.T. Gilbert, *History of the Viceroys of Ireland with Notices of the Castle of Dublin and its Chief Occupants in Former Times* (Dublin, 1865), 560–2.

[61] The language is comparable to the meaning of frontier as an 'uncultivated wasteland' found in the context of the Anglo-Scottish border: see Jackson W. Armstrong, *England's Northern Frontier: Conflict and Local Society in the Fifteenth-Century Scottish Marches* (Cambridge: Cambridge University Press, 2020), esp. 93; and below, Chapter 5. For technical meaning of 'wastes' in the context of the thirteenth-century Irish marches, see Keane, 'Managing a medieval frontier', ch. 2.

[62] The text is printed in Donough Bryan, *Gerald Fitzgerald, The Great Earl of Kildare (1456–1513)* (Dublin: Talbot Press, 1933), 20.

[63] Michael Bennett, 'The *Libelle of English Policy*: The Matter of Ireland', in Linda Clark (ed.), *The Fifteenth Century XV* (Woodbridge: Boydell Press, 2017), 1–22.

by that would-be colonizer, John Rastell (d. 1536), which reflects, ruefully and counter-factually, on the glory that would have redounded to the king had it been the English and not the Spanish whose dominion extended over the oceans:

> Oh what a thynge had be than,
> Yf that they that be Englyshemen.
> Myght have ben furst of all.
> That there shulde have take possession,
> And made furst buyldynge and habytacion,
> A memory perpetuall![64]

Rastell has been described as a 'lone voice crying in the wilderness', and insofar as he was calling for a transatlantic colonizing enterprise by the English he may well have been. But he was not alone in respect of his use of language.[65] His 'vocabulary of colony'—established by inhabiting and building upon the land—is cast in terms that are immediately familiar from the evidence of the previous four centuries.

One word that was *not* part of this cultural lexicon was 'colony'. There is, however, a risk of being dazzled by the arrival of a novel, or newly retrieved, word such as *colonia*, to the neglect of the underlying ideas. As Melvin Richter has noted: 'The presence or absence of such conceptual distinctions in the language of politics reveals much about the government of a society, as well as about the conceptual resources available to those participating in discussions of its arrangements. Yet an individual or group may possess a concept without having a word to express it'.[66] The corollary of this argument is that a new vocabulary may come to infuse or refresh an existing set of ideas.[67] The Tudor humanist scholar, Sir Thomas Smith senior, has been described by D.B. Quinn as England's 'first colonial theorist'.[68] Smith drew extensively and indiscriminately upon classical precedents to extol the virtues of colonization in Ireland. But in doing so, he harnessed his classicizing enthusiasms to a distinctly medieval vocabulary of planting, inhabiting and cultivating

---

[64] Cited in Howard Mumford Jones, 'Origins of the Colonial Idea in England', *Proceedings of the American Philosophical Society*, 85:5 (1942), 448–65, at 449.

[65] D.B. Quinn, 'Renaissance Influences in English Colonization: The Prothero Lecture', *Transactions of the Royal Historical Society*, 26 (1976), 73–93.

[66] Melvin Richter, *The History of Political and Social Concepts: A Critical Introduction* (Oxford: Oxford University Press, 1995), 9.

[67] Skinner, 'The Idea of a Cultural Lexicon', 160: 'The surest sign that a group or society has entered into the self-conscious possession of a new concept is that a corresponding vocabulary will be developed'.

[68] D.B. Quinn, 'Sir Thomas Smith (1513–1577) and the Beginnings of English Colonial Theory', *Proceedings of the American Philosophical Society*, 89:4 (1945), 543–60; Andrew Fitzmaurice, *Humanism and America: An Intellectual History of English Colonisation, 1500–1625* (Cambridge: Cambridge University Press, 2003), 35–39; Hiram Morgan, 'The Colonial Venture of Sir Thomas Smith in Ulster, 1571–1575', *The Historical Journal*, 28:2 (1985), 261–78.

('tilling') as a means of bringing civility. This is most noticeable in an anonymous pamphlet, whose authorship is attributed to Sir Thomas Smith junior,
which sought to advertise Smith's proposal to colonize the Ards peninsula in
county Down. The term 'colony' does not appear. Instead, drawing upon the
language of 'inhabitation', the pamphlet urges Elizabeth I to sponsor an effort
to 'win and replenish with English inhabitantes the country called the Ardes
in the north of Ireland'. Searching for precedents, the author describes how,
in the time of Henry II, Strongbow subdued Leinster, 'which he possessed
and held quietly, plantyng it with Englyshe inhabytants'. Smith describes the
settling and cultivation as a tale of progress 'furthering the inhabiting & ciuil-
itie of the North', and argues that civility increases through cultivation of the
land ('encreaseth more by keeping men occupied in Tyllage'). All this stands
in contrast to the unsettled and uncivil pastoral economy of peoples who
engage in transhumance, 'followyng of heards, as the Tartarians, Arabians, and
Irishe men doo'.[69] Here, beneath the classically inflected contours of humanist
scholarship, we can perceive a late-medieval *pentimento* with persistent traces
of an earlier set of images.[70]

* * *

On his third voyage, Gulliver visited the land of Balnibarbi and its Grand
Academy where the learned and well-funded 'projectors' devised ingenious
schemes to advance the welfare of their country. Among their research projects
was 'a Scheme for entirely abolishing words whatsoever' on the grounds that
words caused a life-shortening corrosion to the lungs. Instead, 'since Words
are only Names for Things, it would be more convenient for all Men to carry
about them, such Things as were necessary to express the particular Business they are to discourse on' (*Gulliver's Travels*, III.5). The drawback of the
proposal was that for onerous and complex matters, the weight of 'Things'
bore down on the academics, causing them to sink.

Colonial situations are complex, politically unstable and culturally
ambiguous: as a result, they are conceptually onerous. We will not necessarily
make the 'thing' easier to describe, interpret or comprehend by abolishing
the keyword, 'colony'. Like the 'projectors' of the Grand Academy, we will
sink to the ground if we accumulate instances without placing them in their
conceptual framework. Drawing on evidence from England's late-medieval
dominions, this chapter has explored the language of inhabitation, cultivation
and edification which described 'the colonial' in Ireland in the later Middle

[69] *A letter sent by I. B. gentleman vnto his very frende mayster R. C. esquire, wherin
is conteined a large discourse of the peopling and inhabiting the cuntrie called the Ardes*
London, Henry Binneman for Anthony K[itson] [1571]: reprinted in George Hill, *An
Historical Account of the MacDonnells of Antrim* (Belfast, 1873), 405–15.

[70] The art-historical metaphor of a 'colonial pentimento' is used to wonderful effect in
Patricia Seed, *American Pentimento: The Invention of Indians and the Pursuit of Riches*
(University of Minnesota Press, 2001), esp. 1–11.

Ages. It has also suggested something of the instrumental and ideological work that this 'vocabulary of colony' performed. Its discursive effect was to advance an argument from improvement which served to vindicate, by virtue of the very terms in which it was couched, the rightfulness and righteousness of the English conquest of Ireland. Both the vocabulary and its associated conceptual schemes were still familiar to England's sixteenth-century humanists, who merged it with the Roman language of *colonia* to formulate the first explicit statements of 'colonial theory'. The more general lesson is that by listening to our sources it is possible to move beyond definitional and taxonomic questions—'What is a Colony?', 'Is this a Colony?', 'What type of Colony?'—to apprehend an underlying and generally unexplored question of how the phenomena which we agree to refer to as 'colonies' were imagined in the Middle Ages. And by listening, we can usefully complicate and perhaps even transcend the modernist position on colonialism—that in the beginning was the word.

CHAPTER 4

Crisis

Carl Watkins

Almost every medieval institution and every medieval social group has had its putative crises: monarchy and church; aristocracy, peasantry, and knightly class. 'Crisis' figures in seemingly almost numberless book titles, article titles, and chapter headings. Howard Kaminsky has gone so far as to say that the term has, through its frequently vague and dramatizing use descended into historiographical cliché.[1] It falls, however, into a large class of concepts that help to structure narrative and guide interpretation and yet, unlike more evidently loaded abstractions (such as 'state' or 'nation', and some of the others tackled elsewhere in this volume, 'magic', 'frontier' or 'colony') is rarely scrutinized. To take just one example: in *Politics and Crisis in Fourteenth-Century England* (1990), the editors, John Taylor and Wendy Childs used their introduction to defend 'the political' from critics keen to champion more fashionable interpretative approaches, but they treated 'crisis' as if the meaning of the term was obvious. To find fuller critical examination of this concept in relatively recent literature one needs to look to the work of German or Scandinavian scholars one of whom, tellingly, felt the need to apologize for entering into a

---

[1] Here following Hans Baron: H. Kaminsky, 'From Lateness to Waning to Crisis: The Burden of the Later Middle Ages', *Journal of Early Modern History*, 4 (2000), 85–125.

C. Watkins (✉)
Magdalene College, University of Cambridge, Cambridge, UK

© The Author(s), under exclusive license to Springer Nature
Switzerland AG 2022
J. W. Armstrong, P. Crooks and A. Ruddick (eds), *Using Concepts in Medieval History*, https://doi.org/10.1007/978-3-030-77280-2_4

preliminary definitional debate that might not be to the taste of Anglophone historians.[2]

A consensus, albeit a hazy one, its assumptions seldom articulated, has nonetheless formed around uses of the word. Crises tend to constitute peaks in patterns of historical explanation, suggesting instants pregnant with potential for change. In a rare direct reflection on the term, Barbara Harvey worked her way to an exact formulation.[3] She set aside definitions that were too constricting or too vague: for her the central meaning of 'crisis' was as a 'turning point' or 'conjuncture', 'the convergence of trends to produce a new situation'. More commonly, however, deployment of the concept has not required a convulsion to be followed by a change in the way that Harvey proposed. This more expansive use owes something to the concept's ancient origins. These lay in the medical writings of Hippocrates and Galen. The 'crisis' was 'the turning point of a disease', but this might be for better or for worse. It need not give rise to transformation: the fever might kill the patient, but it might break, allowing a return to equilibrium. The subsequent evolution of the term in general historical usage expanded on that original sense. Some historians attempted greater precision. Jacob Burckhardt dedicated a chapter to the subject of crises in his *Reflections on History*.[4] He envisioned them as 'accelerations of historical processes'. 'True crises', he thought, were rare. More frequent were 'failed' crises. These were thunderstorms that produced no break in the prevailing weather. Yet when a 'true' or 'genuine' crisis struck, it engendered decisive social and political change. In destroying old structures it made space in which, according to Burckhardt's analysis, 'strong personalities' (the subject of his next chapter) might remake politics within the states in which they operated or in the wider world.

A broadly Burckhardtian conceptualization of crisis, stripped of the somewhat antique contention that they cleared spaces in which strong personalities might act, continues tacitly to inform the term's use in historiography. There is an obvious relation here to other conceptual tools and rhetorical strategies of the historian—the language of 'watersheds' and 'turning points'. These are things that historians almost constitutionally are inclined to seek, springing from a desire to pinpoint moments of change and—simplifying complexity—to isolate prime movers or hierarchize factors giving rise to it. Crises then, contrary to Harvey's formulation, need not imply a transformation. They might be fevers that break or thunderstorms that pass. They might be moments of potential change, but that change need not be realized.

---

[2] See R. Koselleck, 'Crisis', trans. M.W. Richter, *Journal of the History of Ideas*, 67 (2006), 357–400; N. Hybel, *Crisis or Change: The Concept of Crisis in the Light of Agrarian Structural Reorganization in Late Medieval England* (Aarhus: Aarhus University Press, 1989).

[3] B. Harvey (ed.), *Before the Black Death: Studies in the Crisis of the Early Fourteenth Century* (Manchester: Manchester University Press, 1991).

[4] J. Burckhardt, *Reflections on History*, trans. M. Hottinger (London: G. Allen and Unwin, 1943), 213–68.

Crisis then is a capacious concept but in spite, or perhaps because of that it is one with significant ramifications for the arts of historical writing. Embedded in the historiography of the later middle ages is an almost canonical list of political crises, running from Magna Carta through to the Wars of the Roses, implicitly agreed by most historians who have worked on the period. A comparison of the later medieval volumes in the original Oxford History of England authored by Maurice Powicke and May McKisack with the equivalent ones written for the new series by Michael Prestwich and Gerald Harriss indicates that broadly the same climactic events have remained the focus of attention, lending the political history of the later middle ages much of its intellectual bone-structure.[5]

Interpretations of these events, these crises, *have* changed, of course, and so too the ways in which the concept has been implicated in the arts of persuasive argument. For William Stubbs, in his monumental constitutional history, crises became steps in a teleological development, the tectonic forces of struggle between king and nobles eventuating in convulsions that were stages of an evolution, especially of parliament's role, which saw the restriction of royal power.[6] Stubbs ran into difficulties as he applied this analysis to the fifteenth century because those years seemed to him devoid of meaningful change, such that his marginal annotation to the first paragraph of the chapter introducing them noted that this was 'not a period of constitutional development'. In what followed a certain presentational finesse crept into Stubbs' account, for having placed crises centrally in his narrative hitherto, he now used the actual word more sparingly, so co-opting it silently into a rhetoric designed to emphasize the significance of the period down to 1399, while marginalizing the century that followed.

The impulse among those writing against such narratives—perhaps most strikingly K.B. McFarlane and his intellectual heirs—was not so much to revise the 'list' of crises that earlier generations of historians had concentrated on, but rather to re-conceptualize the politics that gave rise to them, reinterpreting their causes and ceasing to assume that each was a consequence of inexorable struggle within the elite. McFarlane was thus disposed to cast these events more as passing thunderstorms than 'true' crises, stripping out much of that constitutional significance with which Stubbs had been keen to invest them, dissolving his teleology and observing deep and durable continuities in the ideas that structured political interactions. Even the striking events of 1399, which witnessed the deposition of Richard II and the seizure of the throne by Henry Bolingbroke, constituted not a 'revolution', an innovation by which a king came to owe his title to parliament, but a more limited development

[5] M. Powicke, *The Thirteenth Century, 1216–1307* (Oxford: Oxford University Press, 1962); M. McKisack, *The Fourteenth Century, 1307–99* (Oxford: Oxford University Press, 1959); M. Prestwich, *Plantagenet England, 1225–1360* (Oxford: Clarendon, 2010); G. Harriss, *Shaping the Nation: England 1360–1461* (Oxford: Clarendon, 2005).

[6] W. Stubbs, *The Constitutional History of England in its Origin and Development* (Oxford: Clarendon, 1880).

in which parliament acknowledged a claim based, altogether less radically, on right.[7] Crises thus came to be seen as eventuating not so much from the working out of structural weaknesses, institutional problems, and political tensions between kings and magnates but rather from 'bad kingship' that the restoration of competent rule might reset. Examining the politics of the period 1369 to 1422, John Gillingham traced 'disturbances on the surface of politics' that some had seen as 'something much more fundamental', that is 'symptoms of a change in the balance of power between king and subjects ... a crisis from which the crown emerged weaker than before'. But for Gillingham this was not crisis followed by change but rather a species of continuity, surface turbulence—a summer storm—rather than a transformation.[8] In similar vein, historians working at the other end of the long fifteenth century have lodged the explanation of the Wars of the Roses not so much in deep structural tensions in the body politic but rather in the spectacular failure of Henry VI's rule.[9] Agreement about the list of crises down the historiographical *longue durée* thus belies the very different ways in which this rather baggy concept has been framed and the very different expectations of the explanatory work it might do.

It is the case, however, that the concept of crisis has the potential to establish its own kind of tyranny. Valerie Flint questioned in a critique of Brian Tierney's *Crisis of Church and State* whether the sum of the individual crises identified by the author amounted to the singular—grander—crisis that he had hypothesized. In such circumstances, she intimated, the concept risked turning from descriptive device into organizing principle and guide for the selection of examples. A much bigger form of that same essential problem is to be found in the historiography—especially but not only the older historiography—of the later middle ages, because this period can be, and has been, conceptualized as an age *of* crisis, in which the word is a shorthand for its essential characteristics. Léopold Genicot contended that 'crisis is the word which immediately comes to the historian's mind when he thinks of the fourteenth and fifteenth centuries ... not necessarily crisis as the word is commonly understood, not regression, absence of creative thought, lack of initiative ... but a break in equilibrium'.[10] Crisis, whether refined in the way Genicot proposed or not, might appear a historiographically antique tool with which to conceptualize the later middle ages. Yet it has proved a surprisingly durable framing device,

---

[7] K.B. McFarlane, *Lancastrian Kings and Lollard Knights* (Oxford: Clarendon, 1972).

[8] J.B. Gillingham, 'Crisis or Continuity? The Structure of Royal Authority in England, 1369–1422', in R. Schneider (ed.), *Das Spätmittelalterliche Königtum im europäischen Vergleich* (Sigmaringen: Thorbecke, 1987).

[9] J. Watts, *Henry VI and the Politics of Kingship* (Cambridge: Cambridge University Press, 1996). See also for a not dissimilar reframing of the recurrent crises of late medieval Scottish political history: K. Stevenson, *Power and Propaganda: Scotland 1306–1488* (Edinburgh: Edinburgh University Press, 2014).

[10] L. Genicot, 'Crisis: From the Middle Ages to Modern Times', in M. Postan (ed.), *The Cambridge Economic History of Europe* (Cambridge: Cambridge University Press, 1966).

even in some recent and cutting-edge work. 'The Late Middle Ages were', Katherine Pribyl has observed, 'a time of crisis'. She contended that 'the heaviest blows were concentrated in the fourteenth century which saw the blossom of the High Middle Ages wither: the Great Famine 1315–1317 was followed by the Great Pestilence 1347–1353...', and she also posited war, heresy, and schism as further dimensions of far-reaching dislocation.[11]

Broad notions of crisis have also become entangled in narratives of 'waning' or 'decline'.[12] Again, these are antique formulations, leading back, in many cases, to the arguments of Johanne Huizinga, but they are nonetheless resilient in their hold on at least some imaginations. Pribyl's words imply a 'falling off' from a medieval politics and society that was in some sense 'mature' in the 'central' (or 'high') middle ages, only to be transformed into something debased, degraded, or senescent during the fourteenth and fifteenth centuries.[13] What follows from such assumptions is the conviction that the period is a prelude to something new, embedding the idea of 'crisis', alongside the still more loaded notions of 'waning' and 'decline', in assumptions about periodization.[14] Thus Genicot observed that the late middle ages was 'not only a time of decadence but also one of preparation, of search for new solutions to enduring problems', so suggesting that in the crucible of crisis were forged new ideas and institutions.

Are we, then, entitled to associate all, or at least many, of the specific late medieval events that might be labelled, often in a loose and commonsensical way, as crises—the famines, epidemics, wars—to postulate a crisis of larger proportions, something that might be construed as a 'general crisis'? And, if so, can we move from that notion of general crisis to make claims about epochal, systemic, and structural change? Those questions tend to lead from politics to economics. When he spoke of late medieval crisis, Genicot had in mind in the first instance the economic sphere, and it is in the economy and society that many other historians sought the origins of such a crisis. It is there, too, that rather sharper conceptualizations of crisis are sometimes to be found. At the heart of the matter are not only, indeed not primarily, the calamity of the Black Death but also a sequence of famines and murrain that struck during the period from 1315 to 1322. Was this a concatenation of essentially distinct events, or are we entitled to connect them in some way to suggest that they are signs of, or a stimulus for, systemic problems?

The historiographical importance of famines, murrains, and epidemics of the fourteenth grew during the twentieth century. This was in part consequent

[11] K. Pribyl, *Farming, Famine and Plague: The Impact of Climate Change in the Late Middle Ages* (Springer, 2017), 2.

[12] For this point see: Watts, *Making of Polities*, introduction. J. Watts, *The Making of Polities: Europe 1300–1500* (Cambridge: Cambridge University Press, 2009), esp. 1–13.

[13] J. Watts (ed.), *The End of the Middle Ages?* (Cheltenham: Sutton, 1998), introduction.

[14] For the concept of 'crisis' in the historiography of late medieval Europe and something of its genealogy in Marxist and non-Marxist approaches, see Watts, *Making of Polities, 1–42.*

on empirical work by historians who disinterred the famines and murrains of
the early fourteenth century from the historical record, but it emerged also
from new ways of thinking about, and modelling, the medieval economy and
society in which these catastrophes were conceived not as falling thunderbolt-
like from without, but rather as emerging from its very guts.[15] For though
historians were divided on the question of causation, Marxists looking to
tensions in the socio-economic order, giving rise, ultimately, to a transition
from feudal to capitalist modes of production, and Neo-Malthusians concentrating on demographic pressure, they converged on the idea that the crisis
at hand had been endogenously generated. The concept of crisis was implicated in these approaches in different ways. But it was in Marxist analyses that
the formulation was the subject of most critical reflection. Here it did more
explanatory work, although the work it did also varied in different Marxist
theorizations, since different causes of crisis, each with social relations at its
heart, were identified.

In thinking about these different approaches the Marxist historians who
stand out are Robert Brenner, Rodney Hilton, and Guy Bois. Brenner stressed
that the nature of the relationship between lord and peasant, in which the
former extracted ever more of the latter's surplus, precluding innovation and
so ensuring a 'productivity crisis *leading* [my emphasis] to a demographic
crisis sooner or later'.[16] Guy Bois attached more significance to upward demographic pressure in the late thirteenth and early fourteenth centuries than
Brenner, but continued to locate tension between lords and peasants at the
heart of the mechanism of socio-economic change: lords extracted peasant
surpluses, but with reducing effect as peasant resistance intensified, encouraging lords to bolster their incomes by carving out new tenements.[17] Yet the
continued rise of population that facilitated the strategy undercut gains made
as land ran short and acute problems engulfed both groups, experienced by
peasants as famine and lords by inescapably constrained revenues. Hilton's
views in his mature work on the crisis of feudalism converged in many ways
with those of Bois. He held that lords looked to grow their incomes not so
much by fruitlessly seeking to annex more of the peasant surplus but rather
by capitalizing on population growth, expanding tenanted lands, and riding
rising markets.[18] This strategy began to founder in the late thirteenth and

[15] H.S. Lucas, 'The Great European Famine of 1315, 1316, and 1317', *Speculum*, 5
(1930), 343–77.

[16] T.H. Aston and C.H.E. Philpin (eds), *The Brenner Debate: Agrarian Class Structure
and Economic Development in Pre-industrial Europe* (Cambridge, Cambridge University
Press: 1985).

[17] G. Bois, *The Crisis of Feudalism: Economy and Society in Eastern Normandy, 1300–
1500* (Cambridge: Cambridge University Press, c.1984).

[18] R. Hilton, *Class Conflict and the Crisis of Feudalism: Essays in Medieval Social History*
(London: Verso, 2nd edn., 1990), ch. 15.

early fourteenth centuries in the face of overpopulation, exhausted opportunities for agricultural extensification, and a depressed economy that in turn saw seigniorial incomes flat-line.

The agrarian and other crises that eventuated in the fourteenth century were for Hilton, as for Bois, elements in, but not the cause of, a fundamental crisis in the mode of production—of feudalism—that subsequently developed. For tension between lords (whose survival depended on the extraction of surpluses) and peasants (whose interests turned on sustaining their families, and who, in pursuing that objective saw in lordship no significant benefit) remained at the heart of the system of relationships, manifested in resistance, whether active or, more commonly, passive in form.

If these analyses were subtly distinct, the centrality of crisis to each of them was a stimulus to reflection on the concept, of which the most explicit instance is to be found in the work of Hilton. He drew out the medical analogy that we have already met because the crisis of a social system was, in his eyes, similar to the crisis of an organism.[19] But Hilton also attended to the analogy's limits: analyzing the crisis of a social system was, in a crucial respect, a very different enterprise, since an organism had self-evident bounds and the social system did not. So when the concept of crisis was transplanted from medical science into historical study, it was essential to be clear about *who* or *what* was in crisis, to define the parameters of the 'system' that was convulsed. Hilton's explicitness about terms, and his return to the concept's linguistic roots was a useful call for precision of a kind that is not often found, and it encouraged him to anatomize the 'system' that he needed to examine in terms of peasant family, landholding, lordship, and more. It also, however, throws into relief certain problems with the Marxist conceptualization of crisis too.

There was a tendency among Marxist historians towards capaciousness when it came to marking the bounds of the 'system' with which they were concerned. Leading Marxists, including Robert Brenner, Guy Bois, and Rodney Hilton himself held that a 'total crisis' was to be found in their period. Thus Guy Bois discerned in the 'long' fourteenth century not only depopulation and 'regression of productive capacity' which was 'without historical precedent', but also 'an atmosphere of catastrophe' not only surrounding but also connected to those economic fundamentals. He pointed to 'ceaseless epidemics, endless war … spiritual disarray, social and political disturbances', and he observed that 'when it had ended, European society was remodelled from top to bottom'. This interpretation suggests how, if the bounds of the 'system' were drawn generously there was a risk of associating phenomena that were not—not demonstrably—causally connected. This danger is perhaps better illustrated not with reference to the work of Bois but rather by turning to the synoptic treatment of the middle ages offered by Perry Anderson.[20] His distinctive—and in many ways imaginative—treatment of the period shared

[19] Ibid.

[20] P. Anderson, *Passages from Antiquity to Feudalism* (London: New Left Books, 1975).

with other Marxist analyses a conceptualization in which agrarian and monetary shocks were related to falling incomes of the seigniorial elite, which in turn had wider social and political ramifications. Yet his eagerness to tie not only seigniorial retrenchment but also other phenomena—from the Hundred Years War, conceived as a route to plunder, and the Wars of the Roses, portrayed as 'gangsterism'—into an account of growing resistance and ultimate crisis produced an explanation that was too schematic and too programmatic.[21]

The consequences of these assumptions are felt not only in the broad-brush claims ventured by Bois in his conclusions, and in the synthesis developed by Anderson, they are also to be detected in empirical work too, in which the commitment to the existence of a crisis was a stimulus to finding one, disparate examples being assimilated to the central explanation. Thus for Rodney Hilton instances of non-performance of labour services became significant as expressions of building peasant resistance in an England in which open rebellion by the lower orders was rare, missing the point that the total number of instances of manorial indiscipline was perhaps not so very great.

The concept of crisis is, of course, not itself the centre or cause of such difficulties, but in elevating the concept to the status of a 'general' phenomenon of the economy and society, it was nonetheless implicated in deterministic and teleological explanation that it helped in turn to reinforce. In some ways it was the marriage of two concepts—'crisis' and 'system'—that was the deeper problem. This might be true in a second sense too, visible especially in the work of Bois. This is because he did not conceive his analysis of late medieval eastern Normandy simply as a patch in a quilt of regional studies, the completion of which might in future reveal broader lineaments of late medieval historical development. Rather, because the crisis he had adumbrated gripped the whole 'feudal world economy', convulsing 'the densely populated core of Europe' (a zone within which 'the contradictions of feudal development reached their peak') and rippling through the 'peripheries', the example of Normandy illuminated the whole. The language here (again) was often organic—society and economy was a body or an organism—or else it was systemic, emphasizing essential interconnectedness not only of society, economy, politics, and church but also of places—or at least those places possessed of the essential characteristics of the feudal order. For Bois it was possible to argue that the 'crisis' he had elucidated in Normandy was 'general' in the geographic sense because of the nature of the 'system' he had postulated.

A further complication in each of these models was that crisis could not be a passing thunderstorm: it needed to occasion a decisive break, a change of climate, so to speak, as the feudal yielded to the capitalist order. Yet here the evidence for the partial and protracted nature of change in the fourteenth and fifteenth centuries was a problem. In light of this Hilton said more about his conceptualization of crisis and its implications, reaching again for

---

[21] Ibid., 200–201.

medical and biological analogies.[22] 'Crises were', he contended, 'by definition turning points in the history of a social system as well as a natural organism'. He explained that 'the organism may die, [or] it may survive more or less intact'. But he added that the organism 'may [also] survive having undergone sufficient changes to enable it to cope with changing circumstances ...'. This specific analogy was one that fitted the later middle ages. He acknowledged that 'after the crisis in the fourteenth century, feudalism had a long, tortured subsequent history', but 'if the crisis of the social system did not end in its demise, we need not pretend it did not happen'. In speaking of 'crisis' in bold socio-economic terms, as a crisis of the whole 'feudal' order, there remains, however, the fundamental problem that change was patchy and drawn out. And if we are to accept a long gap between crisis and ultimate transformation in the seventeenth century, as Hilton invites us to do, one might feel entitled to ask what, exactly, the 'crisis' of the fourteenth century has explained, given that so much often imperfectly explicated history lies in a long period of development. Hilton's refined definition—for all its plausibility in biological terms—raises questions about the usefulness of 'crisis' as a tool of analysis when it is understood to be 'general' or 'total' and thus a mainspring of historical development.

In this context it is interesting that a leading critic of such Marxist analyses, Michael Postan, was rather more circumspect in his deployment of the word, even if the concept is still a presence in his writings. He did not use 'crisis' in his discussion of population in *Medieval Economy and Society*, and in a foundational article treating 'Heriots and Prices' he used it only to label the trauma of 1315–1316, which saw 'a heightened crisis in agriculture and a rise of mortality to unprecedented heights'.[23] It featured rather more in his later summative essays, but only in the company of adjectives that placed careful limits on its bounds: 'agrarian', 'agricultural', and 'economic'.[24] That Malthus had himself largely eschewed the word may have guided Postan's election of terms, but more deeply, in construing positive checks as means by which the demographic 'system' was regulated, returning it to equilibrium, 'crisis' might have possessed certain connotations of transformation that, as a strong critic of Marxist analyses, he was keen to avoid.

'Crisis' remains a central way of thinking about the social and economic history of the fourteenth century, whether historians argue against it or for it. There is a parallel here with the argument about the way in which 'crises' form part of the framework of political narrative, for the 'facts' of the case, so to speak, explain the concept's ongoing centrality, the famines, murrains,

[22] R.H. Hilton, 'Crisis of Feudalism', in Aston and Philpin (eds), *The Brenner Debate*.

[23] M. Postan, *The Medieval Economy and Society: An Economic History of Britain in the Middle Ages* (London: Weidenfeld and Nicolson, 1972); M.M. Postan and J. Titow, 'Heriots and Prices on Winchester Manors', *The Economic History Review*, new series, 11 (1959), 392–411.

[24] M. Postan (ed.), *The Cambridge Economic History of Europe* (Cambridge: Cambridge University Press, 1966), 548–632.

epidemics of the period stimulating its use. Contemporary chroniclers might not have had terms neatly analogous to the modern word, but the language they chose continues to encourage modern historians to have recourse to the concept. Likewise, runs of data extracted from manorial and other records continue to suggest its use too, permitting inferences about spiking mortality from indications of, for example, steep grain price rises and burgeoning post-famine land transfers. What further work on the society and economy has done, however, is to raise questions about the generalizability of claims about crisis. Proliferating research into the fourteenth and fifteenth centuries over the last fifty years has uncovered greater variety and complexity in the economy and society, problematizing approaches that isolated specific prime movers. It has generated doubts, too, about how far one is entitled to move from the particular crises—famine, murrain, epidemic—to larger claims that these sprang from a socio-economic *system* that was in crisis, or that these events precipitated crisis in that system.[25]

The discovery of diversity has been attended by recognition of greater complexity. Neither Marxists nor Neo-Malthusians had paid much attention to the role of the market in their postulations of crisis, but the act of writing markets into the story of the medieval economy and society, so uncovering the extent of its commercialization, raised all sorts of questions.[26] The most confident articulations of a commercialization thesis dissolved the broader historical significance of the famines and murrains that struck in the early four-teenth century. These became functions of exogenous shocks in an economy that was buoyant, stimulated by rising population and broadly able to meet subsistence needs. Crises did not vanish, of course: the famines, murrains, and epidemics could not be argued away. But as historical subjects they shrank in significance.[27] If such radical re-interpretations have not commanded general assent, more mainstream arguments about the importance of land, labour, and commodity markets have had major implications for both conceptualiza-tion and measurement. For example, Malthusian arguments that movement onto agriculturally marginal land indicated demographic pressure were under-mined because such expansion could be a function of the prospects such land afforded lords and peasants as they looked to market opportunities. Morcella-tion of holdings in the later thirteenth and early fourteenth centuries remained

[25] B. Harvey, 'The Population Trend in England between 1300 and 1348', *Transactions of the Royal Historical Society*, 16 (1966), 23–42.

[26] For recent discussion: J. Drendel (ed.), *Crisis in the later Middle Ages: beyond the Postan-Duby paradigm* (Turnhout: Brepols, 2015). See also J. Hatcher and M. Bailey, *Modelling the Middle Ages: the History and Theory of England's Economic Development* (Cambridge: Cambridge University Press, 2001).

[27] G.D. Snooks, 'The Dynamic Role of the Market in the Anglo-Norman Economy and Beyond, 1086–1300', in R.H. Britnell and B.M.S. Campbell (eds), *A Commercialising Economy: England, 1086 to c. 1300* (Manchester and New York: Manchester University Press, 1995), 27–54; K.G. Persson, *Pre-Industrial Economic Growth: Social Organization and Technological Progress in Europe* (Oxford: Blackwell, 1988).

a surer sign of population pressure, but the inability of such small parcels of land to sustain a peasant family also implied the existence of something more complex than the subsistence economy assumed by Postan. Commercialization also had ramifications for understandings of both seigniorial priorities and peasant solidarities and hence for Marxist interpretations too. For in a rather more fluid social world informed by market forces, some peasants rose while others fell, generating stratification and fragmentation of interests, and hence raising questions about whether collective 'peasant' struggle might be so central a mechanism of socio-economic transformation.

What has emerged is the importance of multi-factorial, and hence regionally inflected, explanations of the agrarian crisis, or perhaps more accurately 'crises', since it is clear that the course of events in different local and regional economies often differed. These varied experiences needed to be understood in complex terms, integrating rising population, weather-induced harvest failure and animal disease, and then the effects of these pressures had to be calculated for economies in which land, labour, and commodity markets were developed to differing degrees. War, taxation, and the impoverishing effects of hard lordship also claimed a place in such analyses but, like population, they were not given a determining role. More refined language has, in consequence, spread through textbook syntheses in which the experience of 'crisis' might, it is now recognized, have been a matter of perspective. Thus for Hoppenbrouwers and Brockmans, transformations of labour and commodity markets meant that landlords may indeed have been in such a state, but the later fourteenth and fifteenth centuries could simultaneously be construed as a 'golden age' for a peasantry whose wages tended to rise in a world of diminishing seigniorial authority.[28] As a result, the 'general crises' posited by older models have splintered into many distinct—more sharply defined—crises that are regional or even local in character and are the preserve of particular sectors of the society and economy. Historians, rather than feeling the need to abandon crisis as a concept, have brought the idea under control. Even when more expansive forms are ventured there is now caution: introducing a volume of essays treating the early fourteenth century, Harry Kitsikopoulos, averred that the agrarian shocks might be no 'ordinary crisis', but rather one that 'opened the possibility of fundamental systemic change', and yet he acknowledged that there were now known to be 'different outcomes across different countries and regions'.[29] Moved to resuscitate the notion of general crisis, he drew back. Others have looked to the specific relationships between markets and political structures to develop explanations capable of assimilating the mass of frequently discrepant evidence from different regions. Stephan

---

[28] W. Blockmans and P.C.M. Hoppenbrouwers, *Introduction to Medieval Europe, 300–1500* (London: Routledge, third edition, 2017).

[29] H. Kitsikopoulos (ed.), *Agrarian Change and Crisis in Europe, 1200–1500* (London and New York: Routledge, 2012), 1.

Epstein, in tracing economic change in the later middle ages driven by positive political development (in essence processes of state formation for market integration) sought to re-conceptualize the antecedent traumas that helped to facilitate that shift in narrower terms, arguing for an 'integration crisis' that had convulsed markets, rather than a general crisis that encompassed the economy and society.[30]

Climate has also commended itself as a potential prime mover in resurgent general theories of crisis too. Geoffrey Parker revived the idea of a seventeenth-century 'General Crisis', not in the political terms in which Hugh Trevor Roper originally conceived one in 1959 but rather as a linked cluster of crises across the globe whose origins lay in 'fatal synergies' of climate change and political action.[31] The leading champion of such an approach to the later middle ages has, however, been noticeably more cautious in his election of terms.[32] Bruce Campbell has, like Parker, thought globally about climate and historical development. Such a reframing of debate locates socio-economic change in an ecological setting in which 'crisis'—in its original biological or medical sense—might potentially be applied in a more precise way. But it is striking that Campbell, perhaps alert to the inescapable freightedness of the concept reached for new and more precise wording to capture the implications of climate change for ecosystems and the societies and economies embedded in them. Perhaps the most significant is the idea of the 'tipping point'. This term was generated in the social sciences but Malcolm Gladwell put it into widespread circulation in a popular book about social change. Geoffrey Parker adopted it as a supplement to the concept of crisis but Campbell took it up seemingly as a substitute. The tipping point refers to a moment beyond which a societal system ceases to function (or is transformed in its functioning). The term has also had a life in climate science too, where it is deployed to pinpoint the moment when the climate system goes through irreversible change and it allows for an incremental development to have a disproportionate effect on a system. In Bruce Campbell's work, the 'tipping point' helps him to describe how hitherto resilient socio-economic systems came to be undone during the fourteenth century when deteriorating weather conditions pressed on a society weakened by demographic increases, the negative effects of which neither technological development nor commercialization proved able fully to offset.

Adoption of the 'tipping point' is an attempt to find a more exact language with which to talk about change. A problem is that what works in scientific,

[30] S.R. Epstein, *Freedom and Growth: The Rise of States and Markets in Europe, 1300–1750* (London and New York: Routledge, 2000).

[31] G. Parker, *Global Crisis: War, Climate Change and Catastrophe in the Seventeenth Century* (New Haven: Yale, 2013).

[32] B.M.S. Campbell, 'Nature as Historical Protagonist: Environment and Society in Pre-industrial England', *The Economic History Review*, new series, 63 (2010), 281–314; B.M.S Campbell, *The Great Transition: Climate, Disease and Society in the Late-Medieval World* (Cambridge: Cambridge University Press, 2016).

or even in a social scientific, explanation might work less well in historical interpretation wherein data is uneven and the variables are many and not susceptible to scientific control. The disproportionate effects of any individual incremental change on the larger societal system are, in such a context, inevitably easier to assert than to demonstrate. Isolating one factor that leads a balance to tip becomes as much a matter of personal election as anything objectively extractable from the sources.[33] The risk is that we have contiguities rather than connections, things that may be merely coincidental rather than causally linked, 'tipped balances' that are coextensive with climate change but which may not be functions of it. Nonetheless the new language has the merit of liberating us from the over-used and inherently vague language of crisis. It brings the question of change into sharp focus without denying the complexity of the system in which it takes place. It also makes plain something that 'crisis' tends to cloud: crises might eventuate in the restoration of the original equilibrium, whereas the tipping of a tipping point implies that there can be no return to the *status quo*.

As a minimum proposition the foregoing reflections might suggest that we profit from de-dramatizing language when we are characterizing the later middle ages, such that its undoubted and profound specific crises (of famine, epidemic, violence) do not by default define the period as a whole. New coinages can help. 'Reconversion' and 'transformation' have commended themselves as alternative ways of framing late medieval change to scholars working in Italy.[34] Others, including several prominent historians working in the British Isles, have settled on 'transition'. Bruce Campbell, notably, moved away from explanation in terms of (general) crisis and (epochal) change to a new interpretational framework of just this kind. Chris Dyer also reached for the term in his own synthesis, *The Age of Transition*. Concentrating on the period from 1350 to 1520, he cautioned against a search for turning points around the year 1500 and adumbrated instead a generous intermediate phase extending from the late middle ages to the early nineteenth century, highlighting a series of probably non-reversible—and certainly unreversed—shifts between the thirteenth and the sixteenth centuries that were significant elements in a bigger but slow and uneven transformation.[35] Where Campbell and Dyer focused on society and economy, others concentrating on politics have also stepped back from implicating 'crisis' in a meta-narrative of late medieval change and have similarly set question marks against traditional periodization too. Rather than co-opting the political and dynastic convulsions of

---

[33] For elaboration of this point and further critical comment see P. Warde, 'Global Crisis or Coincidence', *Past and Present*, 228 (2015), 287–301.

[34] For this point see Watts, *Making of Polities*, 16 n. 19; and note also F. Menant, M. Bourin, L. To Figueras (eds), *Dynamiques du monde rural dans la conjoncture de 1300* (Rome: École française de Rome, 2014).

[35] C. Dyer, *The Age of Transition? Economy and Society in the Later Middle Ages* (Oxford: Oxford University Press, 2nd edn., 2007).

the fifteenth century into narratives of malaise, decline, or crisis—which might be held up as a prelude to Tudor transformation—recent work has suggested greater complexity and more continuity. Gerald Harriss has acknowledged the political and military (as well as socio-economic) stresses that characterized his period but ultimately emphasized how institutions and structures evolved and regenerated in response to them, being shaped, and reshaped, rather than transfigured.[36] In these cases 'transition', whether explicit or implicit, might again better capture the complexity of the 'data' now available for late medieval society, creating interpretational space for protracted, multi-layered change. And it speaks also, of course, to problems of political periodization, avoiding overly neat schematizations in which 'the medieval' yields to the 'early modern' (or the 'feudal' to the 'capitalist').

None of this implies that 'crisis' need—or should—be abandoned as a weapon in the armoury of historical explanation. It is merely to suggest that recognizing its limitations as a conceptual tool is important, especially since it has been blunted by mis- and over-use. Indeed, in periods in which it has not become a cliché, 'crisis' might prove a valuable interpretational instrument precisely because it is an unfamiliar means of conceptualization, throwing hitherto unnoticed features of the historical landscape into clear relief. Tom Bisson's *The Crisis of the Twelfth Century* used the concept to detonate a mine beneath comfortable assumptions. He forced rethinking of the period that was at the heart of the 'high' middle ages, one more usually associated with upbeat nouns such as 'renaissance', 'reformation', or 'revolution', and argued instead for deep creative tension between different means to power, constituted by fidelity and force on one hand and politics, policy, and service on the other.[37] In this 'high' medieval setting 'crisis' was not a tired cliché but a provocation to reconsider how new state structures came into being and the circumstances of their production.

More generally, the point is not, perhaps, that this concept—or any other for that matter—need necessarily be retired. There are indeed instances when a more neutral alternative, perhaps a more technical and exact language, might be used with advantage. But, as Rees Davies noted, historians pay a price when they write in accessible terms and this might be a price worth paying if the alternative is to bury the past in jargon. This seems right: for a term is not intrinsically problematic, it is rather the unintended consequences, and sometimes the intended consequences (in that a concept such as 'crisis' is a strong piece of rhetoric) of its deployment that need to be monitored. We must, in other words, be alert to the point that 'crisis' is a term of art, that

[36] Harriss, *Shaping the Nation*, 650; Watts, *End of the Middle Ages*.

[37] T.N. Bisson, *The Crisis of the Twelfth Century: Power, Lordship and the Origins of European Government* (Princeton: Princeton University Press, 2009).

it possesses imaginative power and interpretative potency and rhetorical force when employed in narrative. And so, like 'state' and 'feudalism' and 'frontier'—terms that rightly have caught the eye—we might pause momentarily to wonder what work this concept, and others like it, oft-used but little attended, might be doing in historical explanations.

CHAPTER 5

Frontier

Jackson W. Armstrong

It is the concept of 'Frontier' and its use that will be explored in this essay, and this particular problem will be developed with reference to late medieval Scotland, with regard to the question of how to understand the frontiers of the Scottish kingdom in the fifteenth century. That is, not only to consider the familiar southern frontier with England, but also the kingdom's other frontiers to the west and to the north. If we are to attempt to speak of Scotland's frontiers what, then, are we to look for in late medieval sources as evidence of their existence? In this way the question can be framed as one about the tension between concepts and historical terminology: between the analytical category of 'frontier' that might be adopted as a tool of historical enquiry, and the way the phenomenon we are looking for might have been recorded in sources from the past. This very tension may be put to work for an exercise in thinking about how medieval historians may employ concepts in fruitful and constructive ways as they interrogate the past.

'Frontier' is a well-worn concept in terms of scholarly treatment. More than a century of work has grappled with the idea, building on the foundational efforts of Turner, Febvre, Bolton, and Lattimore which explored modern frontiers as zones, boundary lines, borderlands, and fluid, permeable

J. W. Armstrong (✉)
Department of History, University of Aberdeen, Aberdeen, Scotland, UK

J. W. Armstrong, P. Crooks and A. Ruddick (eds), *Using Concepts in Medieval History*, https://doi.org/10.1007/978-3-030-77280-2_5

spaces of interaction.[1] The investigation of frontiers, borders, and boundaries of all conceivable types has generated an immense literature, and historical approaches to the topic have generally adopted a comparative emphasis (best exemplified in the still indispensable collection edited by Power and Standen). It is fair to say that 'frontier' is a concept in which historians generally have been leading creative voices, and not simply content to import ideas from other disciplines, such as political science and geography.[2] For the middle ages in particular, of course work on frontiers has highlighted the recurring phenomenon of marcher jurisdictions, memorably characterised by Lourie as societies 'organised for war'.[3] And further work on premodern frontiers, led by Abulafia and Berend, has made the point that frontiers may exist in the mind as imagined constructs, more clearly than they might be marked out in the landscape.[4]

Medieval historians, including those of the British–Irish Isles, have readily employed 'frontier' as an analytical tool. This is so with reference to the marcher lordships of medieval Wales, the Tudor state's frontiers with Gaelic Ireland and with Scotland, and Anglo-Scottish march administration, law, and

---

[1] I am grateful for the comments of my fellow editors, and those of Dr Alison Cathcart, Dr Ian Grohse, and Dr Simon Egan who kindly read this essay in draft. I have also benefited from the comments of my colleagues in the University of Aberdeen History Department's work-in-progress seminar in October 2020, and those of participants in the workshop on 'Nobility in Scotland and the Holy Roman Empire during the Later Middle Ages', at Johannes Gutenberg University of Mainz in February 2020.

[2] F.J. Turner, 'The Significance of the Frontier in American History', in F.J. Turner, *The Frontier in American History* (New York: Henry Holt and Company, 1920), 1–38; L. Febvre, 'The Problem of Frontiers and the Natural Bounds of States', in L. Febvre, *A Geographical Introduction to History*, trans. E.G. Mountford and J.H. Paxton (London: Routledge, 1932), 296–314; L. Febvre, '*Frontière:* The Word and the Concept', in L. Febvre (ed.), *A New Kind of History: From the Writings of Lucien Febvre*, trans. K. Folca, ed. P. Burke (London: Routledge, 1973), 208–18; O. Lattimore, *Studies in Frontier History: Collected Papers, 1928–58* (Oxford: Oxford University Press, 1962), esp. 'The Frontier in History' at 469–91; A.L. Hurtado, 'Parkmanizing the Spanish Borderlands: Bolton, Turner, and the Historians' World', *Western Historical Quarterly*, 26 (1995), 149–167.

[2] D.J. Power and N. Standen (eds), *Frontiers in Question: Eurasian Borderlands, 700–1700* (Basingstoke: Macmillan, 1999). See also F. Curta (ed.), *Borders, Barriers, and Ethnogenesis. Frontiers in Late Antiquity and the Middle Ages* (Turnhout: Brepols, 2005).

[3] E. Lourie, 'A Society Organised for War: Medieval Spain', *Past & Present*, 35 (1966), 54–76, esp. 58–59; A. Goodman, 'The Anglo-Scottish Marches in the Fifteenth Century: A Frontier Society?', in R.A. Mason (ed.), *Scotland and England, 1286–1815* (Edinburgh: John Donald, 1987), 18–33, at 18; S.G. Ellis, 'The English State and Its Frontiers in the British Isles, 1300–1600', in Power and Standen (eds), *Frontiers in Question*, 153–81, at 163–64. On 'march' applied to Wales see M. Lieberman, *The Medieval March of Wales: The Creation and Perception of a Frontier, 1066–1283* (Cambridge: Cambridge University Press, 2010), 5–19.

[4] D. Abulafia and N. Berend (eds), *Medieval Frontiers: Concepts and Practices* (Aldershot: Routledge, 2002).

warfare.[5] All the same 'frontier' is a concept that sometimes remains vague and slippery. The possible array of different types is broad, for example, 'political', 'religious', 'cultural', 'linguistic', and 'topographical' frontiers.[6] Moreover, 'frontier' readily elides and intertwines with related concepts (for example, that of periphery and core), and the connotations and assumptions which they bring, which are not always explicitly acknowledged.[7] One aspect of note in relation to the scholarly treatment of premodern frontiers is the classification into those which are 'linear', and those which are 'zonal'. For political scientists and geographers, zonal frontiers are understood to be ambiguous spaces, sometimes no-man's lands 'between' different political powers, and sometimes wildernesses 'beyond' more definitely controlled territory. By contrast, linear frontiers tend to describe artificial lines of separation, as between sovereign territories. (In this regard the related term 'border', marking out the extent of jurisdiction and authority over territory, generally carries with it the meaning of a linear boundary.) However, despite these different classifications, premodern frontiers have been shown to have exhibited features

---

[5] Among the leading examples of such work are: G.W.S. Barrow, 'The Anglo-Scottish Border', *Northern History*, 1 (1966), 21–42; R.R. Davies, *Lordship and Society in the March of Wales, 1282–1400* (Oxford: Clarendon Press, 1978); S.G. Ellis, *Tudor Frontiers and Noble Power: The Making of the British State* (Oxford: Clarendon Press, 1995); S.G. Ellis, *Defending English Ground: War and Peace in Meath and Northumberland, 1460–1542* (Oxford: Oxford University Press, 2015); A. Goodman, 'Religion and Warfare in the Anglo-Scottish Marches', in R.J. Bartlett and A. MacKay (eds), *Medieval Frontier Societies* (Oxford: Clarendon Press, 1989), 245–66; C.J. Neville, *Violence, Custom and Law: The Anglo-Scottish Border Lands in the Later Middle Ages* (Edinburgh: Edinburgh University Press, 1998); A.J. Macdonald, *Border Bloodshed: Scotland, England and France at War 1369–1403* (East Linton: Tuckwell Press, 2000); A. King, 'Best of Enemies: Were the Fourteenth-Century Anglo-Scottish Marches a "Frontier Society"?', in A. King and M.A. Penman (eds), *England and Scotland in the Fourteenth Century: New Perspectives* (Woodbridge: Boydell, 2007), 116–35; E.M. Jamroziak, *Survival and Success on Medieval Borders: Cistercian Houses in Medieval Scotland and Pomerania from the Twelfth to the Late Fourteenth Century* (Turnhout: Brepols, 2011); B. Smith, *Crisis and Survival in Late Medieval Ireland: The English of Louth and Their Neighbours, 1330–1450* (Oxford: Oxford University Press, 2013). For an overview see Jackson W. Armstrong, *England's Northern Frontier: Conflict and Local Society in the Fifteenth-Century Scottish Marches* (Cambridge: Cambridge University Press, 2020), 1–73.

[6] P. Sahlins, *Boundaries: The Making of France and Spain in the Pyrenees* (Berkeley: University of California Press, 1989). For a recent example of a 'cultural borders' approach see M. Andrén, T. Lindkvist, I. Söhrman, K. Vajta (eds), *Cultural Borders of Europe: Narratives, Concepts and Practices in the Present and the Past* (New York and Oxford: Berghahn, 2017).

[7] On conceptual interdependence and intertwinement, see W. Steinmetz and M. Freeden 'Introduction. Conceptual History: Challenges, Conundrums, Complexities', in W. Steinmetz, M. Freeden and J. Fernández-Sebastián (eds), *Conceptual History in the European Space* (New York and Oxford: Berghahn, 2017), 1–46, at 26. On core and periphery see Jackson W. Armstrong, 'Centre, Periphery, Locality, Province: England and its far North in the Fifteenth Century', in P. Crooks, D. Green and W.M. Ormrod (eds), *The Plantagenet Empire: Proceedings of the 2014 Harlaxton Symposium* (Donington: Tyas, 2016), 248–72.

of both, to be hybrid 'linear zonal' boundaries.[8] A helpful illustration of this hybridity, and its historical interest, is the notable effort spent by historians on the identification of so-called 'frontier societies'. In the Anglo-Scottish and Irish cases, for example, the discussion of frontier societies has turned upon the topics of cross-border acculturation, and the complex subject of 'identity', manifested in local and national ties and sentiments.[9] All the same the usefulness of 'frontier society' as a (sub-)category of analysis has been challenged with demands for greater precision.[10]

This essay does not seek to depose 'frontier' as a conceptual tyrant. Despite the many meanings historians have ascribed to frontiers, especially those of a military-social aspect, it has arguably still to mutate into the 'sentient, autonomous agent' whose interference does more harm than good and thus demands outright rejection.[11] Rather, the present goal is to explore how the concept may be harnessed, and still put to work in a rigorous way, 'without distorting and skewing the past'.[12] Those who have considered this challenge explicitly have observed that 'employing concepts is always an exercise in selectivity'.[13] Concepts are naturally slippery, and prone to generate disagreement over the connotations they accrue. It is impossible to use them as a tool for historical analysis without being forced to address what Steinmetz and Freeden have recently called 'conceptual indeterminacy'.[14] So, in what follows 'frontier' as a concept will be explored for the way in which it may be helpful in identifying and exploring inconsistencies, anomalies, ambiguities, and complexities in the past, not least in regard to the tensions between historical terminology and current concepts, and the question of how to address apparent silences in the historical record.[15] It seeks a way to work productively with conceptual indeterminacy, and even use it to our advantage, to give historical treatment greater precision and nuance.

---

[8] Power and Standen (eds), *Frontiers in Question*, 2–3, 5, 9, 13 (and 10, 12, 27 on hybridity); N. Berend, 'Medievalists and the Notion of the Frontier', *The Medieval History Journal*, 2 (1999), 55–72, at 68, 69 (quote).

[9] Goodman, 'Anglo-Scottish Marches'; King, 'Best of Enemies'; S. Booker, *Cultural Exchange and Identity in Late Medieval Ireland: The English and Irish of the Four Obedient Shires* (Cambridge: Cambridge University Press, 2018). L. Dauphant, *Le Royaume des Quatre Rivières: l'espace politique français (1380–1515)* (Seyssel: Champ Vallon, 2012), 233–72, considers the question of frontier societies in late medieval France, and emphasises not their exceptionality but the realm's frontiers as *containers* of the royal *État* (at 262).

[10] Berend, 'Medievalists and the Notion of the Frontier', 68–71.

[11] E.A.R. Brown, 'The Tyranny of a Construct: Feudalism and Historians of Medieval Europe', *American Historical Review*, 79 (1974), 1063–88, at 1088.

[12] R.R. Davies, 'The Medieval State: The Tyranny of a Concept?', *Journal of Historical Sociology*, 16 (2003), 280–300, at 293.

[13] Steinmetz and Freeden, 'Introduction. Conceptual History', 25.

[14] Ibid.

[15] Ibid., 27–28, 31.

SCOTLAND'S FRONTIERS: A CASE STUDY

Frontiers have tended to be understood as landward phenomena, and defined as the limits of territorial jurisdiction, or the zones in which those limits are reached. This tendency is perhaps one of the reasons that Scotland's frontiers have been the subject of less scrutiny than other insular frontiers. The notion of the frontier as a land border fits well with one end of the kingdom, but at the other margins of the realm, frontiers were strongly shaped by the sea. Equally, to the extent that landward frontiers have been understood in terms of control over territory and struggles for that control between competing sovereign powers, work on Scotland's frontiers has been closely tied up with a history of war and diplomacy, particularly with regard to the southern frontier towards England. While Emilia Jamroziak's work on Cistercian abbeys in the Anglo-Scottish marches helpfully opens the topic up in its international religious dimensions, her focus nevertheless emphasises the experience of war and violence in the region in the later middle ages.[16] This prevailing focus on military conflict is why Grohse's more recent work on the Northern Isles as a 'frontier for peace' between Scotland and Norway comes as such a refreshing break from the historiographical emphasis to date.[17]

The following brief case study seeks to identify and compare Scotland's southern, western, and northern frontiers in the fifteenth century, in each instance not in any exhaustive depth but rather through particular illustrative examples. These examples are intended to illuminate the ways in which creative tensions can be found between a current concept or category of analysis like 'frontier' and related historical terms (or their absence). As we shall see, not all of Scotland's frontiers were furnished with a detailed historical terminology. This presents us with a challenge and an opportunity. For the sake of this exercise, the idea of territorial sovereignty will be the principal hook on which we hang the concept of the frontier, to allow us to proceed to all three of Scotland's frontiers with the same questions in mind.[18] In late medieval Scotland sovereignty underwent 'a reinterpretation of public authority in which the crown, comprising both the king and his noble counsellor-administrators, was to have a far greater role in the lives of the governed'.[19] If Robert II's entail of the crown in 1373 had set the rules of succession 'to the kingdom and in the right of ruling' (*in regnum et in jus regnandi*) in fairly undecorated terms, it was in 1469 that James III used parliament to declare his 'ful jurisdictioune and fre impire within his realme', drawing on the jurists'

---

[16] Jamroziak, *Survival and Success on Medieval Borders*.

[17] I.P. Grohse, *Frontiers for Peace in the Medieval North: The Norwegian-Scottish Frontier c. 1260–1470* (Leiden: Brill, 2017), 23–30, and 30–37.

[18] J.P. Canning, 'Ideas of the State in Thirteenth and Fourteenth-Century Commentators on the Roman Law', *Transactions of the Royal Historical Society*, 33 (1983), 1–27, at 16, 23–7.

[19] C. Hawes, 'Community and Public Authority in Later Fifteenth-Century Scotland', unpublished PhD thesis, University of St Andrews, 2015, 132.

maxim *rex in regno suo est imperator regni sui*.[20] Reference to sovereignty, duly acknowledged to be a dynamic and expansive matter in its own right, is a way to observe that concepts do not exist in isolation, but they exist in relation to other concepts. Thus, together with the frontier, territorial sovereignty (alongside other concepts which will become apparent, such as lordship, law, and identity) will serve among our analytical categories of investigation, in an interdependent manner which is only to be expected and which should be recognised at the outset.[21] The goal is to show how being explicit about the challenges of applying 'frontier' as a concept can help us to sharpen our focus and bring out into the open useful historical complexity.

THE SOUTH

It is the southern end of the Scottish realm which has had the greatest attention paid to it with the modern concept of 'frontier' in mind. The good reason for this is that it was well defined in the middle ages, both in terms of international diplomacy and administrative framework. The kingdom's southern limit was clearly agreed as consisting of a borderline stretching from Tweed to Solway in 1237 under the terms of the Treaty of York. And this frontier had its own body of law, known as the 'laws of the marches' or *Leges Marchiarum* which, in the following decade (1249), were first compiled in a text that was to become part of the medieval Scottish legal canon. This was so even as, over the subsequent centuries, march law itself in its international guise would continue to be revised and updated by truce indentures sealed between Scotland and England. It would also continue to evolve in its domestic guise by legislation enacted by parliament. Thus, the late medieval Anglo-Scottish frontier was both linear (in so far as it formed an agreed boundary separating two sovereign jurisdictions), and zonal (in that it applied the framework of the march, on both sides of the border, to denote areas of special jurisdiction arising as a result of proximity to the border). In this way, the Tweed–Solway borderline was principally a political and jurisdictional boundary rather than a religious, linguistic, or cultural divide.[22]

And so the marches and their law offered medieval contemporaries a terminology to describe the frontier; they also featured the officials who administered the march jurisdiction: the wardens. Although adopted much earlier on the English side of the frontier, it was in the 1340s that the office of warden appeared in Scotland in its enduring form, and the term 'warden' was first used there only in 1355. In time it came to be that the marches were

---

[20] *The Records of the Parliaments of Scotland to 1707*, ed. K.M. Brown et al. (St Andrews, 2007–), www.rps.ac.uk [hereafter RPS], 1373/3; RPS, 1469/20. See also N. Macdougall, *James III* (Edinburgh: John Donald, 2009), 88–89.

[21] Steinmetz and Freeden, 'Introduction. Conceptual History', 26. See also Q. Skinner, *Visions of Politics. Volume 1: Regarding Method* (Cambridge and New York: Cambridge University Press, 2002), 43–47.

[22] Armstrong, *England's Northern Frontier*, ch. 2 ('Frontiers and Borderlands').

divided into three, each with its own warden on either side of the border, answerable to their own king.

March administration itself adopted an even more precise terminology to describe the particular boundaries of the marches themselves. For instance, the truce of 1398 made references to 'the bownds of the Marches' and to the responsibilities of each warden to redress breaches of truce '[be]langand to his Bownds'.[23] More particular attention was at times given to the *fines limites terminos et bundas* around the English-held castles of Berwick, Roxburgh, and Jedburgh, which were acknowledged in 1405 to be among those places situated 'on and in the marches shared among [*inter*] the English and Scottish realms and also [*ac*] in the realm of Scotland'.[24] Such contested areas, known as 'debatable lands', were a recurring theme of Anglo-Scottish truce indentures. Most notably this included the substantial stretch of land in the west march between the Rivers Sark and Esk called the 'Batable Landez or Threpe Landez', first addressed in the truce of 1449.[25] In the 1470s, truce commissioners were instructed to proceed by inquiry and perambulation to determine the disputed fishery on the River Esk, and this resumed in the 1480s and 1490s with the additional question of the *metis finibus limitibus et bundis* of the debatable lands [*terrarum batabilium*] in the west marches. They were also to investigate the *metibus finibus limitibus et bundis* of the west marches themselves.[26] This 'metes and bounds' phraseology appears to mirror the language that was typically used, in both realms, to identify the boundaries of private property in this period. Overall, the southern frontier offered late medieval Scots and their neighbours a rich conceptual and terminological framework upon which to draw.

It is notable that ideas of lordship came to be identified with the marches and their legal and administrative framework. This first becomes evident in the later thirteenth century with the earls of Dunbar who, from about 1289, begin to identify themselves as the 'earls of Dunbar or March', presumably to signal their role as landowners on both sides of the frontier, with particular duties in the English lordship of Beanley relating to administering pledges under march law. Although these English lands were lost in the course of Anglo-Scottish conflict, the cross-border identity of the earls endured, and could be activated. It is well known that George, earl of March (d. 1420), chose to adhere to the

[23] *Foedera, Conventiones, Litterae ...*, ed. T. Rymer, 10 vols (The Hague: Neaulme, 1745; reprint, Farnborough: Gregg, 1967), [hereafter *Foedera*], III, iv, p. 153 (1398).

[24] *Rotuli Scotiae in Turri Londinensi ...*, ed. D. Macpherson et al., Record Commission, 2 vols (London, 1814–1819) [hereafter *Rot. Scot.*], ii, pp. 173–74 (1405); *Foedera*, V, i, 50 (1438).

[25] *Calendar of Documents Relating to Scotland ...*, ed. J. Bain, 5 vols (Edinburgh: H.M. General Register House, 1881–88), iv, no. 1221, p. 247; *Foedera*, V, ii, pp. 15–16 (1449). See Armstrong, *England's Northern Frontier*, 56.

[26] *Rot. Scot.*, ii, pp. 450 (1474), p. 452 (1475), p. 479 (1487), p. 491 (1489, quotations), p. 498 (1491), pp. 513–14 (1494).

English king in the period from 1400 until 1409, when he finally returned to Scottish allegiance.[27]

From the later fourteenth century and up until their forfeiture in 1455, the Black Douglas earls of Douglas claimed the mantle of paramount lords of the marches. This magnate dynasty's claims to authority were closely tied to their role as 'wardens and warlords' defending the southern frontier of the kingdom.[28] Indeed, the fourth earl of Douglas held all three wardenships from 1400 to his death in 1424, together with extensive lands in the marches and elsewhere.[29] In 1448 the eighth earl of Douglas and his council went as far as to legislate, overturning parliamentary acts concerning the domestic 'laws of the marches in time of war'.[30] The pinnacle of Black Douglas power was reached in 1450 with the concession by the crown of the earl's extensive land-holdings in free regality and 'regalia'.[31] The identification of military lordship and frontier defence is a phenomenon notable in other parts of the British–Irish Isles in the period.[32] And yet, following the series of clashes with the king and the final forfeiture of the Black Douglas earls in 1455, there was no question that the administrative and official structures of the march remained as the undergirding framework of the frontier. The wardenships came to be held not as hereditary property, but as salaried offices granted by the crown. A mixture of regional nobles served as wardens in the latter decades of the century.[33]

Nevertheless, the idea of the frontier as defined by Anglo-Scottish warfare persisted, and the close identification of lesser inhabitants of the marches with the cause of national defence may be seen in the example of the Grahams of Hutton in Annandale in an undated petition, possibly from the reign of James III (1460–1488). These three minor landowners ('Wylzame the Grame',

---

[27] 'Patricio de Dunbar et Marchia' (RPS, A1296/8/1); Macdonald, 'Kings of the Wild Frontier', in S. Boardman and A. Ross (eds), *The Exercise of Power in Medieval Scotland, c.1200–1500* (Dublin: Four Courts Press, 2003), 139–58, at 140–41, 155–56.

[28] Michael Brown, *The Black Douglases* (East Linton: Tuckwell Press, 1998), 142.

[29] Brown, *Black Douglases*, 95–118, 166–80. James I experimented with advancing the earls of Dunbar and Angus in the marches in the 1430s: Michael Brown, *James I* (Edinburgh: Canongate Academic, 1994), 130–31, 133–35, 139, 145, 150, 154–55.

[30] *The Acts of the Parliaments of Scotland*, ed. T. Thomson and C. Innes, Record Commission, 12 vols (Edinburgh, 1814–1875), [hereafter *APS*], i, app. iv, pp. 714–16. See Brown, *Black Douglases*, 277, 287; C. McGladdery, *James II*, revised edn (Edinburgh: John Donald, 2015), 68–71, 93–95.

[31] RPS, 1450/1/35; RPS, 1450/1/36: '*in puram, integram et liberam regalitatem seu regaliam*'. For further comment on this grant see A.R. Borthwick and H.L. MacQueen, *Law, Lordship and Tenure: The Fall of the Black Douglases*, forthcoming.

[32] R.R. Davies, *Lords and Lordship in the British Isles in the Late Middle Ages*, ed. B. Smith (Oxford: Oxford University Press, 2009), 48, 122, 132.

[33] M.H. Brown, 'The Scottish March Wardenships (c.1340–c.1480)', in A. King and D. Simpkin (eds), *England and Scotland at War c.1296–c.1513* (Leiden: Brill, 2012), 203–29; J.W. Armstrong, 'Local Society and the Defence of the English Frontier in Fifteenth-Century Scotland: The War Measures of 1482', *Florilegium*, 25 (2008), 127–49.

'Richarde the Grame', and 'Henry the Grame') sought royal favour in part by drawing special attention to the fact that they 'ar marche men and dwellys owtmest and may ill be absent owte of our ger for gret scathis apperance tyll us'.[34] Here is a Scottish example of the sort of 'frontier rhetoric' that has been identified on the other side of the English frontier, and also within the English lordship in Ireland.[35] It illustrates the readiness of local landowners to harness the frontier explicitly for their own assertions of identity, loyalty, and defence of property rights. Curiously, that rhetoric also included the geographical idea of distance from royal power (that they dwelled 'owtmest'), whereas in truth the English marches were, of the three frontiers considered here, the closest to the Forth valley hub in which Scottish kings spent the bulk of their time. This is suggestive that perceived (and consciously asserted) distance from the king and his courts, and a need to be physically present and ready to defend the realm, were enduring aspects of how the southern frontier was understood and represented in the fifteenth century. It is also a reminder of the extent to which frontiers existed in the mind. If the Grahams themselves felt distant from royal priorities, they took a convenient opportunity to remind the king and those close to him of the service given by 'marche men', implying that matters relating to the English frontier should not be forgotten on the governmental agenda.

THE WEST

Scotland's western frontier in the later middle ages was framed by another act of thirteenth-century diplomacy, the Treaty of Perth of 1266. By this treaty, the Norwegian king ceded his claims to overlordship of the Western Isles to the king of Scotland. The agreement laid down that Man and the Isles 'shall be subject to the laws and customs of the realm of Scotland and be judged and dealt with according to them henceforth'.[36] What was transferred from one king to another was a temporal dominion, for all the same the diocese of the Isles still remained within the Norwegian archdiocese of Trondheim. This was to last until the see of the Isles passed to the control of the archbishop of St Andrews in 1472.[37] Unlike the southern frontier, the west had no framework like that of the marches which was applied by contemporaries. Thus, in the

---

[34] *Report on Manuscripts in Various Collections,* v, Historical Manuscripts Commission (London, 1909), 77. For comment on this document see H.L. MacQueen, *Common Law and Feudal Society in Medieval Scotland* (Edinburgh: Edinburgh University Press, 1993, 2nd edn. 2016), 112, 215.

[35] Smith, *Crisis and Survival in Late Medieval Ireland,* 183; Armstrong, *England's Northern Frontier,* 90–94.

[36] *APS,* i, pp. 420–21; R.A. McDonald, *The Kingdom of the Isles: Scotland's Western Seaboard, c.1100 – c. 1336* (East Linton: Tuckwell Press, 1997), 131.

[37] The see of the Isles was separated from the diocese of Man during the Great Schism. See J. Munro and R.W. Munro (eds), *Acts of the Lords of the Isles 1336–1493* (Edinburgh: Scottish History Society, 1986) [hereafter *ALI*], lv–lvi; T. Thornton, 'Scotland and the

west, Scotland's frontier lacked a contemporary terminology with which to describe it. This fact forces us to reflect on how far 'frontier' can be applied in the west, and in what historical terms the category of analysis can be situated.[38]

Historians have tended to shy away from identifying Scotland's western 'frontier', perhaps with good reason. Recent work by Egan has sought to treat the Lordship of the Isles instead as part of what he calls a 'wider Gaelic world', with certain shared linguistic and cultural practices, that reached from Ireland, across the Hebrides, and into the Scottish Highlands.[39] In an important article on the Lordship of the Isles some decades ago, Grant preferred to speak of Scotland's 'Celtic fringe'.[40] In the absence of a clearly delineated frontier in historical terms, the tendency has thus been to look for alternative ways to address the problem, and the longer-term picture of a 'Gaelic cultural province' straddling Ireland and Scotland in the premodern period is a useful reference point (which all the same should be seen as nuanced and far from homogenous).[41] However, if in the present exercise we are to apply the concept of 'frontier' in the west in the sense of the limits of territorial sovereignty, we could do worse than look to the phenomenon of lordship as a way to ground the discussion.

The Treaty of Perth of 1266 'effectively killed' off the former kingdom of the Isles, which had been ruled by the *Ri Innse Gall*, the great sea kings like Godred Crovan (d.1095) and Somlered of Argyll (d.1164). In the words of one historian, the phoenix which rose from the ashes of the kingdom's funeral pyre was the MacDonald Lordship of the Isles.[42] The Latin title *'dominus Insularum'* was first used in 1336 by John of Islay, who was great-grandson of Donald, who himself was a grandson of Somerled. The lordship existed for more than a century and a half, descending from John of Islay to his

Isle of Man, *c.*1400–1625: Noble Power and Royal Presumption in the Northern Irish Sea Province', *Scottish Historical Review*, 77 (1998), 1–30.

[38] For brief comment on mainland Argyll as a 'frontier' see I. G. MacDonald, *Clerics and Clansmen: The Diocese of Argyll between the Twelfth and Sixteenth Centuries* (Leiden: Brill, 2013), 6.

[39] S. Egan, 'Richard II and the Wider Gaelic World: A Reassessment', *Journal of British Studies*, 57: 2 (2018), 221–52, esp. 224n 8. See also S. Egan, 'The Early Stewart Kings, the Lordship of the Isles, and Ireland, c.1371–c.1433', *Northern Studies*, 49 (2018), 61–78.

[40] A. Grant, 'Scotland's 'Celtic fringe' in the Late Middle Ages: The MacDonald Lords of the Isles and the Kingdom of Scotland', in R.R. Davies (ed.), *The British Isles 1100–1500: Comparisons, Contrasts and Connections* (Edinburgh: John Donald, 1988), 118–41.

[41] W. McLeod, *Divided Gaels: Gaelic Cultural Identities in Scotland and Ireland, c. 1200–c. 1650* (Oxford: Oxford University Press, 2004). See R.D. Oram, 'A Celtic Dirk at Scotland's Back? The Lordship of the Isles in Scottish Historiography since 1828', in R.D. Oram (ed.), *The Lordship of the Isles* (Leiden: Brill, 2014), 1–39, at 37–38.

[42] McDonald, *The Kingdom of the Isles*, 256.

son, grandson, and great-grandson, before the final forfeiture of the latter in 1493.[43]

The MacDonald Lords of the Isles also held various possessions on the Scottish mainland.[44] Chief among these, held from 1437–1475, was the earldom of Ross which proved to be their eventual 'Achilles Heel' in the view of Macdougall.[45] As a result the Lords of the Isles were hardly confined to the Hebrides, or even to their possessions along the western seaboard. The charters of the fifteenth-century Lords, Alexander and John, as earls of Ross, reveal them to be very active mainland magnates, with landed interests from the earldom reaching from Kincardineshire to Sutherland.[46]

The designation *'dominus Insularum'* was simply adopted by the Lords of the Isles from 1336; it was not bestowed upon them by royal grant.[47] There has been some speculation about the significance of this title, and the extent to which this *'dominium'* might have carried princely connotations, as a Latin translation of the former Gaelic *Ri Innse Gall*.[48] However, it is difficult to find any clear MacDonald pretensions to sovereignty in the fifteenth century. During the period when the Lords also possessed the earldom of Ross, in their *acta* they consistently placed their comital dignity ahead of their other titles, including *'dominus Insularum'*, which suggests at least that they did not view their status as Lord of the Isles to take precedence over their status as a Scottish earl. The 'wider Gaelic world' provided examples of petty kings with whom the Scottish diplomats engaged in the fifteenth century, such as the O'Neill kinglet ['*Regulus Onele*'] in Ireland to whom the sheriff of Wigtown was sent in 1460.[49] Although Irish marriages brought about the MacDonald acquisition of the Glynns of Antrim and thus gave the close kinsmen of the

---

[43] *ALI*, pp. xix–xx, 279; C. Martin, 'A Maritime Dominion – Sea-Power and the Lordship', in Oram (ed.), *Lordship of the Isles*, 176–99, at 192. For a historiographical survey see Oram, 'A Celtic Dirk', 1–39.

[44] For example: RPS, 1372/3/15; *ALI*, nos A6, A9, A10, p. 209.

[45] *ALI*, p. xxxiv, note 54; N. Macdougall, 'Achilles' Heel? The Earldom of Ross, the Lordship of the Isles, and the Stewart Kings, 1449–1507', in E.J. Cowan and R.A. McDonald (eds), *Alba: Celtic Scotland in the Medieval Era* (East Linton: Tuckwell Press, 2000), 248–75.

[46] *ALI*, no. 54, no. 55, pp. 80–83.

[47] *ALI*, pp. xix–xx.

[48] *ALI*, pp. xx, lxxx–lxxxii; Grant, 'Scotland's Celtic Fringe'; W. McLeod, '*Ri Innsi Gall, Ri Fionnghall, Ceannas nan Gàidheal*: Sovereignty and Rhetoric in the Late Medieval Hebrides', *Cambrian Medieval Celtic Studies*, 43 (2002), 25–48.

[49] J. Stuart et al. (eds), *The Exchequer Rolls of Scotland*, 23 vols (Edinburgh: H.M. General Register House, 1878–1908), vii, p. 9. See also E. Curtis, 'Richard, Duke of York, as Viceroy of Ireland. 1447–1460; With Unpublished Materials for His Relations with Native Chiefs', *Journal of the Royal Society of Antiquaries of Ireland*, Seventh Series, 2 (1932), 158–86, at 171–72.

Lords of the Isles possessions in Ireland,[50] *regulus* was never a style the Lords of the Isles bothered to assume.

Even if John, Lord of the Isles (1449–1493) might grant a quasi-royal licence for a tenant to build a fortified residence on the mainland,[51] he was still quite ready to acknowledge the authority of the crown in other transactions,[52] and to serve as royal sheriff of Inverness and justiciar in the north.[53] And in his most famous act, the so-called Treaty of Westminster-Ardtornish of 1462, when he sent his own ambassadors to negotiate with the English king Edward IV in a period of tensions during the early minority of James III, the resulting agreement in no uncertain terms recognised Edward's sovereignty, and required John and his heirs to become 'subjettis and liegemen' of the English king.[54] The provisions of the treaty were never to be realised; but they show a Scottish magnate who flirted with English allegiance (much like other Scottish magnates of the era), not an aspiring prince seeking to make alliance with another sovereign ruler.

Still, as is well known, the Lordship of the Isles had certain special features, such as its own council (which sat at Finlaggan on Islay as a representative assembly of the chiefs of the island kindreds) and legal officers (known as *breves*). All of these features are poorly documented but they attest to an enduring form of lordship grounded in a Gaelic heritage and tradition, not any grant of regalia from the Scottish crown.[55] And these distinguishing features were doubtless part of the consideration of the events of the 1470s. After the fourth lord, John, was eventually forfeited for his treasonable dealings with the English king in the preceding decade, his restoration in 1476 made it plain that although he was to be known again as the Lord of the Isles, he was now a baron and lord of parliament, and nothing more.[56]

---

[50] Egan, 'Richard II and the Wider Gaelic World', 231–32: noting the marriage of Christina, daughter of John, Lord of the Isles (d. 1387), to Robert Savage *c.*1387, and the subsequent marriage of John Mor (d. 1427), brother of Donald, Lord of the Isles (d. 1423), to Marjory Bisset, heiress of the Glynns.

[51] *ALI*, no. 70, p. 102.

[52] *ALI*, no. 69, p. 101.

[53] A.R.C. Simpson and A.L.M. Wilson, *Scottish Legal History: Volume 1: 1000–1707* (Edinburgh: Edinburgh University Press, 2017), 89–95.

[54] *ALI*, nos. 74–5, pp. 110–16 (at 112); *Rot. Scot.*, ii, pp. 405–7. See Oram, 'A Celtic Dirk', 21, 34; Martin, 'A Maritime Dominion', 193; J. Petre, 'Donald Balloch, the "Treaty of Ardtornish-Westminster" and the MacDonald raids of 1461–3', *Historical Research*, 88 (2015), 599–628; R. Nicholson, *Scotland: The Later Middle Ages* (Edinburgh: Oliver & Boyd, 1974), 401–402.

[55] *ALI*, pp. xlii–xlix; J. Bannerman, 'The Lordship of the Isles', in J.M. Brown (ed.), *Scottish Society in the Fifteenth Century* (London: Edward Arnold, 1977), 209–40. See also M. Brown, *The Wars of Scotland 1214–1371* (Edinburgh: Edinburgh University Press, 2004), 255–73 (on the period up to 1350).

[56] RPS, 1476/7/5–9 (10 July 1476); RPS, A1476/7/1 (15 July 1476); *Registrum Magni Sigilli Regum Scotorum. Register of the Great Seal of Scotland*, ed. J.M. Thomson

Thus, on the basis of this cursory overview, is it possible to apply the concept of 'frontier' in the west in the sense of the limits of sovereign control of territory, even if there was no contemporary terminology for the frontier? For this task, our focus may be directed to the lordship exercised in the region. The Isles were an absorbed polity, but the effective absorption into the kingdom of Scotland had happened in the thirteenth century. Prior to 1493 Scottish kings had no direct control in the Lordship of the Isles, and none could have hoped to exercise control even if it had been direct, for they depended on the Lords of the Isles to govern on their behalf. All the same the MacDonald Lords accepted the suzerainty of the Scottish crown, even as they engaged with the politics of the wider Gaelic world. Even considering the treasonous flirtation of 1462, no other sovereign powers were seriously involved in this equation. The Scottish frontier in the west was thus defined by the frequently distressed relationship between these magnates and their kings, and the unresolvable tension between the crown's needs for the Lords of the Isles to be at once obedient vassals and local rulers.

THE NORTH

Scotland's northern frontier is a region where historians have been more comfortable to deploy the category of 'frontier' (or more specifically that of 'border') in their analysis.[57] The joint earldoms of Caithness and Orkney, and the lordship of Shetland, have been the subject of a considerable body of research by Crawford.[58] More recently, Grohse has addressed the medieval Northern Isles explicitly in the framework of a frontier which, he argues persuasively, was characterised by amicable diplomatic intercourse in pursuit of peace, and by generally positive cross-cultural exchange.[59] Of significance once again for our present purpose is the 1266 Treaty of Perth between King Magnus VI and King Alexander III, whose terms also included the provision that Orkney and Shetland would be retained as part of the Norwegian king's domain. The effect was thus to separate sovereignty over the earldoms of Orkney and Caithness, so that henceforth Caithness would be part of the domain of the Scottish king. Thus the earldom of Caithness would be held of Alexander III. In exchange, the Scottish king agreed to make an 'annual'

---

et al., 11 vols (Edinburgh: H.M. General Register House, 1882–1914), Scottish Record Society, reprint (Edinburgh, 1984), ii, no. 1246, p. 253.

[57] S. Imsen, 'The Scottish-Norwegian Border in the Middle Ages', in A. Woolf (ed.), *Scandinavian Scotland – Twenty Years After* (St Andrews: St John's House Papers no. 12, 2009), 9–30.

[58] B. Crawford, *The Northern Earldoms: Orkney and Caithness from AD 870 to 1470* (Edinburgh: John Donald, 2013), 23–26. See also: S. Imsen, 'Public Life in Shetland and Orkney c.1300–1500', *New Orkney Antiquarian Journal*, 1 (1999), 53–65; S. Imsen, 'Earldom and Kingdom: Orkney in the Realm of Norway 1195–1379', *Historisk Tidsskrift*, 79 (2000), 163–80.

[59] Grohse, *Frontiers for Peace*, esp. 25–30, 79, 250, 253, 259.

payment to his Norwegian counterpart. This promised payment was often forgotten over the next two hundred years and it came to a particular pressure point in the mid-fifteenth century, prompted by the financial needs of the Danish-Norwegian monarchs at that time.[60]

Thus, in 1266 the Pentland Firth became a formal sea boundary between Norway and Scotland but, much as in the West, there was no specific name for the frontier that diplomacy had achieved as a conceptual feat. Instead, descriptions of relevant territories were given in terms of the 'lands and islands of Orkney and the lands of Shetland',[61] or the 'mainland of Shetland'[62]; these, for example, were sufficient administrative identifications of territory. And, just as in the west, a focus on lordship is instructive in helping to address the absence of a specific historical terminology for this international frontier.

When the kindred who had held the joint earldoms of Orkney and Caithness died out in 1350, the fortunes of inheritance eventually brought the earldom of Orkney and the lordship of Shetland to the Sinclair family.[63] Henry Sinclair and his successors held the earldom from 1379 as vassals of the king of Norway, whereas the earldom of Caithness was purchased by the Scottish king, Robert II, from the eldest grandson of the last joint earl. King Robert bestowed Caithness on his son David, from whom the Stewart earls of Caithness derived and continued until 1431.[64] Then, in 1455, William Sinclair, earl of Orkney, obtained the earldom of Caithness from the Scottish crown. Thus, about the middle of the century the situation of jointly held earldoms was re-established, this time in the hands of Earl William, holding Orkney from the king of Norway and Caithness from the king of Scotland.

There are a number of illustrations that could be taken from the time of the Sinclairs to illustrate the exercise of lordship in this region. Of particular note are the actions of the bishop of Orkney (1420 and 1422), and the so-called 'complaint of the people of Orkney' (1425), which took the forms of appeals to the Norwegian monarch to intervene against the misrule of David Menzies, who was acting in those years as tutor testamentary to the underage Earl William. In particular the latter document is an instructive vignette of the collective identity of the Orkney elite, and of the Scandinavian legal and administrative structures and the norms associated with them

---

[60] *APS*, i, pp. 420–1; Crawford, *Northern Earldoms*, 23, 301, 332.

[61] '...*terras et insulas Orchadie aut eciam terram Hietlandie...*': C.C.A. Lange and C.R Unger et al. (eds), *Diplomatarium Norvegicum* (Oslo: Riksarkivet, Kommisjonen for Diplomatarium Norvegicum, 1847–) [hereafter *DN*], ii, no. 459, p. 354; J. S. Clouston (ed.), *Records of the Earldom of Orkney, 1299–1614* (Edinburgh: Edinburgh University Press, 1914) [hereafter *Orkney Records*], no. xi, p. 24; Crawford, *Northern Earldoms*, 53–55, 338, 340, 368.

[62] '*Megolande ÿ Hetland*' (Middle Norwegian): J.H. Ballantyne and B. Smith (eds), *Shetland Documents 1195–1579* (Lerwick: Shetland Islands Council Museums and Archives Section and The Shetland Times Ltd, 1999), no. 21, pp. 14–15.

[63] Crawford, *Northern Earldoms*, 320–25, 334, 344–45.

[64] Ibid., 325–26.

during this period.[65] However, it is the 1460s which offer the most instructive example for present purposes. The pledging of the Northern Isles by Christian, king of Denmark–Norway, to James III as part payment of Margaret of Denmark's queenly dowry in 1469 is well known.[66] That eventual arrangement was the result of continued negotiations over the Scottish payment of the 'annual', which some years earlier (in 1460) had been mediated by King Charles of France. The proposal for a Danish–Scottish marriage alliance was a permanent solution put forward by Charles, but negotiations at that time collapsed. Two letters survive which neatly show Earl William Sinclair as a figure whose divided loyalties—bestride two earldoms on either side of the Pentland Firth—put him in a very awkward position between the different ambitions and needs of his two sovereigns in 1461. In the course of events Earl William had been summoned by King Christian to attend him but he refused to go and, in response to this, the bailies of Kirkwall and the bishop of Orkney separately wrote to the king to excuse the earl's absence.[67] These two letters set out that Earl William had been unable to come to Christian because he had been engaged in the vigorous defence of the bishop and the people of Orkney. To this end he had laid himself out '"to no small suffering and loss, bearing the expense, labours and dangers of war" specifically (it is said) in his earldom of Caithness in putting a stop to the malicious and savage attacks there and on the islands by the earl of Ross and Lord of the Isles. Without the earl's "presence and defence we had been utterly lost and destroyed by the sword and the fire"'.[68]

Unlike the situation in the west, there was no question of any ambiguous sovereignty in this northern region (a point to be underscored by the timing later that decade, coincident with the pledging of the Northern Isles, of James III's act of 1469 asserting his 'free empire', already noted). Earl William was a magnate who straddled the frontier between two kingdoms, and who attempted to avoid offending either of his royal masters, in this instance by securing timely good references from the other significant power-holders in Norwegian Orkney, who cited the vigorous defensive actions he had taken in Scottish Caithness. That the Lord of the Isles was truly troublemaking in the Scottish north early in the minority of James III is known from other sources; this was no convenient fabrication.[69] Earl William's solution to the problem of divided loyalties was thus to resort to an assertion of military lordship. In this case, it came in the form of a claim to the defence of the Norwegian frontier against a wayward Scottish magnate. There are resonances here of just the sort of rhetoric that we noted in the south at Scotland's frontier towards England.

---

[65] Ibid., 350–52.

[66] The pledge made to James III was in lieu of 50,000 florins: ibid., 365–66.

[67] Ibid., 37, 362.

[68] Ibid., 37, translating from *Orkney Records,* nos. xxii and xxiii; *DN*, v, pp. 827 and 836.

[69] W.P.L. Thomson, *The New History of Orkney* (Edinburgh: Birlinn Ltd., 2008), 197.

Soon after the superiority of the Northern Isles came to the Scottish crown in 1469, James III sought to buy out William Sinclair from his Orkney earldom, and absorb the Orkneys and Shetlands directly into the crown estate. Still, even some decades later we can see that this new international and national arrangement failed to resolve potential political and cultural ambiguities. In Shetland in 1502 a local chaplain was to be reprimanded by Scottish officers under pain of treason for having 'of temerarite and presumption' purchased the archdeaconry of Shetland from the king of Denmark, in place of the man presented to the office by the Scottish king.[70]

It is notable that, throughout the period from 1266 onwards, and despite a clear articulation of the international boundary at the Pentland Firth, the idea of 'territorial waters'—and their extent or their intersection—was not adopted by either realm in this period. It was only in later years that Scottish maritime boundaries would come to be more clearly articulated, notably by the first Scottish king to navigate by sea his kingdom's coasts, as James V undertook in his famous voyage of 1540. In the 1530s and 1540s fishing disputes with foreign powers (chiefly the Dutch) particularly in waters off the northern mainland and the Orkneys and Shetlands prompted the king to assert his jurisdiction around the coast of Scotland.[71] By contrast, in the fifteenth century, the frontier at the north of the kingdom was one which was understood and expressed in terms of territorial lordship, subject to superior sovereign jurisdictions.

* * *

The application of 'frontier' as a concept in this short comparative exercise to examine the boundaries of the Scottish kingdom in the fifteenth century reveals that in some regions a closely related historical terminology (i.e., the 'march') existed to match our analytical category of 'frontier', whereas in others it did not. This disparity need not pose a barrier to our analysis, and it need not lead us to become 'trapped in [a] game of definitions'.[72] The solution advanced here has been to focus on a particular aspect of the category of frontier (in this case territorial sovereignty), and to pay attention to a related concept (that of lordship) as tools to frame and direct our investigation.[73] In these three brief examples I hope to have shown that being alert to conceptual indeterminacy and making explicit the friction between a chosen concept and what historical terminology may be available to us can be constructive. In this case, the exercise has suggested that fifteenth-century Scotland was bounded

---

[70] Ballantyne and Smith, *Shetland Documents*, no. 35, p. 25.

[71] S. Murdoch, *The Terror of the Seas? Scottish Maritime Warfare 1513–1713* (Leiden: Brill, 2010), 20–25; T.W. Fulton, *The Sovereignty of the Sea* (Edinburgh and London: W. Blackwood, 1911), 78–86.

[72] F. Benigno, *Words in Time: A Plea for Historical Re-thinking*, trans. D. Fairservice (Abingdon: Routledge, 2017), ch. 4.

[73] Davies, *Lords and Lordship*, 1–2.

by three different types of 'frontier'. In the south was a landed frontier heavily defined by a legal-diplomatic framework negotiated over time between two sovereign kingdoms, and with a strong role for lordship, especially lordship defined by military leadership. In the west was a maritime frontier defined by the distressed relationship between Scottish kings and a preeminent magnate dynasty, sitting within the wider context of a Gaelic cultural world. In the north was another maritime frontier clearly set at the Pentland Firth but counterintuitively defined by a dual lordship over landed territory held by a magnate dynasty owing allegiance to two sovereigns, and sitting within the wider context of a Scandinavian cultural world. These different manifestations need not lead to confusion, nor lead us to reject 'frontier' as of limited usefulness because of its multiple meanings; indeed, it is hoped that applying this concept to the challenges of evidence in our sources can be seen to be a positive tool to help us to view our chosen problem, that of understanding Scotland's frontiers, with greater clarity.

There are complexities that arise from this line of analysis. For instance, the focus on the sea in the west and in the north prompts the question of whether a further frontier should be considered as well, in the form of the kingdom's port towns, which dominated the eastern seaboard and engaged in international trade and fishing. In this vein a striking illustration comes in the response made in 1445 by the provost, bailies, and council of Aberdeen to a supplication from a merchant of Lübeck on behalf of the German merchants at Bruges in Flanders. A ship, having sailed from Bruges with cargo belonging to the supplicant, was captured by pirates. It was rumoured to have been wrecked at Aberdeen and its cargo sold there. The merchant was promised by the civic magistrates that if any of the goods were to be found within the town's liberty he would have justice.[74] There are opportunities, too. Crown-magnate relations have been a prominent theme in late medieval Scottish historiography, and this thematic emphasis has come in for criticism in recent years in part for being too narrowly focussed.[75] The preceding discussion focuses attention on magnate lordship and relations with the crown as particularly useful for addressing and understanding Scotland's frontiers. Different types of lordship (i.e., that exercised over a barony, an earldom, or a regality, and other Scottish variants) remain important for a perspective on how the kingdom itself came to be defined by the king's relations with different types of lords including, and perhaps especially, the nobility at the frontiers of the realm.

For the wider insular world this examination encourages our attention to be cast onto a broader array of frontiers than those, chiefly of the English

---

[74] E. Frankot, A. Havinga, C. Hawes, W. Hepburn, W. Peters, J. Armstrong, P. Astley, A. Mackillop, A. Simpson, A. Wyner (eds), *Aberdeen Registers Online: 1398–1511* (Aberdeen: University of Aberdeen, 2019), https://www.abdn.ac.uk/aro [12 February 2020], ARO-5-0693-02.

[75] Hawes, 'Community and Public Authority in Later Fifteenth-Century Scotland', 1–4, 102–6, 173; C. Hawes, 'Reassessing the Political Community: Politics and the Public Domain in Fifteenth-Century Scotland' (unpublished symposium paper, 2019).

kingdom and its external territories, which have been the focus of so much scholarship to date. For instance, to what extent might the concept of 'frontier' be usefully applied to post-conquest Wales, from the perspective of Welsh political society, over and above the political society of the Welsh marches in the fourteenth and fifteenth centuries? To what extent might the Gaelic world straddling Ireland and Scotland continue to develop as a scholarly focus, as a political space with its own frontiers?[76] To what extent might port towns need to be accounted for in our understanding of frontiers not just in Scotland but across various jurisdictions in the British–Irish Isles? And for the study of premodern frontiers generally, the broader point made through the example of Scotland is the benefit of a focus on specific issues which helped to define historical frontiers, and which may encourage historians to work constructively with the tension between modern categories and historical terms—or their absence. In this case territorial sovereignty and lordship have been useful anchor points which have not required us to gesture more generally, and vaguely, at 'cultural' frontiers. Even so the focus on territorial sovereignty has brought us to the sea and to Scotland's maritime boundaries, and for historians of other premodern times and places there is opportunity, it is hoped, to take this late medieval example and use it to expand the discussion of frontiers beyond that of predominantly landward borders and marcher jurisdictions.

[76] For new work in this field see S. Duffy, D. Ditchburn and P. Crooks (eds), *The Irish-Scottish World in the Middle Ages* (Dublin: Four Courts Press, forthcoming, 2022); A. Cathcart, *Plantations by Land and Sea: North Channel communities of the Atlantic archipelago c.1550–1625* (Oxford: Peter Lang, 2021).

CHAPTER 6

Identity

Andrea Ruddick

The Life Cycle of a Concept

The concept of 'identity' has become ubiquitous in modern scholarship, including the work of medieval historians. Even a cursory search of the *International Medieval Bibliography* for the keyword 'identity' reveals hundreds of pieces of scholarship written in the last ten years which examine different forms of identity, including national, regional, communal, ethnic, noble, social, cultural, tribal, colonial, religious, monastic, clerical, episcopal, Christian, Jewish, Muslim, Arab, Roman, royal, authorial, intellectual, political, Mediterranean, female, masculine, chivalric, mercantile, urban and civic identity.[1] Yet 'identity' is also notoriously difficult to pin down. As the Italian scholar Francesco Benigno recently noted: 'It traverses through our public sphere as a category midway between scholarly tool and collective experience'.[2] In addition to difficulties in defining the term itself, 'identity' may present particular problems on account of the frequency with which it is attached to other equally contestable concepts, not least the forms of 'national'

[1] International Medieval Bibliography (Turnhout: Brepols, 2019). http://cpps.bre polis.net.ezp.lib.cam.ac.uk. Accessed 17 August 2019. Search for keyword 'identity' in items published between 2010 and 2019.

[2] Francesco Benigno, *Words in Time*, trans. D. Fairservice (London: Routledge, 2017), 99.

A. Ruddick (✉)
St Paul's School, London, UK

© The Author(s), under exclusive license to Springer Nature
Switzerland AG 2022
J. W. Armstrong, P. Crooks and A. Ruddick (eds), *Using Concepts in Medieval History*, https://doi.org/10.1007/978-3-030-77280-2_6

and 'ethnic' identity which have featured in my own work.[3] In many ways, the evolution of 'identity' as an analytical tool could be seen as representative of other terms and concepts used in academic writing. By taking 'identity' as a case-study, therefore, we can trace more broadly what might be called the 'life-cycle' of a concept.

i. *Stage One: Appearance in Modern Social Sciences*
   As Philip Gleason has noted, current meanings of the word 'identity' are relatively modern. Before the mid-twentieth century, the word 'identity' was primarily used to mean sameness (from its Latin root, *idem*), with restricted technical applications in mathematics and philosophy.[4] However, from the 1950s and 1960s the term began to be used in a more precise way by psychologists to describe a sense of individual self, popularised by Erik Erikson's work on the idea of the 'identity crisis' in adolescents.[5] At the same time, the term was also developed as an analytical tool by sociologists to refer to the idea of collective group identity, particularly in relation to ethnicity.[6]

ii. *Stage Two: Inter-Disciplinary Borrowing, Notably by Historians*
   Historians are notable for their magpie-like tendency to borrow concepts and terminology from other disciplines. By the late twentieth century, 'identity' had been picked up by historians, by whom it was used with increasing enthusiasm. By the mid-1990s, studies of different forms of 'identity' in medieval Europe were flourishing, particularly in the field of national identity amidst contemporary debates about devolution, ethnocentrism and federalism in modern-day Europe.[7] Indeed, as noted above, medieval historians' enthusiasm for 'identity' continues unabated.

iii. *Stage Three: Ubiquity in the Public Sphere*
   At the same time as terms become popular in academia, they frequently pass into the public sphere, where they are widely—and often

---

[3] Example Andrea Ruddick, *English Identity and Political Culture in the Fourteenth Century* (Cambridge: Cambridge University Press, 2013).

[4] Philip Gleason, 'Identifying Identity: A Semantic History', *The Journal of American History* 69:4 (1983), 910–31, at 911. See also W.J.M. Mackenzie, *Political Identity* (Harmondsworth: Penguin, 1978), 19–27.

[5] Gleason, 'Identifying Identity', 914.

[6] Ibid., 915–19.

[7] Example C. Bjorn, A. Grant and K.J. Stringer (eds), *Nations, Nationalism and Patriotism in the European Past* (Copenhagen: Academic Press, 1994); R.R. Davies, 'The peoples of Britain and Ireland 1100–1400. 1. Identities', *Transactions of the Royal Historical Society*. 6th series: 4 (1994), 1–20; S. Forde, L. Johnson and A.V. Murray (eds), *Concepts of National Identity in the Middle Ages* (Leeds: University of Leeds, 1995); Adrian Hastings, *The Construction of Nationhood: Ethnicity, Religion, and Nationalism* (Cambridge: Cambridge University Press, 1997); Thorlac Turville-Petre, *England the Nation: Language, Literature and National Identity* (Oxford: Oxford University Press, 1996).

somewhat uncritically—used in journalism, politics, public policy, ordinary conversation and, increasingly, online. 'Identity' is no exception to this. Gleason explains the rapid rise of 'identity' to ubiquity as a result of the intellectual prestige and 'aura of cognitive authority' that it derived from its association with the well-funded social sciences of mid-twentieth-century America. In addition, he highlights its adaptability for use in discussing the changing issues of the day, from the relationship of the individual to society in the 1950s to the perceived 'identity crisis' over key American values in the 1960s and 1970s.[8] Moving into the twenty-first century, the concept of 'identity' has proved equally adaptable as an analytical tool to express the concerns of a new generation of social commentators in the era of 'identity politics'.[9]

iv. *Stage Four: Criticism of Historians for Borrowing Conceptual Apparatus from other Disciplines*

The appropriation of analytical terms by historians has not gone unnoticed, however. They frequently face the charge that they borrow conceptual apparatus from other disciplines without fully understanding its theoretical framework and intellectual pedigree. The medieval historian Jan Dumolyn notes that historians tend to jump onto theoretical bandwagons that have been fashionable for a decade or so in social sciences or literary theory, and apply what he describes as a 'thin veneer of theory' to their work, borrowing material in an eclectic and superficial way. He memorably describes this as a 'lack of conceptual hygiene'.[10] Historians' use of 'identity' is undoubtedly open to this criticism.[11]

v. *Stage Five: Scholarly Doubts and Deconstruction*

As academics become more conscious of these problems, however, it leads to greater critical engagement with terminology. Among medieval historians, we see this concern, for example, in the work of Peggy Brown on 'feudalism', Rees Davies and Susan Reynolds on the 'state', and many others since.[12] Eventually, however, this can lead to a crisis point, where

---

[8] Gleason, 'Identifying Identity', 922–28, quote at 922.

[9] For a useful bibliography, see Vasiliki Neofotistos, *Identity Politics* (Oxford Bibliographies, 2013). https://www.oxfordbibliographies.com/view/document/obo-9780199766567/obo-9780199766567-0106.xml. https://doi.org/10.1093/OBO/9780199766567-0106. Accessed 17 August 2019.

[10] Jan Dumolyn, 'Political Communication and Political Power in the Middle Ages: A Conceptual Journey', *Edad Media*, 13 (2012), 33–55, at 47. The notion of 'conceptual hygiene' is also noted in relation to historical terms in P. Crooks, D. Green and W.M. Ormrod, 'The Plantagenets and Empire in the Later Middle Ages', in P. Crooks, D. Green and W.M. Ormrod (eds), *The Plantagenet Empire: Proceedings of the 2014 Harlaxton Symposium* (Tyas: Donington, 2016), 23.

[11] As noted in this book review: Peter Crooks, 'English Identity and Political Culture in the Fourteenth Century by Andrea Ruddick', *Scottish Historical Review* 94 (2015), 105–7.

[12] E.A.R. Brown, 'The Tyranny of a Construct: Feudalism and Historians of Medieval Europe', *American Historical Review* 79 (1974), 1063–88; Rees Davies, 'The Medieval

scholars begin to question the usefulness of the concept or term altogether, and to call for its abandonment or replacement, as the sociologist Rogers Brubaker and the historian Frederick Cooper have done in the case of 'identity'.[13]

THE PROBLEM WITH 'IDENTITY'

What, then, are the key problems with historians' uses of terminology that can lead to this crisis point in the life-cycle of concept, particularly in respect of 'identity'? And how successfully have medieval historians, in particular, begun to tackle them?

i. *Anachronism*

Charges of anachronism are often levelled at medievalists, usually in the context of debates with historians of later periods.[14] There are valid questions to be asked about how far medievalists should use terms which originated in the modern conceptual and material world; we might very reasonably ask whether 'identity' was a category in terms of which people thought about themselves in the middle ages, given its relatively recent emergence as an analytical term. Richard Handler has expressed serious doubts about this, noting that historical actors who do not belong to a modern, western, individualistic worldview may have, or have had, very different ideas about the self and personhood to modern western historians.[15] For medievalists, Susan Reynolds' articulation of the distinction between words, concepts and phenomena continues to provide a valuable analytical framework for responding to such concerns.[16] For example, the absence of a precise word for 'the state' in the middle ages, Reynolds argues, does not mean that medieval people had no concept of it, or that the phenomenon itself did not exist.[17] Consequently, medievalists might appropriately use a term such as 'state' in their analysis, even if the word itself was not used in this

State: The Tyranny of a Concept?', *Journal of Historical Sociology*, 16:2 (2003), 280–300 and Susan Reynolds, 'There Were States in Medieval Europe: A Response to Rees Davies', *Journal of Historical Sociology*, 16:4 (2003), 550–55. For further examples, see Introduction, above, n. 15.

[13] Rogers Brubaker and Frederick Cooper, 'Beyond "Identity"', *Theory and Society*, 29 (2000), 1–47, esp. 14–21.

[14] E.g. Len Scales and Oliver Zimmer (eds), 2005. *Power and the Nation in European History* (Cambridge: Cambridge University Press, 2005), 1–29.

[15] Richard Handler, 'Is "Identity" a Useful Cross-Cultural Concept?', in John R. Gillis (ed), *Commemorations: The Politics of National Identity* (Princeton: Princeton University Press, 1994), 27–40.

[16] See Introduction, above.

[17] Susan Reynolds, *Fiefs and Vassals: The Medieval Evidence Reinterpreted* (Oxford: Oxford University Press, 1994), 12–13. See also Willibald Steinmetz and Michael Freeden,

way at the time. However, Reynolds also stresses the need to avoid an implicit teleology, which presents the medieval phenomenon as an embryonic version of a fully developed model that inevitably emerged in the modern world.[18] Danger lies too in the assumption that medieval people thought in exactly the same way as us (although who constitutes 'us' is, of course, itself debatable), even if they lacked precisely the same vocabulary to articulate their thoughts. There will always be an element of historical actors' patterns of thinking and ways of experiencing the world that remain inaccessible to historians. Nonetheless, when used with appropriate caveats, 'identity', along with other 'modern' concepts such as the nation, the state, and the self, can be used convincingly by medievalists as tools of analysis, even while stoking the fires of continued lively debate with modernist colleagues.

ii. *Essentialism*

Another charge levelled at historians' use of concepts, particularly in relation to 'identity'-related fields (most notably the 'big three' of race, class and gender), is that of essentialism. To combat this, scholars have increasingly made a turn towards constructivism. It is now standard practice for any piece of scholarship on themes relating to 'identity' to begin by stressing that identities are socially constructed, unstable, contingent and multi-layered.[19] This new orthodoxy offers a way to escape and critique the essentialising, naturalising assumptions about identity that are frequently found not only in older scholarship but also in present-day public discourse. However, for some this doesn't go far enough. Brubaker and Cooper are critical of what they call 'clichéd constructivism', that is, token statements about the fluid and constructed nature of identity, used more as a way of signalling an author's ideological and methodological stance than because this has any substantial bearing on his or her subsequent analysis.[20]

iii. *Reification*

In relation to this, Brubaker and Cooper also highlight the dangers of reification in academic writing, that is, attributing concrete reality to an abstract concept or classification. They note a tendency, even among avowedly constructivist scholars, to reproduce categories used in contemporary political discourse ('categories of practice') as their

---

'Introduction. Conceptual history: Challenges, Conundrums, Complexities' in W. Steinmetz, M. Freeden and J. Fernández-Sebastián (eds), *Conceptual History in the European Space* (New York and Oxford: Berghahn, 2017), 21–24 for the suggestion that meaningful historical comparisons might be better explored by looking first for analogous historical phenomena rather than for particular words (i.e. an onomasiological as opposed to a semasiological approach).

[18] Reynolds, 'There Were States in Medieval Europe', 553–55.

[19] Brubaker and Cooper, 'Beyond "Identity"', 1, 8, 11.

[20] Ibid., 11.

own objective 'categories of analysis'.[21] Consequently, they argue, these writers end up with 'an uneasy amalgam of constructivist language and essentialist argumentation'.[22] Even using the language of 'identity' itself, Brubaker and Cooper argue, predisposes scholars to think of people in terms of groups with an objective existence—as a 'Thing' with a capital 'T'.[23] 'Identity' is assumed to be something that simply *is*, or that people simply *have*, even if it is conceptualised in a constructivist way.[24] Moreover, echoing Bourdieu, Brubaker has noted in his work on ethnicity that language choices can have a constitutive performative dimension. For example, by invoking ethnic groups—'the French', 'the English', 'the Russians'—academics help to call them into being, inadvertently reinforcing and even contributing to the processes by which these group identities are reified and essentialised.[25]

Medieval historians who use 'identity' as an analytical tool face a slightly different issue to academics who comment on present-day politics; it is in our sources, rather than in contemporary political discourse, that we encounter essentialist assumptions about group identity (although not the word 'identity' itself). But we similarly need to exercise scrutiny over our chosen terms of analysis and be careful not to import the essentialism of our primary sources. By uncritically accepting the categories used by our subjects and treating them as homogeneous, objective entities with collective agency, historians too can end up unintentionally reproducing the reifying assumptions of our sources.

iv. *Over-extension*

Over-extension occurs when a term is used so often, to describe such a wide range of phenomena, that it loses any specificity of meaning that makes it a useful as a tool of analysis. As a term accrues multiple, sometimes contradictory, meanings, both in public discourse and in academic writing, scholars become increasingly doubtful about its usefulness. Gleason noted that, as early as the 1970s, the use of 'identity' had reached a 'level of generality and diffuseness' that threatened to render it meaningless, a problem that some scholars recognised at the time.[26] He concluded: 'As *identity* became more and more a cliché, its meaning grew progressively more diffuse, thereby encouraging increasingly loose and irresponsible usage'.[27] More recently, Brubaker and Cooper have voiced similar concerns about the increasingly elastic definition of the term, commenting that: 'It does not contribute to precision of analysis

[21] Ibid., 4–6.

[22] Ibid., 6.

[23] Ibid., 27–28.

[24] Ibid., 10.

[25] Rogers Brubaker, 'Ethnicity Without Groups', *European Journal of Sociology* 43:2 (2002), 163–89, esp. 166.

[26] Gleason, 'Identifying Identity', 914. See also Mackenzie. *Political Identity*.

[27] Gleason, 'Identifying Identity', 931.

to use the same words for the extremes of reification and fluidity, and everything in between'.[28]

They identify at least five different current meanings of 'identity' and argue that the term has now become so vaguely defined and ambiguous that it would be better to stop using it altogether and find more precise alternative terminology for each of the conceptually distinct phenomena it is used to describe.[29] While the particular concern of Brubaker and Cooper is with scholars who use 'identity' in relation to more recent history and contemporary politics, we might equally ask whether, in the context of medieval history, the elastic has now been stretched so far in the definition of 'identity' that it is no longer useful as an analytical tool. Moreover, Brubaker and Cooper have also suggested that the current obsession with 'identity' may even be blinding scholars and policy makers to 'other, looser forms of affinity and commonality'.[30] Furthermore, this leaves people who do not fit easily into clear group identities at risk of falling between the cracks of our analysis by conceptualising the world in terms of 'flat, reductive accounts of the social world as a multichrome mosaic of monochrome identity groups'.[31]

Some Possible Solutions

This leaves us with a dilemma. It is relatively easy to identify a list of problems with the use of a particular concept or word by historians. What is more difficult is finding a solution. So, what are our options?

i. *Ditch and Switch?*
    That is, replace the problematic term with more specific alternatives, as suggested by Brubaker and Cooper in respect of 'identity'. The danger here is that we simply exchange one under-conceptualised term for another one, on an endless quest for the holy grail of an unproblematic word. Often, historians laudably seek to replace an older term with one deemed to be less ideologically problematic. However, this has limited effectiveness if it has little or no impact on our approach to the subject. Simply replacing the word 'race' with 'ethnicity', for example, or 'nationalism' with 'national sentiment', achieves little if our underlying conceptual framework remains unchanged. Public engagement also needs to be borne in mind here; it is possible to produce such specialised vocabulary that it becomes unintelligible to anyone outside our immediate field of expertise.

[28] Brubaker and Cooper, 'Beyond "Identity"' 35–36.

[29] Ibid., 6–8, 14–21 and on 27: 'it blurs what needs to be kept distinct: external categorization and self-understanding, objective commonality and subjective groupness'.

[30] Ibid., 30.

[31] Ibid., 31.

ii. *Define, Define, Define?*

Another option is to re-define existing terms in increasingly narrow and specialised ways. One problem here is that an overly narrow definition may lead to the opposite problem to over-extension: terms that are so restrictively applied that it prevents meaningful comparison and dialogue across different time periods, places and disciplines.[32] In addition, as with new words, specialist definitions can create difficulties communicating in the public sphere if academics end up with a definition that is too far removed from the everyday 'lay' understanding of a word's meaning. Scholars in all fields face the challenge of finding ways to communicate a more nuanced understanding of their subject to wider audiences in a way that is accessible and yet conceptually rigorous. Ever more convoluted re-definitions of existing terminology may produce longer introductions to our books and articles, but seem unlikely to improve our public engagement.

iii. *Plough on Regardless?*

In fact, most of the time, historians neither completely reject problematic concepts nor create new ones. More often in practice, we dutifully note the theoretical problems with our terminology in the introductions to our books and articles and then plough on regardless, perhaps surrounding our chosen vocabulary with knowing but potentially irritating quotation marks to signal our continuing unease. As a result, 'identity' remains a central analytical tool in historical scholarship but one that is frequently under-defined, despite well-established concerns about its usage.

iv. *Another Option?*

This essay proposes an alternative to this impasse. I want to ask whether we can, in fact, work productively with conceptual indeterminacy, and even use it to our advantage, to give our work greater depth and nuance. Historians from Koselleck onwards have recognised that both words and concepts consist of aggregative meanings that build up layer by layer in different times, places and languages.[33] There is never just one universally accepted, hermetically sealed definition of each word or concept. It is simply not realistic, therefore, to think we can pin down a single meaning and control it when we employ it in our writing, however hard we try. Nor, as George Orwell might have pointed out, is total restriction of meaning necessarily desirable.[34] As

[32] Of course, over-extension can also lead to problems in making comparisons: when so many different forms of group, label, collectivity or self-perception are classified as forms of 'identity', for example, it becomes very difficult for scholars to be sure they are comparing like with like.

[33] Steinmetz and Freeden, 'Introduction. Conceptual History', 2.

[34] As Syme, the editor of the 'Eleventh Edition of the Newspeak Dictionary' observes to Winston Smith in *Nineteen Eighty-Four*: 'Don't you see that the whole aim of Newspeak is to narrow the range of thought? In the end we shall make thoughtcrime literally impossible,

medieval historians, we encounter a double layer of multivalence—not only do the analytical terms we employ have multiple accrued meanings, but so too did—and do—the historical terms used in our primary sources. Thus, while it is tempting to think that it might be less problematic to restrict ourselves to contemporary medieval terms untroubled by modern connotations, medieval terms are just as difficult to pin down, shifting in meaning over time and in different contexts.[35] Recently, however, there has been a recognition by conceptual historians that this is something we need to accept and work with, rather than fight against. As Willibald Steinmetz and Michael Freeden recently put it:

> Employing concepts is always an exercise in selectivity, whether deliberate or unintended, not an exercise in generating the totality of meanings. Disagreement, however gentle, over their connotations is invariably built into the very existence of social and political concepts, because conceptual indeterminacy is their norm, not the exception.[36]

Every time a concept is used, Steinmetz and Freeden argue, some meanings are suppressed and others given greater weight—not only by journalists and politicians, and in everyday talk, but also by historians. We need to recognise this and work with it.

At the same time as acknowledging that multiple meanings are inherently built into concepts, however, Steinmetz and Freeden note that societies cannot cope with permanent contestability—and nor, we might wish to add, can academic writing. Put simply, at some point we need to choose a word and go with it if we want to communicate our ideas meaningfully to a wider audience. Otherwise, it is possible to reach such a state of semantic paralysis that we lose all confidence in our ability to call anything anything.[37] With this pragmatic agenda in mind, therefore, I shall spend the remainder of this paper exploring some ways in which the vocabulary of 'identity', for all its problems and inherent ambiguities, might remain useful to historians.

---

because there will be no words in which to express it. Every concept that can ever be needed will be expressed by exactly *one* word, with its meaning rigidly defined and all its subsidiary meanings rubbed out and forgotten'. George Orwell, *Nineteen-Eighty-Four* (London: Penguin, 1949, 2013 edn.), 60.

[35] As demonstrated in modern dictionary projects for medieval languages, e.g. Anglo-Norman Dictionary. 2019. Universities of Aberystwyth and Swansea. http://www.anglo-norman.net/; Dictionary of Medieval Latin from British sources. 2012. Oxford: University of Oxford. http://www.dmlbs.ox.ac.uk/web/index.html.

[36] Steinmetz and Freeden, 'Introduction. Conceptual History', 25.

[37] I have rather inelegantly dubbed this the 'your boyfriend's mother' conundrum; if you are not sure what to call something, you will tend to avoid calling it anything at all. The end result of this prolonged state of semantic uncertainty is impeded communication, which is unsatisfactory for everyone concerned.

'Identity' in Medieval Britain: Some Case-Studies

Of the different phenomena identified by Brubaker and Cooper as being subsumed under the heading of 'identity', three are commonly used by medieval historians. First, identity as a process of 'identification' or categorisation, usually according to some shared categorical attribute such as nationality, class, race, gender, sexuality or a person's position in a web of social relationships such as the family or workplace. This can be further subdivided into self-identification, and an external categorisation imposed on a person by others, such as the state.[38]

Secondly, identity can be conceptualised as a form of self-understanding, a subjective sense of who one is and one's place in the world—which may, of course, be influenced by external categorization.[39] This is perhaps the meaning most often intended by medieval cultural historians. 'Identity' thus becomes a subset of historiography on notions of the self and related debates about medieval and modern concepts of the self. Miri Rubin's rich essay on *Identities*, for example, takes 'identity' almost entirely to mean self-understanding, offering a robust defence of medieval concepts of the self and the possibilities of 'self-fashioning'. 'Identity' itself is lightly theorised in the essay and described as 'a cluster of co-existing attributes' and 'the result of a complex interplay between personal and social forces, or between the individual and the community'.[40]

Thirdly, identity can be used to describe a group—real or imagined—with a sense of collective solidarity and distinctiveness, which may also form the basis for social and political action.[41] This all sounds very neat. These distinctions can certainly be useful in reminding us not to take for granted the categories presented to us by our sources. They prompt us to ask useful questions, such as: Who is doing the identifying here? And for what purposes? Yet this neat subdivision of categories is also where the notion of a total conceptual distinction falls apart in practice. Often, 'identity' can be both an externally attributed category imposed on a person *and* a subjective lived experience. Indeed, what is perhaps most interesting to the historian is the creative space in which these dual perspectives interacted and overlapped with one another, as I hope to illustrate in the case-studies that follow, drawn from my own work on 'national identity'.

i. *Resident Aliens: Identity as External Categorisation?*

From 1440 onwards, the resident alien population of England was regularly assessed for tax as a way of raising money for the war with

---

[38] Brubaker and Cooper, 'Beyond "Identity"', 14–17.

[39] Ibid., 17–19.

[40] Miri Rubin, 'Identities', in Rosemary Horrox and W. Mark Ormrod (eds), *A Social History of England, 1200–1500* (Cambridge: Cambridge University Press, 2006), 410, 412.

[41] Brubaker and Cooper, 'Beyond "Identity"', 19–21.

France. With varying degrees of detail, tax commissioners in each county duly reported back to the government with a list of resident aliens, providing a vast repository of data on foreigners living in later medieval England which has recently been collected together as part of the *England's Immigrants* database project.[42] One of the striking things about these alien subsidy records is the way in which they show how nationality categories were attributed to people by the tax commissioners. The documents themselves are fairly dispassionate lists of names, along with place of origin, town or village of residence and sometimes additional information such as occupation and marital status. The 'identities' attributed to these people, therefore, were very much the creation of the state. These nationality labels also frequently formed the basis of surnames recorded by the tax commissioners: 'John Frensshman', a name which appears over one hundred times in the records, 'Walter Ducheman', 'Elizabeth Scot', 'John Iryssh' and so on.

It is also notable that some of the nationality labels attributed to resident aliens changed between tax assessments. One of the most notoriously loose categories in the records is the label 'Doche', roughly translatable as 'Dutch', which was applied to a variety of people from different parts of the Low Countries.[43] In Rutland, for example, which has unusually detailed records, an inhabitant of Oakham described as Nicholas Ducheman was assessed for the alien subsidy five times between 1440 and 1457. In 1440, 1446, 1455 and 1457, he was recorded as 'Dutch'. In 1449, however, when the same man was listed as 'Nicholas Taillour', he was recorded as a 'Fleming'.[44] Similarly, people listed as 'French' in one assessment show up as 'Norman' in another, or 'Norman' men are listed alongside (usually unnamed) wives and children who are more generically described as 'French'.[45]

What these records cannot, by themselves, tell us much about is the extent to which these labels reflected the assessed aliens' own self-understanding. Is this kind of external categorisation, indeed, anything to do with 'identity' at all? Certainly, this would be the line taken by Brubaker and Cooper, who argue: 'The formal institutionalization and

[42] England's Immigrants 1330–1550: Resident Aliens in the Late Middle Ages. 2015. University of York, The National Archives and Humanities Research Institute, University of Sheffield. https://www.englandsimmigrants.com/. See also W.M. Ormrod and Jonathan Mackman, 'Resident Aliens in Later Medieval England: Sources, Contexts, and Debates', in W.M. Ormrod, Craig Taylor and Nicola McDonald (eds), *Resident Aliens in Later Medieval England. Studies in European Urban History (1100-1800), Vol. 42* (Turnhout: Brepols, 2017), 1–32.

[43] Ibid., 18–19.

[44] England's Immigrants. https://www.englandsimmigrants.com/person/34472. Accessed 17 August 2019.

[45] See also Christopher Linsley, 'The French in Fifteenth-Century England: Enmity, Ubiquity, and Perception', in Ormrod et al. (eds), *Resident Aliens*, 147–62.

codification of ethnic and national categories implies nothing about the depth, resonance, or power of such categories in the lived experience of the persons so categorized'.[46] Nonetheless, it is at least plausible to suggest that these designations reflected the names by which the listed aliens were known in their local communities; it is unlikely that the tax commissioners were the first to describe the many men listed as 'John Frensshman' in this way.

ii. *William ap Gwilym ap Griffiths: Identity as Self-Understanding?*

With a few notable exceptions, medieval archives are notoriously short on 'ego-documents' of the kind used by modern historians of the self: diaries, autobiographies, memoirs and so on.[47] Medieval historians therefore need to use other types of primary source imaginatively to infer the self-understanding of historical subjects. One such example is the case of William ap Gwilym ap Griffiths, recorded on the Parliament Rolls of 1439.[48] As the document is a petition, we might reasonably expect that the vocabulary used at least partly reflects the petitioner's own views and self-perception, even if the petition is recorded in the third person.[49] William, as the rest of his name suggests, was Welsh— or, to use the more specific wording of his petition, 'English on his mother's side… and Welsh on his father's side'.[50] It was this English heritage that prompted William to petition parliament that they might 'make the said William an English man (*de faire le dit William Engloys*)'. Technically, this was not a request actually to change nationality. In this context, to be 'made English' meant being granted denization, that is, the right to be treated *as if* fully English in certain legal and political contexts. From the late fourteenth century onwards, denization was most commonly granted in the context of exemption from alien taxation or wartime orders for the expulsion of foreigners.[51]

There are further reasons for exercising caution before viewing this simply as a statement of personal English self-identification. It is possible

---

[46] Brubaker and Cooper, 'Beyond "Identity"', 26–27.

[47] Rubin, 'Identities', 386–89.

[48] Parliament Rolls of Medieval England, Henry VI: Parliament of November 1439, Text and translation, item 29, Anne Curry (ed), Leicester: Scholarly Digital Editions. http://www.sd-editions.com.ezp.lib.cam.ac.uk/. Accessed 17 August 2019. For further discussion of the case, see Andrea Ruddick, '"Becoming English": Nationality, Terminology, and Changing Sides in the Late Middle Ages', *Medieval Worlds*, 5 (2017), 57–69, esp. 62–64.

[49] On petitions, see Gwilym Dodd, *Justice and Grace: Private Petitioning and the English Parliament in the Late Middle Ages* (Oxford: Oxford University Press, 2007).

[50] Parliament Rolls of Medieval England, Henry VI: Parliament of November 1439, Text and translation, item 29, Curry (ed), http://www.sd-editions.com.ezp.lib.cam.ac.uk/. Accessed 17 August 2019.

[51] Ruddick, '"Becoming English"', 59–60, 62–67; W. Mark Ormrod and Bart Lambert, 'Friendly Foreigners: International Warfare, Resident Aliens and the Early History of Denization in England, c. 1250-c. 1400', *English Historical Review*, 130 (2015), 1–24.

that his anglicised forename—William—represented a conscious preference for an English self-identification over a Welsh one. Alternatively,
it could have been a calculated way of playing up his English ancestry
for an English audience, or more simply a designation chosen by the
parliamentary scribe. More importantly, this petition was not primarily
a matter of personal sentiment. The reason for William's request was
specific and practical: he wanted to be declared legally English to gain
exemption from the restrictions on land tenure and office-holding that
had been imposed on the Welsh since the Glyn Dŵr revolt in Henry
IV's reign.[52] In the event, he was granted the right to buy and bequeath
lands and to use English courts, but he was still banned from holding
office. In addition, the grant was made on condition that he did not
marry a Welsh woman, in line with restrictions in place since the Glyn
Dŵr revolt against Englishmen with Welsh wives holding office in Wales.
Thus one man's attempt to define himself as English, for practical
purposes if not for reasons of sentiment, came up against the external
categorisation attributed to him by the government on the basis of his
ancestry, which ultimately counted for more than his personal feelings
or individual claims.

This is highlighted by William's second attempt at getting permission
to hold office in 1442. This time, he appears to have tried to beef up
his claims to English nationality by making his father sound less Welsh.
His English-language petition now described him as 'Englissh of his
moderside… and aparte Englissh on his faderside'.[53] He also emphasised his father's faithfulness to Henry IV during the Welsh rebellion,
in a seeming attempt to make political allegiance count for more than
birth. This time, he had more success; he was granted permission to
hold office for life or for a fixed term, although his request to hold
hereditary office was referred for a later decision. It seems unlikely that
William ap Gwilym felt any more or less 'English' than he had before,
simply as a result of acquiring the right to hold office; again, his petition
was evidently motivated more by pragmatism than by national sentiment. Nonetheless, William's case shows that there could be a conscious
and creative interaction between externally imposed nationality labels
and self-selected forms of national identity which makes them difficult
to separate out in analysis. As a man of mixed Anglo-Welsh heritage,
his case also illustrates the difficulties faced by those who do not fit
easily into clear 'identity' categories. The practical problems that this
ambiguity caused for both William and the English government are
evident from the sources; his case also serves as a reminder not to force

[52] Ivor Bowen, *The Statutes of Wales* (London: T.F. Unwin, 1908), 33–36.

[53] Parliament Rolls of Medieval England, Henry VI: Parliament of January 1442,
Text and translation, item 16, Curry (ed), http://www.sd-editions.com.ezp.lib.cam.ac.uk/.
Accessed 17 August 2019.

our subjects into 'monochrome identity groups' which Brubaker and Cooper warn may result from the overuse of identarian language.[54] Yet, far from undermining the analysis of medieval Anglo-Welsh relations in the fifteenth century by forcing the historian to shoehorn the evidence artificially into restrictive categories, here the concept of 'identity' is helpful in exploring the inconsistencies and anomalies in medieval English government attitudes towards nationality and race in ways which deepen and enrich our historical understanding.

iii. *'The English' and their Enemies: Identity as the Basis for Collective Solidarity?*

Even the medieval English government itself recognised that nationality labels had a basis in the lived experience of the peoples it governed. The issue of restrictions on office-holding for men of Welsh ancestry (and those with Welsh wives) came up again in a parliamentary petition in 1445, with the added request that no more Welshmen 'shall be made denizen or English'. The reason for this request, the petition explained, was fear that if the Welsh were made equal to Englishmen in Wales through denization, they might use their new powers to take revenge on the English, 'for whom they have great hatred in heart, countenance and word… on the grounds of the slaughter and destruction of their rebel ancestors in the time of rebellion'.[55] Here, nationality represents far more than an arbitrary label imposed on a social actor by the state. Being Welsh is described as a matter of the heart, of belonging to a distinct national group who share collective memories and a strong sense of collective solidarity, defined against and hostile towards an equally solid, bounded 'other' in the shape of 'the English'. This certainly fits many modern sociological definitions of ethnic identity. But, of course, the very use of this vocabulary in official documents itself helped to call into being the idea of 'the Welsh' as a coherent entity; in reality, not all Welsh people had supported Glyn Dŵr's revolt.[56] Yet, in the view of the English parliament, nationality was expected to coincide both with political allegiance and with powerful subjective feelings of ethnic identity and collective solidarity—even as they made decisions about what nationality label to award anomalous individuals such as William ap Gwilym ap Griffths. The different types of 'identity' listed by Brubaker and Cooper were not hermetically sealed phenomena in medieval England and Wales, but merged, overlapped and interacted with each other.

---

[54] Brubaker and Cooper, 'Beyond "Identity"', 31.

[55] Parliament Rolls of Medieval England, Henry VI: Parliament of January 1445, Text and translation, item 26, Curry (ed), http://www.sd-editions.com.ezp.lib.cam.ac.uk/. Accessed 17 August 2019.

[56] Rees Davies, *The Revolt of Owain Glyn Dŵr* (Oxford: Oxford University Press, 1995), 103–26.

iv. *Accusations of Scottish Nationality in Fifteenth-Century York: Over-lapping Forms of Identity?*

A final example will help to illustrate this point further. In the late fifteenth and early sixteenth centuries, the records of the city of York contain around thirty cases of men who were accused of being Scottish.[57] These cases are well-known and come in the context of the continuing hostilities between England and Scotland, which had led to demands that no Scotsmen should be made freeman of the city. This led to a number of men facing the accusation of being Scottish and having to produce proof in court that they had been born in England. In 1477, for example, John Saunderson, a fisherman, complained that 'he of late ayanest right and gude consciens by the children of wekydnes was wrongfully noysed, slaundered and defamed that he shold be a Scotissheman and born in Scotland'.[58] Saunderson, 'willyng to subdieu and avoid the said noise and slaunder, and declare and prove hym self a trewe Englissheman', appeared before the city authorities with witnesses who were able to vouch that 'they verelie knewe the said John Saunderson for a trew Englissheman, and at he was born in Cheswyk in Northumbreland, and son to John Saunderson of the same'.[59]

This, and other cases like it, repeatedly refer to the applicants in question as 'trew Englisshemen', largely on the basis of their birthplace and parentage. They act as another example of how different forms of 'identity' could interact. On the one hand, we have an officially sanctioned identity created by the apparently objective criteria of birthplace and parentage. These were the criteria used by the English government to decide who qualified for English nationality, with its attendant rights and privileges, as well as its political and financial obligations. On the other hand, the language of the petitioners is suggestive of a self-identification as a 'trew Englishman', supported by the use of official criteria. It would be a mistake to read too much emotional resonance into this phrase. The opposite idea in the documents is to be a 'fals Scot', that is, someone who has been incorrectly identified as a Scot. It is also worth noting that there is a strong element of convention in the phrasing of the complaints; the same phrases come up repeatedly over a period of thirty years. The main thrust of the word 'trew', therefore, seems to be factual and concerned with correctness of identification rather than with conveying strength of feeling. Nonetheless, the context shows that this was still an identity which mattered to people.

---

[57] James Raine, *A Volume of English Miscellanies Illustrating the History and Language of the Northern Counties of England* (Durham: Surtees Society, 1890), 35–52. See also J.A.F. Thomson, 'Scots in England in the Fifteenth Century', *Scottish Historical Review*, 79 (2000), 3–4; David M. Palliser, *Medieval York, 600–1540* (Oxford: Oxford University Press, 2014) 268.

[58] Raine, *Miscellanies*, 36.

[59] Ibid., 36.

As with the case of William ap Gwilym ap Griffiths, there is clearly an element of pragmatism in these complaints—being a suspected Scot not only disbarred a man from the freedom of the city but it was bad for business and could lead to physical harassment as well as reputational damage. It seems that many of these accusations were motivated by commercial and personal rivalries, as they involve key figures in local industries. One such example is the draper Bartram Dawson, who complained in 1506 that he 'is senysterly defamed that e shulde be a Scottysshman borne, wherby he is grievously hurt in his name & goodes'.[60] This was particularly important to Dawson, as he was one of the ruling Twenty-Four in York's civic government and due to be elected as an alderman.[61] Politically, therefore, it was essential to establish his English credentials to counter what looks like a strategy by rivals to discredit him. In Dawson's case, he was able to call upon friends and supporters to testify that he had been born in Bamburgh, Northumberland, and thus demand that the city authorities should 'admit, repute, & take the sayd Bartrame as a Ynglesman, not yevyng credence to suche defame & detraction in hurtynge the same person in his good name & goodes'.[62] However, pragmatic motives such as this do not preclude the possibility that this coexisted with a genuine sense of Englishness in the affiliations and affections of these men who were so concerned to define themselves as 'trew Englishmen'.

In respect of political and legal status, the identity label that mattered most in medieval England was usually the one attributed to a person by the government, as the 1440 alien subsidy records show. However, historical actors were not simply passive recipients of the nationality labels imposed on them by the authorities. Rather, as in the cases of William ap Gwilym ap Griffiths or Bartram Dawson and his enemies, people interacted with and even attempted to manipulate these labels and categories, which had a real impact on their daily lived experience. This is also a reminder to historians seeking to counter the essentialism of our sources with a constructivist approach; even as we acknowledge the constructed nature of these categories and labels, we need to acknowledge that these forms of identity were 'real' and meaningful to people at the time, and had a material impact on their social, emotional, economic and political lives as they lived inside these categories.

* * *

Are Brubaker and Cooper therefore correct to argue that the term 'identity' is trying to do too many different things? Should we do away with the vocabulary of 'identity' altogether and instead write about 'categorisation', 'identification', 'self-understanding' and 'collective solidarity'? I have argued in this essay that it is not always necessary to insist on an absolute analytical

---

[60] Ibid., 51–52.

[61] Palliser, *Medieval York*, 268.

[62] Raine, *Miscellanies*, 52.

distinction between the different meanings of 'identity', helpful as these analytical subdivisions can be. It need not automatically lead to conceptual confusion to use the word 'identity' to express the multiple ways in which people in medieval society used and interacted with categories such as nationality labels. In fact, the multiple meanings of 'identity' may be positively useful, capturing something of the different facets of a person's status in society, which is always, after all, a combination of self-perception, external labels and a creative interaction between the two. If we take our quest for 'conceptual hygiene' too far, we risk losing sight of some of the ambiguities and complexities inherent in our sources and in the lived experience of historical actors that we are trying to recover—an ambiguity which may also be usefully present in our choice of terminology.[63] In historical research and writing, it is not always easy—or indeed desirable—to separate out the attributed label from the lived experience when these interacted in reality. This doesn't mean we become lazy or complacent about the concepts and categories that we use. As Francesco Benigno has insisted, our own categories of analysis need to be subject to the same levels of scrutiny as the historical terms and interpretive categories we study—the language used by academics in the social sciences and humanities is not, he argues 'epistemologically privileged' and therefore exempt from such scrutiny.[64] Is 'identity' therefore an indispensable part of the historian's conceptual toolkit? Clearly not. Do its more problematic dimensions require rigorous and thoughtful handling by scholars who choose to deploy 'identity' as an analytical tool? Clearly they do. Does it, however, remain useful to scholars despite—or even because of—its ambiguities? Yes, I still think so.

[63] The same is also true of terms and concepts used in historical sources, as noted in Crooks et al., 'The Plantagenets and Empire', 23: 'the conceptual world of the late Middle Ages was anything but hygienic'.

[64] Benigno, *Words in Time*, 117.

CHAPTER 7

Magic

Sophie Page

The history of magic became in the 1990s an increasingly important field of medieval history. New scholarship was able to show that magic was practised at every level of medieval society and engaged the greatest minds of the time. Contrary to a previous historiographical focus on crude superstitions, historians have demonstrated that magic texts reveal medieval people's syncretic, sophisticated and morally ambiguous understanding of their universe, and that learned magic was tolerated or even valued by diverse people and institutions, including religious insiders. The concept of magic can reveal the interior lives and lived experience of medieval people because magical activities express the desire to have agency over daily or emotional challenges, familiarity or experimentation with rituals and an interest in having spiritual experiences and investigating the uses of natural objects.

The category of medieval magic—*ars magica*—is capacious. This is firstly because it includes many analogues and subcategories, such as natural magic (*magia naturalis*), necromancy (*nigromantia*) and sorcery (*sortilegia*), that demarcate different techniques, sources of power, types of practitioner and degrees of social approval. Secondly, the spectrum of practices that could be classified by medieval observers as magical ranges from the recitation of words or incantations over everyday objects like knots, bread and cloth, to complex ritual magic texts like the *Ars notoria*, whose full complement of

S. Page (✉)
Department of History, University College London, London, UK

© The Author(s), under exclusive license to Springer Nature
Switzerland AG 2022
J. W. Armstrong, P. Crooks and A. Ruddick (eds), *Using Concepts in Medieval History*, https://doi.org/10.1007/978-3-030-77280-2_7

ascetic preparations and rituals took at least three years to perform.[1] Thirdly, the diversity of types of source means that the historian of magic needs to build connections between the visual and material culture of magic that was part of its ritual performance, and the 'ritual residues' and 'odd deposits' studied in the separate field of archaeology.[2] Finally, the views of readers and authorities as to what constituted magic and what should be condemned changed over the course of the Middle Ages, from the embrace of occult knowledge and its possibilities in the period immediately following the translating movement (twelfth to mid-thirteenth centuries), to the increasingly hostile fifteenth-century scrutiny of charms, curses, amulets and other forms of common magic, as the mythology of witchcraft began to take a more defined shape and anxieties about harmful magic increased.[3]

It is important to view medieval belief in the reality of magic as rational because attempting to conjure spirits, channel celestial power into objects or manipulate occult properties in natural objects made sense within the medieval understanding of the cosmos.[4] Nevertheless, some medieval authors expressed scepticism about the claims of magical and other occult practitioners and viewed their apparatuses of occult names, images and qualities as arbitrary human constructions that expressed fake knowledge that was unconnected to the accepted domains of knowledge expressed by mainstream religion and science.[5] Recent historiography, not always uncontroversially, has also approached the question of belief in magic by unpacking the psychological and cognitive conditioning and deliberate deceit and sleight of hand that contributed to subjectively convincing experiences of magic.[6] Finally, before we distance ourselves from superstitious ignorance and non-modern ways of thinking we should note that many contemporary psychologists have argued

[1] Burchard of Worms, *Corrector* (c.1008–12), book XIX, 63; Julien Véronèse, *L'Ars notoria au Moyen Age. Introduction et edition critique* (Florence: Sismel, 2007).

[2] Alejandro García Avilés, 'The Visual Culture of Magic in the Middle Ages'; Sophie Page, 'Medieval Magical Figures: Between Image and Text' and Roberta Gilchrist, 'Magic and Archaeology: Ritual Residues and "odd" Deposits', in Sophie Page and Catherine Rider (eds), *The Routledge History of Medieval Magic* (London: Routledge, 2019), 383–458.

[3] Jean-Patrice Boudet, *Entre science et nigromance: Astrologie, divination et magie dans l'Occident médiéval (XIIᵉ–XVᵉ siècle)* (Paris: Sorbonne, 2007); Michael Bailey, *Fearful Spirits, Reasoned Follies: The Boundaries of Superstition in Late Medieval Europe* (Ithaca, NY: Cornell University Press, 2013).

[4] Richard Kieckhefer, 'The Specific Rationality of Medieval Magic', *American Historical Review*, 99 (1994), 813–36; Nicolas Weill-Parot, 'Astrology, Astral Influences, and Occult Properties in the Thirteenth and Fourteenth Centuries', *Traditio* 65 (2010), 201–230.

[5] Sceptics (or authors presenting sceptical positions) include William of Auvergne, Bishop of Paris (c.1180–1249), the natural philosopher and theologian Nicole Oresme (ca.1320–1382) and the legal scholar Ulrich Molitoris (ca.1442–1507). On Augustine's view of magic as fake knowledge see Claire Fanger, 'For Magic. Against Method', in *The Routledge History of Medieval Magic*, 28–29.

[6] See the special issue on 'Magic and Cognition', in *Magic, Ritual, and Witchcraft*, 7: 1 (2012), and the discussion of Nicole Oresme's attack on magicians below.

that magical thinking (the belief that our thoughts or wishes may influence the world around us or that one event happens as a result of another with no plausible link of causation) is an integral part of human cognition and part of our current lived experience too.[7]

From the Middle Ages to the present, the concept of magic has been applied to texts, images and objects that observers find challenging to place, understand or approve of, and how to approach it continues to provoke lively discussion among historians. In the recent *Routledge History of Medieval Magic*, Richard Kieckhefer argued that 'magic' was too general and ambiguous a term to permit rigorous analysis and instead proposed that scholars view it as an 'aggregative term' and focus their energy on identifying and refining its 'constitutive' terms, such as 'conjuration', 'symbolic manipulation' and 'directly efficacious volition'.[8] In the same volume, Claire Fanger engaged positively with the challenge of magic as a large, abstract and ambiguous term that can 'make reality manageable in conversation'.[9] For Fanger, the value of magic lies in its marking a particular kind of problem in medieval thought: how to deal with phenomena whose causes were mysterious or opaque.

It is possible to study and write about medieval magic using only the 'emic' concepts of medieval writers. These are found in both the 'insider discourses' articulated by those who theorised about, practised or read and collected magic texts, and those of the clerics and lay writers who condemned them. Although historians have tended to specialise in either the pro-magical or anti-magical genres, it can be useful to view these as part of the same conversation engaged in by members of the same social order.[10] In the case of necromancy (*necromantia* or *nigromantia*), for example, a category of ritual magic that involved conjuring demons to do the operator's will, authors, practitioners and critics alike were mainly drawn from the clerical class, although some historians think that enthusiasts for this kind of magic belonged to a 'clerical underworld' of clerics with minimal training and education, and unfulfilled ambitions.[11]

Historians also use 'etic' concepts and categories, that is those created by historians to address particular challenges in the sources or to enable a comparative history of magic that is (in theory) more free of value judgments than

---

[7] See, for example, Eugene Subbotsky, *Magic and the Mind: Mechanisms, Functions, and Development of Magical Thinking and Behavior* (Oxford: University Press, 2010) and Sophie Page and Marina Wallace (eds) *Spellbound: Magic, Ritual and Witchcraft* (Oxford: Ashmolean Museum Press, 2018).

[8] See also Bernd-Christian Otto and Michael Stausber's proposal that scholars identify the 'patterns of magicity' particular to their sources from a catalogue of features of magic: *Defining Magic. A Reader*, 1–4 (Sheffield: Equinox Publishing, 2013).

[9] Fanger, 'For Magic', 34.

[10] Ibid., 27. See also Martine Ostorero, 'Witchcraft', in *The Routledge History of Medieval Magic*, 502–22 on the need for dialogue between historians of magic and historians of witchcraft.

[11] Richard Kieckhefer, *Forbidden Rites* (University Park, PA: Penn State Press, 1998).

contemporary sources.[12] For example, 'common magic' and the 'common tradition of magic' have been used by historians to demarcate magical practices that were widely known, rooted in everyday life, did not require a high degree of education and did not necessarily make use of religious rituals or language.[13] Richard Kieckhefer's use of 'the common tradition of magic' was an explicit rejection of the problematic concept of 'popular magic' in order to draw attention to shared magic practices across social groups, such as making rings and talismans, inscribing knives and pieces of clothing, preparing ritual concoctions and performing rituals which drew on the natural powers of celestial bodies, herbs, stones and animal parts. The neutral associations of the term 'common magic' for practices carried out by non-literate people appealed to Catherine Rider as a counterbalance to hostile terms such as superstition (*superstitio*) and sorcery (*sortilegium*) that dominated discussion of magic in the surviving sources she was using: statutes of Church councils, penitentials, sermons and devotional treatises.

For historians of learned magic, 'etic' concepts can be used to focus on 'insider discourses' rather than on critical perspectives. In her introduction to the first collection of studies on ritual magic texts intended to persuade angels to confer knowledge and spiritual benefits, Claire Fanger proposed using the concept 'theurgy' (in summary: practices that engage with the divine) to give validity to authors who used or adapted magic rituals to initiate spiritual experiences.[14] Another influential 'etic' concept in the recent historiography of medieval magic is Nicolas Weill-Parot's category of 'addressative magic'. 'Addressative' here refers to any ritual elements—prayers, invocations, inscriptions and other magical signs—that were, or were assumed to be, addressed by the human practitioner to another Intelligence (angels, demons or other spirits).[15] The concept of 'addressative magic' engages in a helpful way with the thought processes behind medieval thinkers' assessment of magic texts, to demonstrate why texts from diverse traditions—Arabic, Jewish and Christian—were condemned in similar ways. It also explains the strength of the emic category of 'natural magic' (*magia naturalis*), a category of texts in which no

---

[12] For an example of using 'ideal types' to compare magic in different chronological and cultural contexts, see D.L. d'Avray, 'The Concept of Magic', in *The Routledge History of Medieval Magic*.

[13] Catherine Rider, 'Common Magic', in David J. Collins (ed.), *The Cambridge History of Magic and Witchcraft in the West* (Cambridge: Cambridge University Press, 2015), 303–31; Richard Kieckhefer, *Magic in the Middle Ages* (New York: Cambridge University Press, 1989), 56–90.

[14] Claire Fanger (ed.), *Invoking Angels: Theurgic Ideas and Practices, Thirteenth to Sixteenth Centuries* (University Park, PA: Penn State Press, 2012), 1–33, and Julien Véronèse's chapter in the same volume.

[15] Nicolas Weill-Parot, 'Astral Magic and Intellectual Changes (Twelfth-Fifteenth Centuries): "Astrological Images" and the Concept of "Addressative" Magic', in Jan N. Bremmer and Jan R. Veenstra (eds), *The Metamorphosis of Magic from Late Antiquity to the Early Modern Period* (Leuven: Peeters, 2002), 167–86.

magical signs were identified by critics and which tends to survive in larger numbers than other genres.

Medieval magic has been described as 'a point of intersection between religion and science', and the concept has attracted the interest of both historians of science and historians of religion. For Lynn Thorndike, one of the earliest historians of magic, it was part of the history of 'experimental science': that is, it represented an early branch of knowledge that identified natural properties and tested their effects through observation and experience.[16] Other historians, however, have interpreted magical practice as a religious activity that expressed a human desire to engage with the numinous, and aimed, like other sacred rituals, to strengthen or sever relationships between people, overcome material obstacles and spread good or evil by protecting a community or introducing sickness and death.[17] To some extent these divergent views of magic can be explained by the fact that they focus on different genres of magic, as texts that describe how to conjure spirits may be more 'religious' than the more 'scientific' endeavour of exploiting occult properties in nature. But too strong a division between these two types of magic obfuscates that many learned magic texts include elements of both and that the two genres were often compiled together in manuscripts, suggesting they were of interest to the same collectors and practitioners. In the current state of the field it is worth noting that studies putting magic in its religious context predominate, but this is primarily a reflection of the expertise of historians, many of whom are based in religious studies departments, rather than a rejection of the importance of the relationship between magic and science. In the rest of this chapter I will show the ways in which the concept of magic can provide insights into medieval life and thought through a discussion of its relationship with religion, science, politics and society.

MAGIC AND RELIGION

The close relationship between mainstream Christianity and ritual magic can be seen most clearly in magic texts authored, collected and practised by Christians, usually grouped by historians under the categories 'angel magic' and 'necromancy'. Christian ritual magic texts were influenced by Arabic astral magic and Jewish angel magic, and the ways in which these traditions had already adapted rituals to engage with spirits to a monotheistic world view, for example, by emphasising that the success of the operation depended upon the will of God. After the mid-thirteenth century, the identification, circulation and condemnation of learned magic texts was such that it would have been difficult to claim ignorance of the opprobrium and risk attached to them.

[16] Lynn Thorndike, *History of Magic and Experimental Science*, 8 vols (New York: Colombia University Press, 1923–1958).

[17] Richard Kieckhefer, 'The Holy and the Unholy: Sainthood, Witchcraft, and Magic in late Medieval Europe', *Journal of Medieval and Renaissance Studies* 24 (1994), 355–85.

Nevertheless, many Christian authors claimed that their souls (though not those of all potential users) were not sullied by an interest in magic, and some clearly believed that magic was a practice good Christians could engage in.[18]

Angel magic involved performing rituals to persuade angels to help the practitioner achieve various pious goals, notably the acquisition of knowledge, an increased likelihood of salvation and the vision of God.[19] Necromancy was the practice of safely conjuring and gaining control over demons in order to compel them to perform tasks such as revealing buried treasure or bringing a desired partner into the practitioner's presence.[20] Texts belonging to both these genres involved wholesale adaptation of mainstream Christian practices (such as fasting, meditation and prayer), texts (for example, liturgical prayers, exorcism rituals and sacramental language) and goals (such as salvation, the beatific vision and exercising control over demons). There were also more subtle Christian sensibilities embedded in the texts: respect for the efficacy of ritual actions and objects, awe of God's power and the purity of angels, a longing for spiritual experience and fear of the malignity of demons. Finally, while it is the case that most magic rituals were performed for the personal benefit of the practitioner, some angel magic texts—notably the *Liber Razielis* and the *Liber de essentia spirituum*—exhort magical practitioners to act explicitly as instruments of God's will: following their ascent to the level of angels using magical techniques, they are to return to the earth with a prophetic message and gather followers.[21]

In addition to their adaptation to the needs, habits and desires of Christian authors and practitioners, the cosmologies of learned magic texts in circulation in late Medieval Europe were by their nature syncretic and allusive because they had originated in Greco-Roman, Arabic and Jewish traditions. To some extent of course these allusions were intentional. Flexible and ambiguous rationales, mythologies, and cosmological foundations meant that rituals were adaptable to each practitioner's own cosmological certainties (of angels, demons, God, nature, spirits, stars and so on). The authors of magic texts introduced cosmological elements, not primarily in order to elucidate or endorse a particular view of the universe but rather to map which elements in the universe could be manipulated by the practitioner and how this could be done. Inevitably this ambiguity and flexibility provoked critics, who saw demonic languages in magical characters that imitated the constellations, idols in astrological images and delusion in the idea that one could control spirits.

---

[18] See for example the note added to the image magic text entitled, the *Glossulae*: 'whoever you are who has found these <words> , I ask through Christ that you do not reveal them unless by chance to a good and benevolent man, and if you do the contrary, may your soul be imperiled and not that of the writer. Amen'. Sophie Page, *Magic in the Cloister* (University Park, PA: Penn State Press, 2013), 146.

[19] See Fanger, *Invoking Angels*.

[20] Kieckhefer, *Forbidden Rites*.

[21] See Sophie Page, Sophie 'Uplifting Souls: *The Liber de essentia spirituum* and the *Liber Razielis*', in Fanger (ed.), *Invoking Angels*, 79–112.

Critics of magic perceptively identified other emotions and desires mingling with the appropriately Christian attitudes of awe of God, deference to angels, purification rituals and performative piety. In necromantic rituals, the basic Christian framework of requesting the aid of God and the saints to subdue demons is combined with exhortations to secrecy, the aesthetics of grand court illusions, curiosity about spirits, thrill seeking and clerical longing for the secular trappings of success (horses, lovers and the favour of princes).[22]

Angel magic texts defended their art in ways that were positive but distinct from mainstream Christian practices and sensibilities, especially in their capacious category of good or neutral spirits with whom the practitioner had ambiguous relationships, sometimes including the ability to constrain them. In this respect, this genre may have been influenced by Arabic astral magic, in which a spirit's malice or benevolence depended on its planetary ruler.[23] The Christian author of the early fourteenth-century *Liber iuratus* presents magic as the practice of a virtuous Christian using a consecrated book to compel good and evil spirits to do his bidding.[24] Similarly, Antonio da Montulmo, a fourteenth-century Italian theorist of magic, identified magical practitioners as special and often especially virtuous individuals (in his case virgins, old women and men who had been born with exceptional nativity horoscopes) who worked with a set of universal rules and occult operations to compel spirits in the order Intelligences.[25] The idea and practice of necromancy has particular interest for the student of medieval religion. It is important as an adaptation of a mainstream ritual—exorcism—to personal and unorthodox ends.[26] The image of the necromancer was prominent in anti-magical literature, where it often stood for the whole concept of magic and certainly its most transgressive sense.[27] Finally, the circulation, practice and representation of necromantic rituals contributed to the development of and belief in witchcraft mythologies and is thus part of the origins of the witchcraft persecutions.[28]

The idea that a belief in magic might, counter-intuitively, be useful to the Church is expressed by the influential theologian Thomas Aquinas, who thought that stories about necromancers provided to sceptical lay people

[22] Frank Klaassen, 'Learning and Masculinity in Manuscripts of Ritual Magic of the Later Middle Ages and Renaissance', *Sixteenth-Century Journal* 38:1 (2007), 49–76.

[23] See Weill-Parot, 'Astral magic'.

[24] See the chapters by Katelyn Mesler and Jan R. Veenstra in Fanger, *Invoking Angels*.

[25] Antonio da Montolmo, *De occultis et manifestis*. Edited and translated by Nicolas Weill-Parot and Julien Véronèse, in Fanger, *Invoking Angels*, 238–87.

[26] See especially, Julien Véronèse, and Florence Chave-Mahir, *Rituel d'exorcisme ou manuel de magie? Le manuscrit Clm 10,085 de la Bayerische Staatsbibliothek de Munich (début du XVᵉ siècle)* (Florence: Sismel-Edizioni del Galluzzo, 2015).

[27] Avilés, 'The Visual Culture of Magic'.

[28] See, for example, Michael Bailey, *Battling Demons: Witchcraft, Heresy, and Reform in the Late Middle Ages* (University Park, PA: Penn State Press, 2002).

persuasive evidence for the existence of demons.[29] By the fifteenth century, however, necromancy had become an inconvenient model for the idea of humans entering into willing relationships with demons because it remained— by reputation and probably in practice—the preserve of elite male specialists trained in rituals. Eventually the idea that the necromancer's 'cursed imagination' foolishly led him to believe that he controlled spirits rather than that he was being deceived by them was superseded by the idea of the demonic pact, in which men and women actively entered into relationships with demons and in exchange for their souls gained the ability to wield harmful magic.[30] One of the most important questions faced by the historian of medieval magic is the question, still in its historiographical infancy, of how this concept contributed to the origins of witchcraft mythologies and persecutions.[31]

Magic and Science

Natural philosophy (natural science in our modern terminology) and magic had a close relationship in the late Middle Ages. The translation of Greek and Arabic scientific and philosophical texts into Latin in Spain, Sicily and the Middle East from the late eleventh century influenced medieval Christian conceptions of nature and the cosmos and provided scholars in the Latin West with a new technical vocabulary to describe their universe. In Muslim Spain the exact sciences were inextricably mixed up with astrology and magic and this pattern of interests was continued by Latin translators, debated by scholastic thinkers and embraced by the collectors of texts in both genres. The new university-based discipline of natural philosophy developed its own literature to describe and analyse the structure and operation of the cosmos with all its objects and creatures. Learned magic texts claimed to reveal the occult properties of natural objects and living beings, and their instructions for using these in rituals, recipes and crafted objects signalled their aspiration to be a technology.

Medieval critics of magic texts were aware of their claims to reveal hidden knowledge of the natural world. In her *Liber vitae meritorum* of 1158 the Abbess, visionary and author Hildegard of Bingen personified Magic (*maleficium*) as a monstrous hybrid creature with the body of a dog, the head of a wolf and the tail of a lion.[32] Magic argues that her disciples, Hermes and

---

[29] Thomas Aquinas, *De malo*, Q. 16, article 1.

[30] Michael Bailey, 'The Feminization of Magic and the Emerging Idea of the Female Witch', *Essays in Medieval Studies*, 19 (2002), 120–134; Alain Boureau, *Satan the Heretic*, trans. Theresa L. Fagan (Chicago: University of Chicago Press, 2006). On the cursed imagination see John Lydgate, *The pilgrimage of the life of man* (1426), l.18609.

[31] A good place to start with this question is Boudet *Entre science et nigromance*, 431– 508.

[32] *Liber vitae meritorum*, Angela Carlevaris (ed.) (Turnhout: Brepols 1995), 222–23. The animal parts of the personification are explained as follows: the wolf devours lambs

other philosophers, were wise men (*sapientes*) who through their investigations of the cosmos learned how to harness the elements.[33] They became (Magic declares) pre-eminent experts in the arts of the planets, trees, herbs and all animals, and their study of natural causes was a worthy enterprise because God had created all natural things to benefit humankind.[34] Hildegard does not deny the knowledge of these wise men, but asserts that their learning was acquired only partly from God and partly from evil spirits. Here Hildegard touches on a theme common to arguments defending magic and arguments condemning it: that the *scientia* of ritual magic was acquired through a constant process of revelation and communication with spirits.

In the *Picatrix*, a Latin translation (ca 1256) of pseudo-al-Majriti's *Ghayat al-hakim* and one of the most complex magic texts in circulation in late Medieval Europe, magic is presented as the culmination of human knowledge. The ideal practitioner of magic is a *philosophus perfectus* who has mastered natural philosophy, metaphysics, arithmetic, geometry, music and astronomy.[35] His goal is to use his investigation of the cosmos to create tools for magical practice, for example, by identifying significant shapes in the heavens and then using them in rituals to draw down celestial power.[36] This exemplary magician has acquired his wisdom from a study of the cosmos and books but derives his power from the planets dominant in his nativity (the astrological chart drawn up for the moment of his birth) and the aid of celestial spirits. Indeed, the founder of magic, Caraphzebiz, is said to have had a 'familiar' (a spirit who remained with him as his companion) who performed marvels for him, helped him understand the secrets of nature and the sciences and came when invoked with sacrifices.[37]

Magic could also be thought of as one of the branches of science. In the twelfth and early thirteenth centuries, the period in which Greek and Arabic philosophy and science were being translated and assimilated in the Latin West, some medieval thinkers gave the name 'necromancy' to 'the science of properties of natural things' when these derived from occult causes.[38] This term, probably originating in Isidorian traditions, first became prominent as a Latin translation of the Arabic word *sihr* that designated magic in the *Picatrix* and

like the devil devours sinners; the lion's tail stirs up hatred and tyranny and the dog chases evil things.

[33] *Liber vitae meritorum*, 222.

[34] Ibid., 222.

[35] *Picatrix Latinus*, II, ii, 3.

[36] Ibid., II, v, 2.

[37] Ibid., III, vi, 3.

[38] Isabelle Draelants, 'The Notion of "Properties": Tensions between *Scientia* and *Ars* in Medieval Natural Philosophy and Magic', in *The Routledge History of Medieval Magic*, 169–86.

other texts.[39] In some Latin texts on the classification of the sciences, necromancy was grouped with other practical sciences that involved the study of the four elements such as medicine, agriculture, astrology, alchemy, optics and navigation, even though its activities were classified as unlawful when they were suspected of operating by means of evil spirits. Necromancy thus lay on the borders of natural philosophy because it could be considered either natural (in accord with nature) or supernatural (involving rituals directed to spirits).

The most important development for the classification of some kinds of magic as part of natural science, however, was the appearance of the concept of natural magic (*ars magica naturalis*) in the work of the Parisian Bishop William of Auvergne. Natural magic was the study of surprising natural phenomena whose effects could (in theory) be experienced by the senses, such as the power of the peony to prevent epilepsy, the magnet to attract iron or the basilisk to kill with its gaze. These extraordinary effects were caused by 'occult' properties in nature, that is those whose causes were invisible, but which natural philosophers explained with reference to the heavens or the 'substantial' form of the matter itself.[40] For William these natural wonders originated in the creative power of God, and the concept of 'natural magic' was part of a new and positive approach to nature, inspired on the one hand by enthusiasm for Aristotle and on the other by the desire to emphasise the goodness of Creation and God's creative versatility in the wake of the threat of the Cathar heresy and its hostile approach to the physical world.

The new concept of magic provided legitimisation for the authors, collectors and practitioners of texts compiling the properties of stones, plants and animals. These were sometimes called books of *experimenta*, and included both a 'native' heritage of Latin magic and newly translated texts of Arabic and Greco-Roman magic. Some works of natural magic incorporated scientific theories in order to make their claims for efficacy and orthodoxy more persuasive, such as concepts of celestial influence, the placebo effect and similarity and universal sympathy.[41] The magnet's ability to attract iron was a popular example in magic texts of a striking property that could be experienced by the senses but was difficult to explain. Indeed, the idea that magicians were 'maystres by experience'—that is that their art had progressed through experimentation and observation—is expressed by the messenger of Necromancy in John Lydgate's *Pilgrimage of the Life of Man*, as he tries to disrupt the journey of the pilgrim to the heavenly city, declaring moreover that Solomon,

[39] Draelants, 'The Notion of "Properties"', 176.

[40] Nicolas Weill-Parot, *Points aveugles de la nature: l'occulte, l'attraction magnétique et l'horreur du vide (XIIIᵉ–milieu du XVᵉ siècle)* (Paris, Les Belles Lettres, 2013).

[41] For example, Antonella Sannino (ed.), *De mirabilibus mundi Il "De mirabilibus mundi" tra tradizione magica e filosofia naturale* (Florence: Sismel (2011); Judith Wilcox (ed.), Qusta ibn Luqa's *De phisicis ligaturis*; John M. Riddle 'Qustâ ibn Lûqâ's Physical Ligatures and the Recognition of the Placebo Effect', *Medieval Encounters* 1:1 (1994), 1–25.

Virgil, Saint Cyprian and Abelard had all been practitioners of this art.[42] In theory, natural magic did not involve ritual, craft or the invocation of spirits, but in practice many books of *experimenta* included such human interventions in their instructions on how to collect, prepare and activate natural substances for use. Although some medieval thinkers thought that it was not possible for humans to craft magical objects without the assistance of demons, others allowed for the natural power of words and astrological images.[43]

Even when they accepted that some natural knowledge was part of magical practice, critics argued that powerful natural substances were combined with the arts of illusion to provoke harm and confusion. In his *Treatise on the Configurations of Qualities and Motions*, the natural philosopher and theologian, Nicole Oresme (c. 1320–1382), described how magicians used psychoactive substances, powerful odours, music, dramatic shifts in light and darkness and tricks with mirrors to create terrifying and discombobulating illusions that their audience interpreted as supernatural manifestations.[44] Moreover, to increase the success of their performances, he declared that magicians deliberately targeted those likely to be most vulnerable to their trickery: male adolescents and old women, and more generally the melancholy, weak, imprudent, credulous and infirm.[45] Oresme's critique of magical deceit draws attention to the real effects of substances (such as plants, roots and seeds) given to victims to ingest or anoint on their bodies so that they became confused about the true colour, figure, motion or characteristics of things.[46] He calls this harmful application of natural substances *veneficia* or *maleficia* and contrasts it with the positive use of stones, plants, seeds by other experts, such as surgeons or goldsmiths, to help humans live well.[47]

In conclusion, for medieval people there remained substantial differences between the natural philosopher's attempt to understand nature and the magical practitioner's aim to harness its power and exert control over it. The philosopher and the magus are paired and contrasted on Chartres Cathedral in famous sculptures produced after the 1250s. The philosopher holds a stone, which he scrutinises intently, a representation of the careful study of nature. The magus is represented in the famous pose of the enchanter and the asp, holding a scroll with which he tries to charm into submission the asp crouching below him. In most versions of this story and image, the snake

[42] John Lydgate, *The pilgrimage of the life of man*, ll.18731–39.

[43] Nicolas Weill-Parot, *Les «images astrologiques» au Moyen Âge et à la Renaissance: spéculations intellectuelles et pratiques magiques (XIIᵉ–XVᵉ siècle)*(Paris: Honoré Champion, 2002), 303–40.

[44] Nicole Oresme, *Tractatus de configurationibus qualitatum et motuum*, II xxvi–xxxii.

[45] Ibid., xxvi–xxx.

[46] The use of psychoactive and poisonous substances in medieval magic is little studied but see Dan Attrell and David Porreca, trans. *Picatrix*, 26–30 (University Park, PA: Penn State Press, 2019), on references to such ingredients in the *Picatrix*.

[47] Oresme, *Tractatus de configurationibus*, II, xxxi.

resists the enchanter's charms by inserting his tail in his ear, though in this sculpture the message (as well as the identification of the allegory) has been compromised by the asp's broken and absent tail. In spite of this loss, we should read the intended meaning of this representation as the active resistance of nature, God's good creation, to the seductions of magical ritual.

Magic, Social History and Politics

Magic was a marginal activity in late Medieval Europe, but it was accessible to all social groups and transmitted between them. If we take a step back from the complexity of the concept and define magic as an instrument, a practical art that claimed to offer the tools to manipulate the cosmos, we can gain insights into medieval lived experience. When a medieval man or woman chose to use magic to address a daily or emotional challenge, a fantasy or an aspiration, we can observe their interest in natural forces and spiritual influence, reason and imagination, and effective and merely symbolic ritual action. In the fourteenth-century monk John of Morigny's autobiographical account of his experimentation with magic and his subsequent visionary experiences, the reflections and doubts of a user are vividly expressed.[48] In addition to discovering and editing learned magic texts, historians have explored their readership and circulation among physicians and in the clerical underworld, competitive court circles and the monastic cloister.[49] It has become increasingly clear that manuals of ritual magic were tailored to the individual interests of their owners, whether this was talking to spirits or having success in love.[50] Magical items also appear in lay household books alongside instructions for such things as preparing leather, grafting trees, making soap, glue and ink, washing clothes, curing fevers and catching fish.[51] It is artificial to entirely separate the realms of the mundane and the fantastical, however. The fifteenth-century occult miscellany, Wellcome MS 513, has magical experiments for flying horses and

[48] Nicholas Watson, and Claire Fanger (eds), *John of Morigny's Liber florum celestis doctrine* (Toronto: Pontifical Institute of Medieval Studies, 2015); Claire Fanger, *Rewriting Magic: An Exegesis of the Visionary Autobiography of a Fourteenth-century Century French Monk* (University Park, PA: Penn State University Press, 2015).

[49] On the reception of Arabic image magic by learned physicians see Weill-Parot, *Les images astrologiques*, part 3 and his chapter on Jérôme Torrella in *The Routledge History of Medieval Magic*. Monastic collectors of magic texts are discussed in Page, *Magic in the Cloister*, Fanger, *Rewriting Magic* and Véronèse, *L'Ars notoria au Moyen Age*.

[50] For the former see Oxford, MS Rawlinson D 252 and for the latter Bibliothèque nationale de France, MS italiano 1524, edited by Florence Gal, Jean-Patrice Boudet and Laurence Moulinier-Brogi. *Vedrai mirabilia. Un libro di magia del Quattrocento* (Rome: Viella, 2017).

[51] For discussion of magic in a household book see Kieckhefer, *Magic in the Middle Ages*, 2–6.

invisibility but also for making a lamina (a small square magical figure usually inscribed on metal) to keep mice out of the house.[52]

In learned magic, the personalisation of magical instruments to fit the interests of a new practitioner involved making new copies of texts, incorporating personal names into images (of the user or victim) or even summoning one's own angelic tutor. These actions encouraged practitioners to feel that they were joining a select elite of magical experts. The 'common tradition of magic' offers examples of users adapting magical items to fit a range of budgets. For example, surviving instructions to make laminas for conception and childbirth range from a lead exemplar that could be wrapped in leather and silk to silver, tin and paper versions.[53] Magical figures (large two dimensional diagrams that were assigned an instrumental power) were collected by literate users into their manuscripts and inscribed onto pieces of parchment (textual amulets) or other objects where their power could be accessed by illiterate owners.[54] Surviving examples demonstrate how individual owners elaborated, simplified and recomposed figures, including by the simple action of erasing dubious names and drawing crosses over them.[55] Creative interventions could thus express positive engagement with magical concepts or anxieties about orthodoxy.

Historians in this field are aware that, broadly speaking, medieval magic has two quite different trajectories. On the one hand, the translation and dissemination of learned magic texts from the Greco-Roman, Arabic and Jewish traditions, and the recognition of their intellectual resonances with Greek and Arabic philosophy and science, led to more positive attitudes to magical texts and ideas. More than one hundred distinct texts and several hundred surviving manuscripts with magical contents have been identified by scholars. From the thirteenth-century magic texts were reaching ever wider audiences through vernacular translations, and the appeal of learned magic to readers from the court to the cloister meant that many condemned texts circulated widely under the radar.[56] In the fourteenth and fifteenth centuries some authors of magical texts also, for the first time, allowed their works to circulate under their own name rather than ascribing them to legendary figures such as Hermes or Solomon. Since theological condemnation made it dangerous to claim authorship of a magical text, the fact that authors were becoming confident enough to put their real names to works of magic is a striking development and is

---

[52] Sophie Page, 'Love in a Time of Demons: Magic and the Medieval Cosmos', in Page and Wallace (eds), *Spellbound*, 57–58.

[53] Page, 'Medieval Magical Figures', 435–38.

[54] Dan C. Skemer, *Binding Words: Textual Amulets in the Middle Ages* (University Park, PA: Penn State Press, 2006).

[55] See Page, 'Medieval Magical Figures' and, in particular, London, British Library, Sloane MS 513, f. 199v.

[56] Sebastià Giralt, 'Magic in Romance Languages', in *The Routledge History of Medieval Magic*, 99–111.

evidence of a gradual shift towards more positive attitudes towards certain magical texts and ideas in Western Europe.

On the other hand, magic was condemned with increasing vigour and precision in ecclesiastical sources. The development of the concept of the demonic pact and the involvement of the Inquisition in investigating magical practices widened the scope of persecution and contributed to the emerging theology of witchcraft. Clerical writers used the concepts of magic and superstition to define and control the boundaries of legitimate religious practice and repress dangerous errors, even as they tried not to stifle genuine (if from their perspective often confused) expressions of lay piety.[57] Because the legitimacy of practices was hard to discern, the focus often shifted to the legitimacy of the practitioner, a scrutiny to which women were particularly vulnerable. Before the fourteenth century it had been difficult for clerics to believe that women, who were deemed physically, mentally and spiritually weaker than men, could control powerful, threatening demons. But this paradox was resolved by the increasing theological emphasis on the satanic pact. It was thought that in exchange for surrendering their souls, witches could call on the assistance of demons using only simple gestures or spells.[58]

The relationship between magic and gender is an established topic in the historiography of magic, though until recently most research has focussed on understanding why a disproportionate number of women were put on trial and executed for witchcraft in the early modern period. Medieval historians have shown that writings by learned clerics on canon law, theology and pastoral care were more likely to associate women with the sins of 'magic' and 'superstition', partly because of an association between magic, love and sex and partly because of the misogynistic stereotype that women were more easily deceived by the devil.[59] The practitioners of 'common magic' are often represented in medieval sources as illiterate women who had learned their trade through an apprenticeship and worked closely with natural materials, especially herbs and animal parts.[60] Clerical writers attempted to undermine the reputation of such practitioners by emphasising that they used their powers for profit and could not heal or predict the future by channelling the power of God as saints did.[61]

Although arguments condemning magic dominate the sources on 'common magic', pastoral literature in particular has been mined for evidence of real magical activities.[62] It is likely that there were many local specialists in magic

[57] Bailey, *Fearful Spirits*; Catherine Rider, *Magic and Religion in Medieval England* (London: Reaktion, 2012).

[58] Bailey, 'The Feminization of Magic', 120–34.

[59] See Catherine Rider, 'Magic and Gender', in *The Routledge History of Medieval Magic*, 343–54 for an overview.

[60] Laine E. Doggett, *Love Cures: Healing and Love Magic in Old French Romance* (University Park, PA: Penn State Press, 2009).

[61] Rider, *Magic and* Religion, 61–69.

[62] Ibid.

who offered help with everyday problems such as lost objects, telling fortunes, identifying thieves or attracting a lover. These local practitioners need to be distinguished from early modern 'cunning folk', however, since the latter flourished in the era of anxiety provoked by widespread belief in the powers of malefic witches.[63] A large part of the services of cunning men and women involved helping people to escape bad luck or suspected spells and it is possible they increased in popularity after reforming fifteenth-century writers designated protective practices employed against witchcraft the only 'legitimate superstition'.[64] The medieval manuscript evidence suggests, however, that occult services were frequently offered by medical practitioners, both in the form of magical remedies, protective charms and amulets and as more proactive experiments to achieve victory, fine weather or success in love.[65]

Individuals offering occult services, including physicians, clerics and members of religious orders, flourished in the *demi-monde* of the court as well as among common people, and many magic texts seem intended to facilitate courtly services: gaining the help or favour of social superiors, producing spectacular illusions, causing the destruction of enemies or predicting the outcome of a battle.[66] Occult expertise was attractive in highly competitive sociopolitical contexts, and magic in medieval courts offers interesting perspectives for historians: the study of rulers who collected magic texts, patronised their production or used occult knowledge to enhance their reputation; or the accusations, scandals and paranoia about magic to which courts were particularly prone, with their layers of formal and informal sources of power, frequent political tensions and succession problems.[67] Accusations of magic provided a way to indirectly criticise the king (censuring his advisors, mistresses or relatives) or explain misfortunes such as infertility or madness, or could even be an ingenious device for attacking a pope (who was protected from other charges,

[63] Owen Davies, *Popular Magic. Cunning-folk in English History* (London: Hambledon, 2003).

[64] Bailey, *Fearful Spirits*, 194.

[65] For physicians offering magical remedies see Peter Murray Jones and Lea T. Olsan 'Medicine and Magic', in *The Routledge History of Medieval Magic*, 304–7. For other magical services see Page, 'Magical Figures', 440–41 and Laura Mitchell, Cultural Uses of Magic in Fifteenth-Century England, ProQuest Dissertations and Theses (2011), 166–203.

[66] Edward Peters, *The Magician, the Witch and the Law* (University Park, PA: Penn University State Press, 1978) on the demi-monde; Kieckhefer, *Forbidden Rites* and Conrad Kyeser, 2 vols, *Bellifortis*, Götz Quarg (ed.) (Düsseldorf: Verlag des Vereins Deutscher Ingenieurie, 1967).

[67] Peter Brown, 'Sorcery, Demons, and the Rise of Christianity from Late Antiquity into the Middle Ages', in Mary Douglas (ed.) *Witchcraft: Confessions and Accusations* (London, Tavistock, 1970), 17–45; Jean-Patrice Boudet, 'Magic at Court', in *The Routledge History of Medieval Magic* and Jean-Patrice Boudet, Martine Ostorero and Agostino Paravicini Bagliani (eds), *De Frédéric II à Rodolphe II: Astrologie, Divination et Magie dans les Cours (XIIIe–XVIIe Siècle)* (Florence: Sismel, 2017).

including heresy).[68] Noting twenty cases of magic during a twenty-year period in the reign of Charles VI of France (himself subject to magical attempts to cure his madness), Jean-Patrice Boudet has argued that, on this occasion, magic did not merely play an instrumental role but had 'a central function in the exercise of power'.[69]

Magic at court intersects with many other themes relating to this concept, such as the literary image of the magician, anti-magical arguments, the relationship between magic and gender and the origins of witchcraft. When deciding whether or not to consult a practitioner of magic, rulers might follow the example of romance literature, in which professional magicians like Merlin were 'elegant, learned and powerful' or heed the warnings of a court cleric like John of Salisbury or Nicole Oresme who linked magic to fraud, frivolity and the schemes of demons.[70] In the thirteenth century, a period relatively open to its intellectual and practical potential, magic was promoted at the courts of two princes who were in close contact with Arab-Muslim culture: Frederick II Hohenstaufen and Alfonso X of Castile.[71] As fear of magic grew in the late thirteenth and fourteenth centuries, however, many rulers became paranoid about magical attacks. In the case of Pope John XXII, this had serious repercussions for the repression of magic and divination, leading eventually to the Inquisition treating magical practices as heretical.[72] Women at court were particularly vulnerable to allegations that they had used magic to cause impotence or ensnare with love, and fourteenth-century political trials for magic contributed to the idea of a real sect of sorcerers and sorceresses who were participating in a vast plot against Christianity.[73]

* * *

Magic is not a tyrannous concept if it is freed from anachronistic associations with crude superstition, non-modernity and irrationality. Of course, other challenges are still present: some historians are uneasy about the fact that magic is general, ambiguous and has no single agreed definition but is a word still actively in use. Although definitions of magic always apply better to some practices, objects, practitioners, periods or cultures than others, there is something appealing about the familiarity historians of magic feel when encountering the

[68] Jean Coste (ed.), *Boniface VIII en proces. Articles d'accusation et depositions des temoins, 1303–1311* (Rome: Ecole Francaise, 1995).

[69] Boudet, 'Magic at Court', 338.

[70] Stephan Maksymiuk, *The Court Magician in Medieval German Romance* (Frankfurt and Berlin: P. Lang, 1996).

[71] Boudet, 'Magic at Court', 332–36.

[72] Boureau, *Satan the Heretic.*

[73] Jan Veenstra, *Magic and Divination at the Courts of Burgundy and France* (Leiden: Brill, 1997); Hilary Carey, *Courting Disaster: Astrology at the English Court and University in the Later Middle Age*s (London: Palgrave, 1992), 138–53.

concepts of others.[74] It is not simply that medieval magic should be studied in all its rich, complex diversity and its multivalent relationships with religion and science, but that sophisticated concepts, including those from outside our period, can provoke an intellectual response that helps us shape and refine our own definitions. In my current work, I am thinking through the implications of two perspectives on magic, one emic and one etic. The first is John Lydgate's characterisation (mentioned above) of the practitioner of magic as having a 'cursed imagination' and the second is the idea that magic is found at the intersection of ritual and cosmology (a distilling of religion and science). What are the implications of the fact that magic rituals rarely have an audience or communicate doctrine, and that their cosmologies are syncretic, allusive and pragmatic rather than explanatory?

In this paper I have explored some of the ways medieval magic expresses, elucidates and enriches our understanding of contemporary thought and practice of religion, science, politics and culture. Though there is also a very real sense in which medieval magic was a self-contained and self-referential discipline or practice, and is illuminative of magic only, I have pointed towards some methods for using the concept of magic to reveal the interior lives and lived experience of medieval people and their attempts to understand and describe their social, political and spiritual environments, and the observed and imagined cosmos.

---

[74] This is put very well by Claire Fanger in her 'Response', in *The Routledge History of Medieval Magic*, 66.

CHAPTER 8

Networks

Eliza Hartrich

NETWORKS AS CONSTRUCTS

THE CASE OF JOHN SHILLINGFORD

On 24 October 1447 the mayor of Exeter, John Shillingford, went to London. The city of Exeter was engaged in a long-running dispute with its bishop and cathedral chapter, who claimed that the small area around St Stephen's Church was under ecclesiastical jurisdiction and exempt from the laws of the city.[1] Shillingford was accompanied by William Hampton and John Fagot. In Shaftesbury on the following day they met with one of Exeter's councillors, Richard Druell, who had been advancing the city's cause in London already. At nine o'clock on 28 October, the whole company proceeded to Westminster. Shillingford immediately went to the Star Chamber, where he waylaid the Lord Chancellor (John Stafford, archbishop of Canterbury) as he exited the building. Shillingford knelt before the Chancellor, who then twice bade him welcome and took him by the hand to an awaiting barge, where there were 'a grete presse, lordis and other, &c., and yn especiall the tresorer of the kynges housholde, w^t wham he was at right grete pryvy communicacion'. The

---

[1] For details of this dispute, see Muriel E. Curtis, *Some Disputes between the City and the Cathedral Authorities of Exeter* (Manchester: Manchester University Press, 1932), and Lorraine Attreed, 'Arbitration and the Growth of Urban Liberties in Late Medieval England', *Journal of British Studies*, 31 (1992), 205–35.

E. Hartrich (✉)
School of History, Faculty of Arts and Humanities, University of East Anglia, Norwich, UK

© The Author(s), under exclusive license to Springer Nature Switzerland AG 2022
J. W. Armstrong, P. Crooks and A. Ruddick (eds), *Using Concepts in Medieval History*, https://doi.org/10.1007/978-3-030-77280-2_8

Chancellor promised to speak with Shillingford again and recommended that Shillingford pay a visit to the Lord Chief Justice (Sir John Fortescue), as well. At 8 am the next day, the Exeter contingent went to the Chancellor's archiepiscopal palace at Lambeth, but Stafford declined to meet with them. Shillingford feared that he had incurred the Chancellor's displeasure by his eagerness, but the Chancellor gave assurances that he had not, and Shillingford was offered lavish hospitality by the Chancellor's steward and household. Shillingford declined the food on offer, and instead the group ventured across the Thames to meet with Fortescue. That same afternoon, Shillingford returned to Lambeth. He had heard that the Chancellor was to have a Friday dinner of salt fish with the duke of Buckingham, the marquis of Suffolk, the Lord Treasurer (Marmaduke Lumley, bishop of Carlisle), the under-treasurer, the Lord Privy Seal (Adam Moleyns, bishop of Chichester), 'dyvers abbottes and pryours, and meny strangers aleyns of other londys', and Shillingford sent ahead four salted fish for the Chancellor to serve to his distinguished guests. When Shillingford arrived on the Friday evening, the Chancellor again fobbed him off, saying that he was dealing with important business and needed to travel to see the king early the next morning. The following Monday (30 October), Shillingford returned again to Lambeth with five members of the Exeter city council and five of the city's lawyers, where he presented Exeter's case before the Chancellor and the two Chief Justices of England.[2]

Such comings-and-goings represent only a small part of Shillingford's longer campaign in defence of the rights of Exeter. He would spend much of his time in London and Westminster until February 1448, when he returned to Exeter and appointed a deputy to lobby on his behalf in London. I begin this chapter with a short account of Shillingford's activities over a six-day period in October 1447 not because they are in any way extraordinary or because they form the kind of robust data set suitable for meaningful Social Network Analysis. The Shillingford example instead serves as a convenient way to illustrate the level of complexity involved in applying modern concepts of 'networks' to late medieval England.

Before attempting to draw Shillingford's network, a historian would need to make a series of decisions that would have significant consequences for the 'network' then outlined. Most importantly, what kinds of entities are part of Shillingford's network? Historians influenced by historical geography and the central-place theory of Walter Christaller might be tempted to reconstruct a network of linked *places*, demonstrating the well-worn transport routes of the period and the role of government administration in shaping an individual's zone of travel.[3] By such a definition, Shillingford's network would be relatively

---

[2] S.A. Moore (ed.), *Letters and Papers of John Shillingford, Mayor of Exeter 1447–50* (Camden Soc., New Ser., 2, 1871), 4–12.

[3] For a combination of central-place theory and networks in a historical context, see Paul M. Hohenberg and Lynn Hollen Lees, *The Making of Urban Europe, 1000–1994* (Cambridge, MA: Harvard University Press, 1995), 4–5.

small, consisting principally of Exeter, Westminster, London, and Shaftesbury. Shillingford's network could also be a network of *people*. His letters could be the basis for analysing an 'ego-network', a method used by social scientists to trace the myriad personal connections of a particular individual.[4] This type of analysis could be used to determine the extent or size of Shillingford's network (the number of people he encountered), the density of his network (the number of connections already existing between the individuals Shillingford encountered), the strength of ties within the network (the frequency of contact between particular individuals or 'nodes' in the network), or the extent of homophily in the network (the degree to which people from similar backgrounds tend to group together socially). It would also be possible to identify the 'brokers' in Shillingford's network: that is, the people who link otherwise unconnected groups. In this case, the Chancellor seems to be the key broker connecting Shillingford and the Exeter councillors to a variety of Westminster-based individuals. Ambiguities arise immediately, though, when we try to determine who should be included as a 'node' in Shillingford's network. What should we do with the 'grete presse, lordis and other' that Shillingford met on 28 October 1447? Does Shillingford's decision not to name these individuals render them unimportant to his experiences? Or would excluding these individuals from our reconstruction of Shillingford's network potentially conceal intermediaries who could have passed on new information or ideas to Shillingford? A third approach would be to follow the precepts of Actor-Network-Theory and highlight the agency of *objects* in forming Shillingford's social relationships.[5] Non-human items allowed Shillingford to forge ties with new people and altered the actions taken by the human participants. His extensive communication with the treasurer of the household (Sir John Stourton) was made possible by the presence of a barge, and it was through gifts of salt fish that Shillingford attempted to make contact with the duke of Buckingham, the marquis of Suffolk, and other powerful men in Henry VI's government.

Sociologists, anthropologists, and geographers have pioneered a number of different ways for analysing networks, but there remains no consensus about what a 'network' actually *is* and what things a network analyst studies. As a result, ten different historians analysing the Shillingford letters could easily produce ten different 'networks' from the same evidence. Further complicating the use of 'networks' in the study of late medieval history is, of course, the fact that fifteenth-century England had no concept of 'networks' or words to describe them. Shillingford does refer to a 'feloship', but the term is used solely to signify the city councillors of Exeter and not in any looser sense.[6]

---

[4] See Christina Prell, *Social Network Analysis: History, Theory & Methodology* (London: Sage, 2012), ch. 5.

[5] See Bruno Latour, *Reassembling the Social: An Introduction to Actor-Network-Theory* (Oxford: Oxford University Press, 2005), 70–86.

[6] E.g., *Letters and Papers of John Shillingford*, 5–6, 11, 14, 20, 32, 48.

On other occasions, Shillingford mentions a 'partie' of people, but again this word refers not to a matrix of social relationships but to a group of specific individuals who opposed the city of Exeter in its legal case against the bishop and cathedral.[7] The word in Shillingford's letters that probably comes closest to twenty-first-century conceptions of 'network' is 'laboure'. It is used as both a noun and a verb to indicate Shillingford's efforts on the city's behalf, but is most often mentioned in reference to face-to-face meetings between Shillingford and individuals with whom he sought to curry favour.[8] 'Laboure' is thus perhaps a rough equivalent to the twenty-first-century notion of 'networking'.

Yet another obstacle confronts anyone attempting to use Shillingford's letters to reconstruct his social network: the evidence itself. The letters span a fairly short period of time (October 1447 to August 1448), and we cannot assume that they represent a complete collection. Stuart A. Moore in his 1871 introduction to the printed edition reported that the letters were found stashed in different cubby-holes throughout Exeter's civic building: in the council chamber, the gallery of the Guildhall, and many under the Guildhall's roof tiles.[9] With such haphazard archiving, undoubtedly many letters were lost, meaning that the surviving letters provide only a partial picture of Shillingford's world. What has survived intact are the city of Exeter's Receiver's Accounts for dates coinciding with the Shillingford Letters.[10] These records detail the expenditure of the Exeter civic government in 1447–1448 and, in some respects, provide a better source for network analysis: they cover a longer period of time and provide a more complete record of spending and travel than the letters. But any 'network' reconstructed from the Receiver's Accounts would look very different to the 'networks' deduced from the Shillingford Letters. The most obvious difference is that the Shillingford Letters are best suited for tracing an ego-network (i.e., the connections stemming from an individual) while the Receiver's Accounts trace the relationships formed by a whole group of individuals comprising the Exeter civic government. There are subtler distinctions, as well. Because the Receiver's Accounts trace payments from the civic government, people from outside Exeter traditionally feature because they have received gifts from the mayor and councillors. Objects, therefore, feature strongly in the financial accounts; a thorough Actor-Network-Theory analysis could be constructed using the Receiver's Accounts and detailing the many gifts of fish and wine that Exeter sent to Westminster-based officials. A network analysis based on the Receiver's Accounts would also highlight the significance of administrators and go-betweens. When the civic government paid people to advance

[7] E.g., ibid., 12–13, 18, 21.

[8] E.g., ibid., 5, 9, 18, 22.

[9] Ibid., xiii.

[10] Material pertaining to the period around October 1447 is contained in Devon Record Office, Exeter City Archives, Receiver's Accounts, 25–26 and 26–27 H VI. Extracts are printed in *Letters and Papers of John Shillingford*, 146–52.

their cause, they typically targeted not the figures of greatest influence, but rather those individuals' clerks and servants. The Receiver's Accounts record payments of 6s. 8d. to servants (*administrallis*) of the duke of Suffolk, a gallon of wine to a gentleman (*uno generoso*) of the duke of Suffolk, and 8d. to servants (*administrallis*) of the duke of Buckingham.[11] These types of officials often go unnoticed in Shillingford's letters, as he focussed on reporting his contacts with the great and the good. This discrepancy poses a further dilemma: should we rely on quantitative methods that indicate the centrality of administrators and go-betweens to the formation of social links and the dissemination of information, or should we consider qualitative evidence that pays less attention to such individuals? Furthermore, a network analyst using the Receiver's Accounts would no doubt assume that all the gifts and payments recorded represent the successful formation of social ties between the Exeter civic government and the chosen beneficiaries. Even a cursory reading of the Shillingford letters, however, demonstrates that such offerings failed as often as they succeeded. Shillingford had hoped that his gift of salt fish would gain him an audience with the Chancellor and his distinguished guests, but in the end it provided no such social *entrée*.

This lengthy digression into John Shillingford's activities in London and Westminster illustrates that, like any other concept (be it the 'state' or 'feudalism' or 'identity'), a 'network' is not a thing that actually existed in the past.[12] In the words of a recent text on network analysis in humanities research, 'Nothing is naturally a network'.[13] 'Networks' are a variety of tools employed to visualise or find patterns among social relationships, or they can represent an approach to the past that highlights the importance of influence, imitation, trust, and the dissemination of information when considering why particular historical events occurred or why certain people made particular choices. As such, there is no one 'correct' way to conduct a historical network analysis, particularly as there are inherent problems in applying any of the many methodologies of Social Network Analysis (or SNA, as developed by twentieth- and twenty-first-century sociologists, mathematicians, and physicists) to an era that neither had a word for 'networks' nor left behind particularly extensive or uniform sets of data through which 'networks' can be reconstructed retrospectively.

Rather than assessing the application of SNA methods to historical research, this chapter considers 'networks' as a *concept*: what assumptions about society

[11] Devon Record Office, Exeter City Archives, Receiver's Accounts, 26–27 H VI; *Letters and Papers of John Shillingford*, 149–50.

[12] On 'identity', see Andrea Ruddick's chapter, above. For further discussion of the concepts of 'state' and 'feudalism', see Introduction, above.

[13] Ruth Ahnert, Sebastian E. Ahnert, Catherine Nicole Coleman, and Scott B. Weingart, *The Network Turn: Changing Perspectives in the Humanities* (Cambridge: Cambridge University Press, 2020), 43.

do historians make when using the term 'network', and how do these assumptions vary among historical sub-fields?[14] First, the chapter traces the ways in which the concept of 'networks' developed in the historiography of late medieval England between the 1940s and 1990s, even though few of these historians employed mathematical, graphic, or digital SNA methods. Then, it argues that this lineage has made many of today's historians of fourteenth- and fifteenth-century England hesitant to use SNA methodologies (in contrast to early modern, imperial, and global historians who have embraced these tools in greater numbers and more wholeheartedly). The result is that our historical sub-field has an understanding of 'networks' peculiar to itself, one that pays keen attention to the power dynamics of informality.

The chapter that follows does not present a guide to using SNA or a discussion of the opportunities and dangers that the application of SNA methodologies can bring to the study of history. I have tried, where possible, to avoid duplicating the excellent (and much more theoretically grounded) discussion of the relationship between SNA and history found in recent articles by Kate Davison and Joanna Innes.[15] Nor do I advocate for more methodological rigour in tracing historical networks or denigrate the contributions that SNA methodologies have made to historical scholarship over the past few decades. Instead, I propose that we should consider the ways in which the *concept* of networks as employed by late medieval historians can complement and nuance the more rigid *methodologies* of SNA pioneered in the social sciences.

The Origins of a Concept, 1940–1994

Linton C. Freeman, the foremost authority on the history of SNA, writes that it is an approach to human behaviour consisting of four essential components: an assumption that it is worthwhile to trace links between individuals; the assembly and interpretation of data recording links between individuals; the visual representation of data through graphs to identify patterns; and the creation or use of mathematical or computing models to analyse data.[16] Even the most cursory of glances at the historiography of fourteenth- and fifteenth-century England reveals that the vast majority of historians working in this

[14] For 'network' as a concept and its changing meaning over time, see ibid., ch. 1.

[15] Kate Davison, 'Early Modern Social Networks: Antecedents, Opportunities, and Challenges', *American Historical Review*, 124 (2019), 456–82; Joanna Innes, '"Networks" in British History', *The East Asian Journal of British History*, 5 (2016), 51–72. Nevertheless, the reader should note my debt to these two articles. I have cited their work in this chapter when I make direct reference to it in the text, but to avoid excessive footnoting I have not indicated all the occasions on which Davison and Innes's pieces have proved helpful.

[16] Linton C. Freeman, 'The Development of Social Network Analysis—With an Emphasis on Recent Events', in John Scott and Peter J. Carrington (eds), *The SAGE Handbook of Social Network Analysis* (London: Sage, 2011), 26.

field since 1940 have conducted research centred around the first two of Freeman's criteria: most late medieval historians affirm that connections between people were socially and politically meaningful and they have poured painstakingly over records to identify and analyse these connections. But while our academic sub-discipline is dominated by a socially networked understanding of human behaviour, very few of its practitioners fulfil the latter two of Freeman's SNA criteria.

This hesitance to visualise or mathematically analyse findings cannot be attributed solely to conservatism within the history profession or its alleged aversion to 'theory'. Plenty of other historical sub-fields embrace SNA modelling wholeheartedly, using SNA terminology (e.g., 'density', 'centrality', and 'structural holes'), computerised methods of data collection and analysis, and visualisations (most prominently the 'sociogram' with lines connecting a series of nodes). Surveys by Kate Davison and Joanna Innes on historical applications of SNA show just how prominent these methods have become in works on early modern history and British imperial history, but one would be hard pressed to find a similar range of studies for late medieval England. Both Davison and Innes distinguish between historians who engage with the methodology of SNA and those who use networks as a 'metaphor' for society's interconnectedness; the implication is that while the latter approach can be useful, it is less precise and less revelatory than the analysis of whole systems that can be performed digitally and visualised by sociogram.[17] My contention, however, is that 'networks' as employed by some historians of later medieval England are not simply metaphors, even if they largely eschew the language and data analysis tools of SNA. In these works, the 'network' instead represents a *concept*, in that the term conjures up a series of associations, assumptions, and abstractions that historians impose on a past in which there were no recognised 'networks'.

Indeed, the 'network' was a concept that transformed the study of late medieval English history. Famously, in the mid-twentieth century K.B. McFarlane shifted the studies of the fourteenth and fifteenth centuries from a focus on the development of governing institutions (e.g., parliament, the royal council, the Exchequer) to relationships between people. In a 1944 article, he used an analysis of fifteenth-century parliamentary elections to lay out his vision of late medieval England.[18] In it, individuals gained power not just through the offices they held or even the lands they inherited, but also through their ability to attract and maintain a group of retainers, allies, and associates. This version of politics was a 'joint-stock enterprise', with nobles, gentry, lawyers, and civil servants all competing to gain influence over policy by attempting to accrue as many inter-personal connections as possible—albeit with nobles having a natural advantage in this regard. Interestingly, though,

---

[17] Davison, 'Early Modern Social Networks'; Innes, '"Networks" in British History'.

[18] K.B. McFarlane, 'Parliament and "Bastard Feudalism"', in *England in the Fifteenth Century: Collected Essays* (London: Hambledon Press, 1981), 1–21.

McFarlane believed that his version of late medieval England would emphasise the significance not of nobles, but of their councillors, estate managers, and other middling administrators. It was these men who sat in parliament, and who were most familiar with the documentary culture of wills, enfeoffments, and contracts through which social ties were formed or tightened. Crucially, McFarlane ended the article with a sentence featuring an early use of the word 'network': 'The ramifications of that intricate *network* of personal relationships, constantly changing and forming fresh patterns, will never be fully traced, but as we make ourselves familiar with the lives and achievements of the county gentry...the main outlines of local and central politics may be expected to emerge'.[19] It is apparent from this quotation that McFarlane's 'network' was not simply another word for the bastard feudal 'affinity' or 'retinue' (i.e., the relatives, neighbours, legal counsellors, estate officials, and local gentry who could be deemed loyal to a particular lord, whether or not they were formally contracted to his service). Inter-personal networks, in McFarlane's view, were not institutionalised and never had a fixed presence or identity, making any attempt to capture them at a moment in time difficult or even misleading. They were ever in a state of flux—a transience essential to his vision of late medieval England as a competitive but not necessarily ruthless society.

McFarlane's influence remained dominant in late medieval English history well after his death in 1966. The defining spirit of McFarlanite historiography was its attention to the activities of the aristocracy and nobility rather than royal institutions, and its tendency towards prosopography (i.e., assembling collective biographies of men and women from a particular social milieu to ascertain their motivations, influences, and loyalties). In the 1970s two main streams in McFarlanite historiography emerged: 'vertical' studies based on hierarchies within aristocratic retinues and 'horizontal' studies examining gentry communities in a particular county.[20] From the 1980s, the word 'network' began to appear in works on late medieval England, often as a vague referent to social relationships that existed outside the retinue or county under discussion. Susan Wright, writing in 1983 on fifteenth-century Derbyshire, referred to a 'network of connections' to describe an amorphous series of social relationships that often fortified an aristocratic affinity but nevertheless extended well beyond it or even linked together different affinities.[21] In the same year, Michael Bennett's work on Cheshire and Lancashire similarly used

---

[19] Ibid., 20–21. The italics are my own.

[20] For the 'retinue' approach, see e.g., Carole Rawcliffe, *The Staffords: Earls of Stafford and Dukes of Buckingham, 1394–1521* (Cambridge: Cambridge University Press, 1978), ch. 4. For the 'county' approach, see e.g., A.J. Pollard, 'The Richmondshire Community of Gentry during the Wars of the Roses', in Charles Ross (ed.), *Patronage, Pedigree, and Power in Later Medieval England* (Gloucester: Sutton, 1979), 37–59.

[21] Susan M. Wright, *The Derbyshire Gentry in the Fifteenth Century* (Chesterfield: Derbyshire Record Soc., viii, 1983), 144.

'network' to indicate social relationships that did not fit neatly into bounded entities such as the retinue, county, or village.[22]

This consolidation of what 'network' meant in the historiography of late medieval England occurred mostly without a concrete methodology or theoretical framework. One of the few historians of late medieval England who did consistently register an interest in social science models for human relationships was Christine Carpenter. Carpenter's *magnum opus*, 1992's *Locality and Polity: A Study of Warwickshire Landed Society, 1401–1499*, explored the bonds of trust between members of local society, the sense of identity that grew from membership of a 'network', and, principally, the role that informal networks played in underlying or supplementing formal institutions of law and government.[23] Change over time was also key to her study: politics in fifteenth-century Warwickshire, she wrote, was affected considerably by which type of inter-personal tie (whether kin group, neighbourhood, or lordship) was most prominent at any given time. Indeed, the second half of the book charted the transformation of the nature of elite social networks in Warwickshire between 1401 and 1499—resulting, during the reign of Henry VII, in a shift from noble-dominated 'lordly' networks to horizontal, 'neighbourhood'-based gentry networks. But, as with other late medieval scholars studying elite networks, there is not a sociogram in sight in Carpenter's book. Nor is the absence of these visualisations simply the result of limited access to and training in computer-assisted graphics in the early 1990s. For one thing, *Locality and Polity* did not cite the sociological studies of networks that tended to rely on graphs and mathematics. The works of social science Carpenter cited tended instead to be anthropological studies of individual communities, often written in the 1960s. Unlike sociological studies of networks, network analyses from social anthropologists of this period were not based on the crunching of 'big data' but rather on ethnographic fieldwork observing how a community functioned. *Locality and Polity*'s nearest modern analogue may be J.K. Campbell's *Honour, Family and Patronage* (1964), based on Campbell's embedded field study in Sarakastani shepherd communities in Greece in the mid-1950s. Campbell explored the relationship between kin networks, communities, and patronage networks, as well as the institutional structures and moral values that provided a framework within which inter-personal networks operated. The book contains no graphs, charts, or quantitative methodologies, and is cited in *Locality and Polity* as work of 'peculiar interest to the late-medieval historian'.[24]

---

[22] Michael J. Bennett, *Community, Class and Careerism: Cheshire and Lancashire Society in the Age of Sir Gawain and the Green Knight* (Cambridge: Cambridge University Press, 1983), e.g., 52.

[23] Christine Carpenter, *Locality and Polity: A Study of Warwickshire Landed Society, 1401–1499* (Cambridge: Cambridge University Press, 1992), esp. ch. 9.

[24] J.K. Campbell, *Honour, Family and Patronage: A Study of Institutions and Moral Values in a Greek Mountain Community* (Oxford: Clarendon Press, 1964); Carpenter, *Locality and Polity*, 287 n. 21.

Carpenter's engagement with network theories from social anthropology continued in her 1994 article 'Gentry and Community in Medieval England'.[25] Carpenter framed the piece as a counterpoint to scholarship on the gentry 'county community' produced by historians like Wright and Bennett, arguing that the term promoted a misleadingly harmonious and enclosed picture of elite relations within a county. She turned to social anthropologists' network models as an attractive alternative. Citing the work of Jeremy Boissevain and J. Clyde Mitchell among others, Carpenter wrote that 'historians wishing to escape from the tyranny of the structural-functionalist community may be able to exploit their treatment of *networks*'.[26] Boissevain, in particular, had studied networks to emphasise that community structures did not manifest organically as a means of preserving equilibrium within a society; instead, individuals exercised their own agency to form social links and accumulate power and influence.[27] Carpenter's preference for 'networks' over 'community' as the dominant concept in late medieval English political history stemmed from the same impulses: that 'networks' allowed for more rapid change of over time, acknowledged the existence of disorder, engaged more critically with the realities of power, and recognised the importance of brokering cross-class and cross-county relationships for the acquisition and maintenance of power. To illustrate how historians could use a network approach, she employed a computer to construct an ego-network tracing the different people connected to thirteenth-century Staffordshire gentleman Philip Chetwynd of Ingestre and the 'strength' or 'weakness' of their ties. Even so, the article remained without diagrams, and Carpenter expressed a healthy dose of scepticism when it came to mathematical reconstructions of networks: 'Network analysis has now become big theoretical and mathematical business, but historians need not be too concerned with most of this. Our information is too haphazard for us to want to generate a spurious mathematical precision'.[28]

Of course, not all historians of late medieval England in the 1940s to early 1990s were writing about the aristocracy and gentry. Over that same period there was a boom in studies of the medieval English peasantry. In the 1960s and 1970s, historians of the 'Toronto School' began to use manorial records as the basis for in-depth quantitative analysis of the peasantry, often focussed on reconstructing a peasant 'community' in aggregate and demonstrating that peasant 'communities' were not in an inherently antagonistic relationship to their lords.[29] Just as Carpenter used 'networks' in the early

[25] Christine Carpenter, 'Gentry and Community in Medieval England', *Journal of British Studies*, 33 (1994), 340–80.

[26] Ibid., 365. Italics my own.

[27] Jeremy Boissevain, *Friends of Friends: Networks, Manipulators and Coalitions* (Oxford: Blackwell, 1974).

[28] Carpenter, 'Gentry and Community', 366.

[29] E.g., J.A. Raftis, *Warboys: Two Hundred Years in the Life of an English Medieval Village* (Toronto: Pontifical Institute, 1974).

1990s as a means of challenging a 'community'-based approach to gentry studies, so Judith Bennett in the 1980s pioneered 'networks' as a conceptual and methodological alternative to studies of peasant 'communities'. Bennett's approach culminated in a 1987 monograph on women in the Northamptonshire village of Brigstock.[30] The book was based on quantitative analysis of data mined from manor court rolls, but she differed from predecessors such as Zvi Razi and J.A. Raftis in stressing that a complete reconstruction of a medieval community through aggregate statistical analysis of manor court rolls was impossible due to the difficulties in identifying individuals without conducting painstaking research across several archives. Bennett's solution to this problem was to supplement larger-scale statistical analysis with in-depth studies of certain individuals, allowing her the time to gain a fuller picture of their life experiences. For these case-studies, Bennett used ego-networks. Taking methodological inspiration from the same social anthropologists cited by Carpenter, Bennett traced interactions between members of the Kroyl and Penifader families in the court records of Brigstock and nearby settlements; her conclusions stressed how gender and marital status helped to determine the number and range of social ties a person could form. But Bennett maintained that a computer was not helpful for conducting social network analysis on her sources, as fragmentary and complex archives required a good deal of detailed primary source study and could not be reduced to a collection of data points. There are tables but no sociograms in her work, and she made a deliberate point of saying that any numbers cited were far from definitive.

By the early 1990s, then, among historians of late medieval England a 'network' represented an assemblage of associations, often but not exclusively informal, that could not easily be defined by an institution or administrative unit (be that village, manor, parish, county, or affinity). There was also an implicit assumption, drawn from social anthropology, that 'networks' highlighted the exercise of power, in opposition of the concept of 'community' which emphasised collectivity and cohesion. Close observation of evidence at a micro-level, rather than computer-assisted statistical analysis of large data samples, was the preferred method when it came to studying networks, and visualisations were avoided, as they were believed to convey an impression of precision and finiteness unwarranted by the haphazard survival of medieval source materials.

DIVERGING FROM THE NORM, 1995–2021

The concept of the 'network' employed by historians of late medieval England in the early 1990s, however, was no longer in keeping with the ideas, methods, and connotations associated with this term in other academic disciplines.

---

[30] Judith M. Bennett, *Women in the Medieval English Countryside: Gender and Household in Brigstock before the Plague* (Oxford: Oxford University Press, 1987), esp. 'Appendix: A Note on Method'.

The influence of fieldwork-based social anthropology on the development of SNA in the social sciences had diminished by the 1980s and 1990s—at the same time as it was being embraced in the historiography of late medieval England.[31] From the 1970s, sociological models of social networks were becoming more widely accepted. The work of Harrison White and his students employed more mathematical precision and visualisations. It was also distinct from social anthropology in that it analysed a larger data set to depict a 'complete network' of social relationships rather than focussing on ego-networks or small communities.[32] J. Clyde Mitchell, one of the social anthropologists cited by both Carpenter and Judith Bennett, resisted this drive in the social sciences to create codified theories or models for analysing human behaviour. In a 1974 article, Mitchell wrote that sociological surveys and mathematical equations could supplement but not replace fieldwork; the social scientist needed to observe what social interactions, gestures, and ideas were meaningful to the group in question before seeking to measure social ties and their effects on human behaviour.[33] Mitchell's scepticism extended to visualisations:

> A network diagram purporting to represent the set of linkages in some social situation has an immediate visual appeal and can be used to convey a statement about the social relationships eloquently and succinctly. But before the diagram gets to the paper the fieldworker must have decided to represent some abstract property of the social relationships by lines linking points representing persons. There is the distinct risk here that the diagram may take on greater reality than it really merits.[34]

Mitchell, however, was fighting a losing battle, and from the 1990s mass sociological modelling of networks was kickstarted by advances in digital technology and by the work of physicists, mathematicians, and biologists eager to analyse network data on a larger scale than ever before.[35] In particular, since the new millennium scholars from a number of fields working on SNA have been intrigued by tracing the 'small worlds' phenomenon: that is, by assembling very large data sets to observe the number of steps needed to connect people geographically distant from one another or with very different backgrounds. This type of inquiry involves large-scale data collection, computerised visualisations, and models that simulate how networks *might* evolve over time (as opposed to models that present how an observable network operates).[36]

[31] Prell, *Social Network Analysis*, 35.

[32] E.g., Harrison C. White, Scott A. Boorman, and Ronald L. Breiger, 'Social Structures from Multiple Networks. I. Block Models of Roles and Positions', *American Journal of Sociology*, 81 (1976), 730–80.

[33] J. Clyde Mitchell, 'Social Networks', *Annual Review of Anthropology*, 3 (1974), 295–96.

[34] Ibid., 292.

[35] Freeman, 'Development of Social Network Analysis', 26–39.

[36] See brief summaries in ibid., 28–30, and Prell, *Social Network Analysis*, 46–47, 173.

In many sub-fields of history, large-scale 'small worlds' analyses struck a chord. Recently, some early modern and modern historians have used SNA software and computer-generated visualisations to chart extended networks.[37] To cite only a couple examples, in a 2014 article Emily Buchnea employed computer programming and insights from social network physicists to construct visualisations of Liverpool–New York trading networks in the late eighteenth and early nineteenth centuries.[38] Networks have also become prevalent in work on intellectual and cultural history as a means of tracing communication and the transmission of ideas.[39] The 'Mapping the Republic of Letters' project at Stanford University has produced computer-generated maps and sociograms based on metadata extracted from digitised texts relating to the correspondence between key figures of the Scientific Revolution and Enlightenment across the Mediterranean and Atlantic world.[40] Even when historians of early modern and modern history have not created visualisations, the concept of 'networks' they have employed since the year 2000 has associations and connotations rooted in the 'small worlds' paradigm of sociologists and physicists. 'Networks' are, more often than not, used to describe migration patterns, global business transactions, or transnational communication, especially in studies of the British Empire in the seventeenth to twentieth centuries. Early twenty-first-century scholars of the early modern British Empire saw 'networks' as a useful way to consider the role of trust in risky long-distance trading ventures and migration.[41] Around the same time, Alan Lester, Zoë Laidlaw, and others embraced 'networks' as a way of modifying metropole-periphery distinctions within the nineteenth- and twentieth-century British Empire; information, policy, and ideas of 'British' identity did not simply radiate from institutions in London, but were shaped by individuals across the Empire through their own informal connections.[42] Critical responses to the work of Lester, Laidlaw, and other scholars working in this vein demonstrate that 'networks' have assumed connotations of neo-liberal globalisation—a discourse whose emphasis on informality and privatisation often obscures

---

[37] Davison, 'Early Modern Social Networks', and Innes, '"Networks" in British History'.

[38] Emily Buchnea, 'Transatlantic Transformations: Visualizing Change over Time in the Liverpool-New York Trade Network, 1763–1833', *Enterprise & Society*, 15 (2014), 687–721.

[39] Ahnert et al., *Network Turn*, ch. 3.

[40] Dan Edelstein, Paula Findlen, Giovanna Ceserani, Caroline Winterer, and Nicole Coleman, 'Historical Research in a Digital Age: Reflections from the Mapping the Republic of Letters Project', *American Historical Review*, 122 (2017), 400–24.

[41] E.g., Natasha Glaisyer, 'Networking: Trade and Exchange in the Eighteenth-Century British Empire', *Historical Journal*, 47 (2004), 451–76.

[42] E.g., Alan Lester, *Imperial Networks: Creating Identities in Nineteenth-Century South Africa and Britain* (London: Routledge, 2001); Zoë Laidlaw, *Colonial Connections 1815–45: Patronage, the Information Revolution and Colonial Government* (Manchester: Manchester University Press, 2005).

the power exerted by institutionalised interests.[43] In 2012, Stephen Howe observed that historians of the British Empire who work on 'networks' have a tendency to attach positive connotations to the world and ignore the structural imbalances in power that underlie and determine access to informal social networks.[44] Most recently, Davison has pointed out that visualisations of networks often struggle to communicate the importance of status and hierarchy in forming and maintaining social relationships: 'it is not clear how to account for power effectively amid the dots and lines'.[45]

So, where do historians of late medieval England stand in relation to this transformed concept of 'networks' that employs metadata-driven visualisations and carries with it connotations of decentralisation and globalisation? It is telling that the surge of publications in the last twenty-five years on the 'Plantagenet Empire' of England, France, Ireland, Wales, and (sometimes) Scotland in the fourteenth and fifteenth centuries has not brought with it the wholesale adoption of network visualisations and globalisation-tinged concepts of networks found in historiographies of early modern and modern empires. While the concept of 'networks' has been employed and criticised ad nauseam by imperial historians of those eras, those studying English dominions in the late medieval period have instead debated the 'tyrannous constructs' of 'empire' and 'state'.[46] Studies of the late medieval 'Plantagenet Empire' that do engage with 'networks' do not employ visualisations or SNA methodologies and their idea of 'network' remains very much informed by generations of late medieval scholars past. Michael Bennett, whom we last met writing about the Cheshire and Lancashire gentry in 1983, published a piece in 2016 on military and economic networks within the 'Plantagenet Empire' in the first half of the fifteenth century. He does mention the 'new imperial history' of early modernists and modernists and its use of networks to emphasise the decentralisation of empires and the agency of people outside formal institutional structures, but equally he frames the piece as part of a McFarlanite tradition of studying non-institutional power relations in the later Middle Ages.[47] Is this situation about to change? In the same volume as Bennett's

[43] Esp. Simon J. Potter, 'Webs, Networks, and Systems: Globalization and the Mass Media in the Nineteenth- and Twentieth-Century British Empire', *Journal of British Studies*, 46 (2007), 621–46.

[44] Stephen Howe, 'British Worlds, Settler Worlds, World Systems, and Killing Fields', *Journal of Imperial & Commonwealth History*, 40 (2012), 699–701.

[45] Davison, 'Early Modern Social Networks', 477.

[46] See, e.g., Rees Davies, 'The Medieval State: The Tyranny of a Concept?', *Journal of Historical Sociology*, 16 (2003), 280–300; Peter Crooks, 'State of the Union: Perspectives on English Imperialism in the Late Middle Ages', *Past & Present*, 212 (2011), 3–42; Peter Crooks, David Green, and W. Mark Ormrod, 'The Plantagenets and Empire in the Later Middle Ages', in iidem (eds), *The Plantagenet Empire, 1259–1453: Proceedings of the 2014 Harlaxton Symposium* (Donington: Shaun Tyas, 2016), 1–34.

[47] Michael Bennett, 'The Plantagenet Empire as "Enterprise Zone": War and Business Networks, c. 1400–50', in Crooks et al. (eds), *Plantagenet Empire*, 335–58.

piece, a chapter by Jackson Armstrong called for historians of the late medieval
'Plantagenet Empire' to move away from 'centre-periphery' models of political
power. He wrote that late medievalists would gain from reading works on early
modern and modern empires that employ SNA and examine the roles played
by both aristocratic and non-aristocratic members of society in a dispersed
polity. Consideration of this network-based and methodologically informed
scholarship, Armstrong contended, may encourage historians of the British
Isles in the fourteenth and fifteenth centuries to abandon the idea of 'core'
and 'periphery' cultural zones for a more 'cellular' and regionalised vision of
how decentralised polities operated.[48]

But historians of late medieval England have continued to study 'networks';
they just rarely look to empires and long-distance relationships when doing
so. Some late medievalists even refer to works on network theory from the
social sciences and employ computer-generated visualisations. As early as 1996,
David Postles used SNA software to analyse personal pledging in the Leicestershire manor of Kibworth Harcourt during the late thirteenth and early
fourteenth centuries.[49] Although no visualisations feature in his article, Postles
constructed sociograms and used graph theory to produce precise calculations
of network block density and centrality. Postles's work contains none of the
hesitance expressed by Carpenter or Judith Bennett about the theoretical and
mathematical aspects of network analysis, but in other regards his article is
very much in line with their concept of 'networks', reflected by the thanks to
both historians in his acknowledgements. Like Carpenter and Bennett, Postles
concluded that the analysis of networks disproved assertions by other scholars
about the cohesion of medieval 'communities'. He found that a fairly narrow
range of people acted as pledges for others in Kibworth Harcourt, and that
pledging seemed to be used as a way for an elite to determine what would
be deemed acceptable behaviour in the village and to discourage the integration of outsiders. Nearly a decade later, David Gary Shaw employed some
rudimentary visualisations (but rather more extensive statistical analysis) of
networks found in records of court cases that went to arbitration in the city of
Wells between 1377 and 1429. He concluded that the highest-status citizens
tended to have less dense but more extensive networks, acting as intermediaries linking together most groups within the city. Shaw argued that by making
themselves essential go-betweens in the workings of urban life, such elite citizens were able to augment their power and justify its extension.[50] It is also
telling that the works from the social sciences cited by Shaw include J. Clyde
Mitchell and J.A. Barnes, both social anthropologists and key influences on

[48] Jackson W. Armstrong, 'Centre, Periphery, Locality, Province: England and its Far
North in the Fifteenth Century', in Crooks et al. (eds), *Plantagenet Empire*, 248–72.

[49] David Postles, 'Personal Pledging: Medieval "Reciprocity" or "Symbolic Capital"?',
Journal of Interdisciplinary History, 26 (1996), 419–35.

[50] David Gary Shaw, 'Social Networks and the Foundations of Oligarchy in Medieval
Towns', *Urban History*, 32 (2005), 200–22.

Carpenter and Judith Bennett. Shaw and Postles were both operating within a distinctly 'late medieval' concept of 'networks': they saw networks as a way of investigating the workings of power, not as an approach that might potentially obscure it or as a method that emphasised the maintenance of social ties across distance.

The same concepts of networked power as exclusive power, and of the inherent ways in which informal networks fortify institutional power structures, also pervade recent works of late medieval history that do not employ computer-assisted SNA or visualisations. In 2018's *Trustworthy Men*, Ian Forrest writes that in thirteenth- to fifteenth-century England poorer members of the parish rarely travelled far and needed to rely on local communities for support, while the power of churchwardens was extended by the fact that they had social links to a 'network' of powerholders in other localities. These more wide-ranging connections allowed the 'trustworthy men' the opportunity to obtain additional information and to cultivate a greater number of people able to vouch for their reputations, both factors that entrenched their authority locally.[51] While Forrest uses the word 'network' itself sparingly, the book's premise is that parish elites (or 'trustworthy men') gained power within the medieval English Church through their capacity as intermediaries between local communities and ecclesiastical authorities. The Church itself was an institution based on social networks maintained by powerful brokers and dependent on the information conveyed through these networks. My own work on urban political networks in fifteenth-century England similarly focuses on the collection and dissemination of information by urban elites as a source of power, inspired both by social anthropology and by sociological theories about the 'diffusion of innovations' through networks. This work demonstrates that certain indicators (such as the adoption of particular chartered liberties) can be used to trace the flow of information between English towns. It shows that information spread through the institutional channels of borough governments was passed on to a wider range of actors. Information conveyed more informally through mercantile networks and lawyer-brokers, however, tended to reach fewer towns and to result in a more restricted wealthy elite of townspeople entrenching their own power at an institutional level.[52]

There is an implicit assumption in the works of all four of these late medieval historians (Postles, Shaw, Forrest, and Hartrich) that informal 'networks' feed into and are fed by institutional power, and that institutional systems that rely on informal 'networks' often serve to concentrate authority in an ever-smaller number of people able to access information from diverse

---

[51] Ian Forrest, *Trustworthy Men: How Inequality and Faith Made the Medieval Church* (Princeton: Princeton University Press, 2018), esp. 225–26.

[52] Eliza Hartrich, 'Charters and Inter-Urban Networks: England, 1439–1449', *English Historical Review*, 132 (2017), 219–49; Eliza Hartrich, *Politics and the Urban Sector in Fifteenth-Century England, 1413–1471* (Oxford: Oxford University Press, 2019), ch. 3.

sources. This tendency to associate the concept of 'networks' with structural inequalities and the accumulation of power stands in stark contrast to the 'globalisation' concept of networks prevalent in other historical subfields, which is often accused of concealing the relationship between informal connections and institutional authority. The interest in power displayed by late medieval historians studying networks may stem from the fact that even the scholars who have engaged most with mathematical and computer-assisted SNA (such as Postles and Shaw) still cite social anthropologists like Mitchell rather than the more data-minded 'small world' sociologists and physicists. It also bears testimony to the continuing legacy of Christine Carpenter and Judith Bennett, who were attracted to the concept of 'networks' as a means of lessening the dominance of the concept of 'community' (with its connotations of inclusivity and social harmony) in late medieval historiography.

* * *

Armstrong's statement that 'late medievalists stand to benefit from renewed engagement with debates on interpretative models which historians of other periods are conducting with vigour' is undoubtedly true.[53] Much excellent, theoretically informed, and methodologically sophisticated work has been done in early modern and modern history on the ways in which human social relationships are reconfigured over time, and how those structural reconfigurations affect the functioning of society. In this chapter, however, I have illustrated that we should not view 'networks' as a single accepted methodology that historians in other fields have embraced and historians of late medieval England have shunned. Over the last eighty years, historians of late medieval England have developed their own *concept* of what a network means. It is a concept rooted in McFarlane's understanding of 'networks' as informal power structures that did not map easily onto government or social institutions (such as the county court or affinity), and then developed through engagement with social anthropology. The assumption eventually arose that 'networks' stood in opposition to the idea that fourteenth- and fifteenth-century England consisted of organic 'communities'; informal and 'networked' society served the interests of a narrow social elite and erected barriers to those who wished to join. Indeed, these exclusive networks could then form the basis for institutional power in villages, cities, and parishes, making elites the sole intermediaries between locality and higher authorities. These types of associations have become attached to the way late medieval historians approach 'networks', whether or not they engage with theory from the social sciences or employ SNA software.

Such connotations contrast with the concept of 'networks' that has emerged in other fields, a concept informed by sociological 'small world' and 'whole

[53] Armstrong, 'Centre, Periphery, Locality, Province', 251.

system' analysis based on meta-data rather than by ethnographic social anthropology. In particular, the concept of 'networks' has evolved in imperial and intellectual history to emphasise long-distance relationships and the types of social formations and individuals that enable those relationships to be maintained. It is also commonly viewed to be decentralising and 'decidedly democratic', in that it recognises the importance of middlemen and subalterns in the communication of news, creation of trust, and evolution of discourse.[54] In these fields, there has also been a greater willingness to employ SNA digital methods, visualisations, and terminology, partly because network visualisations arrange data points in a way that is overtly non-hierarchical.[55] But, again, the *concept* of 'networks' often overrides its methodologies. Imperial historians such as Alan Lester do not adopt many of the statistical or visual tools employed by social scientists of networks, but nevertheless their work is informed by the 'small worlds' and 'big data' approach of post-1990s SNA.

These generalisations are painted with a very broad brush. I have neglected to discuss many important works of network-influenced historical scholarship, and I have stereotyped nuanced methodological approaches in the social sciences and in different fields of history. I hope to have illustrated, however, that reflection on the *concepts* of 'network' that we employ in the study of history is as important as reflection on the *methodologies*. Whether or not historians employ particular statistical or digital tools, the data they analyse and the conclusions they draw from it are moulded by their pre-conceptions about what, exactly, 'networks' are, what kinds of entities belong to them, how big or small a functioning 'network' can be, which relationships within a 'network' are worthy of investigation, and which types of behaviour they consider typical of certain social configurations. Undoubtedly, a concept such as 'networks' is, in the famous words of E.A.R. Brown, a 'tyrannous construct'—a word and a set of ideas that we unwittingly impose on a past society to which they would have been alien. But if concepts can be tyrannous, their tyrannies often operate over quite small jurisdictions; it is an enlightened despotism on the scale of a petty German principality rather than Catherine the Great's Russia. Each field of history has its own peculiar intellectual traditions, which can lead the same word to develop different meanings or valences in these different contexts. As the John Shillingford example showed, there are no 'real' networks that existed in the past, and as such no one concept of a 'network' and how it functions is more or less accurate than another. What is important is that we recognise the assumptions that inform how we interpret the past and do not mistake our analytical approximations for measurable and incontestable realities.

Is there much for historians of late medieval England to learn by breaking away from a McFarlanite and social anthropology-driven concept of 'networks'? Certainly. For example, visualisations depicting changes in the structure of cloth trading networks in the fifteenth century could contribute

---

[54] The quotation comes from Ahnert et al., *Network Turn*, 39.

[55] Ibid., ch. 2.

to debates about the rise of capitalism and the 'putting-out' system, the changing role of women in the economy, and the re-orientation of English commerce towards the Atlantic. Moreover, in re-conceptualising 'networks' as longer-distance formations connecting a more diverse range of people, late medieval English history could become less isolationist in its approach and more willing to see the island as part of European or global trends. Equally, though, imperial and intellectual historians studying other periods of history would benefit from further acquaintance with the late medievalists' concept of networks. Embedding the 'dots and lines' of network visualisations within a social anthropology tradition of network analysis might make such historians more cognisant of the ways in which particular configurations of informal connection amplify the more authoritarian or exclusionary aspects of political institutions, rather than bypass or democratise them.

Acknowledgements I am grateful to my colleagues Jayne Gifford, Joel Halcomb, and Samantha Knapton for their helpful comments on the text and their suggestions for improving its intelligibility to non-medievalists.

CHAPTER 9

Politics

Christopher Fletcher

The later Middle Ages did have a concept of 'politics' and the 'political', but not one which corresponds to most ways in which historians have discussed 'politics'. Using modern frames of reference, historians have identified phenomena in late medieval England which they describe as 'politics' or as 'political'. But this is not, in fact, the vocabulary which contemporaries applied to the same phenomena. Historians and late medieval actors used words with similar morphology, but not in the same ways, nor in the same contexts, nor with the same connotations. Over the past century, the meaning of 'politics' and 'political' has evolved both within and outside the discipline of medieval history, from one in which competition for control of the institutions of the state was the definition of politics itself, to another in which competition for influence within many different human groups can be described as 'political'. This has had a tangible impact on what historians consider politics to be and thus on how they interpret medieval phenomena. That said, there is no need to conclude that, since our vocabulary does not correspond to medieval vocabulary, and is in itself shifting, then it can only lead us into anachronism: that there is 'no such thing as politics' in late medieval England. If we shift our view slightly, we can see that although in late medieval England the vocabulary of 'politics' was largely confined to expert discourse until the fifteenth century, and included a slightly different range of phenomena from those we most strongly associate with 'politics', similar sets of ideas, arguments and assumptions are also found in contexts where this language did not occur. There are

C. Fletcher (✉)
CNRS/IRHiS, Université de Lille, Lille, France

© The Author(s), under exclusive license to Springer Nature
Switzerland AG 2022
J. W. Armstrong, P. Crooks and A. Ruddick (eds), *Using Concepts in Medieval History*, https://doi.org/10.1007/978-3-030-77280-2_9

moreover clear overlaps between these contemporary categories and our own. Given movements in the historiography of late medieval England in recent decades, concerned not only with the politics of the kingdom and the nobility but also with the politics of counties, towns, villages and parishes, another way seems gradually to be opening up.

By way of counterpoint to what can seem very English debates, it is also encouraging that recent historians of late medieval Europe have been increasingly tempted by the invocation in a modified form of what Jürgen Habermas, talking of a later period, calls *Öffentlichkeit*, translated into English as 'the public sphere'.[1] This model, and the fundamental notions of publicity, information circulation and opinion it contains, has much to recommend it as a means of conceiving of politics which does not simply impose what seems to us most obviously political, nor lead us into an unhelpfully baggy concept of politics as the competition for power in any context. It is also possible to talk of 'state formation' and 'political culture' or 'political society' as historians habitually do, focussing on the way that local elites act as officers for different forms of 'state' power. In these cases, however, there is arguably a stronger risk of teleology, although not an unavoidable one, since contemporaries did not divide the former from forms of rule which have nothing to do with what we would call the 'state'. The 'cultures' or 'societies' which we identify as 'political' were not described as such by contemporaries. Other concepts, both 'public' as opposed to 'private', but also 'common' as against 'singular', for example, suggest models of politics which strike a middle ground between medieval perceptions and our own preoccupations. There is a caveat for the practice of conceptual history here. It is not necessarily the word whose morphology most resembles our own which necessarily gives the best clues to understanding what we are hoping to analyse.

MEDIEVAL CONCEPTS OF THE POLITICAL

Later medieval English writers were well aware of the Aristotelian division, known to Latin writers since the early twelfth century, between ethics, economics and politics, respectively the art of ruling oneself, a household

---

[1] Nicolas Offenstadt and Patrick Boucheron (eds), *L'espace public au Moyen Âge: Débats autour de Jürgen Habermas* (Paris: PUF, 2011); Hipólito Rafael Oliva Herrer, Vincent Challet, Jan Dumolyn and María Antonia Carmona Ruiz (eds), *La comunidad medieval como esfera pública* (Seville: Universidad de Sevilla, 2014); Jan Dumolyn, Jelle Haemers, Hipólito Rafael Oliva Herrer and Vincent Challet (eds), *The Voices of the People in Late Medieval Europe: Communication and Popular Politics* (Turnhout: Brepols, 2014). The key work is Jürgen Habermas, *Strukturwandel der Öffentlichkeit: Untersuchungen zu einer Kategorie der bürgerlichen Gesellschaft* (Berlin: Luchterhand, 1962), published in English as *The Structural Transformation of the Public Sphere: An Inquiry into a Category of Bourgeois Society*, trans. Frederick Lawrence and Thomas Bürger (Cambridge: Polity, 1989). It has been highly influential on students of the eighteenth century, less so of the Middle Ages. See esp. Nicolas Offenstadt, 'Le Moyen Âge de Jürgen Habermas: Enquête sur une réception allemande', in Offenstradt and Boucheron (eds), *L'espace public*, 77–96.

and a community.[2] For Hugh of Saint-Victor, in his *Didascalicon* (before 1137) the division of the practical art into 'ethical, economic and political' (*ethicam, oeconomicam et politicam*) corresponded to the division between 'individual, private and public' (*solitariam, privatam et publicam*), which in turn mapped onto the 'moral, administrative and civil' (*moralem et dispensativam et civilem*).[3] From the second half of the twelfth century, this understanding of politics acquired a more precise Aristotelian flavour in the *Policraticus* of John of Salisbury (1159).[4] This was developed in scholastic discourse later in the thirteenth century following the Latin translation of Aristotle's *Politics* by William of Moerbeke (1268–1269)[5]; in subsequent commentary upon it, notably by Thomas Aquinas and Albert the Great[6]; before being adapted for lay audiences initially in 'mirrors for princes' and encyclopaedic works, before Nicole Oresme's French translation of 1370–1377.[7] The message common to all of these works, and one which had an enormous impact across Europe, was that good government pursued the common profit, which could overrule even legitimate individual or group interests, and that tyranny was rule for the particular interest of the ruler, not of the community.[8]

Yet although, as we shall see, arguments in terms of the common good and mutual profit were established early in what we would call the politics of late medieval England, the terminology of 'politics' and the 'political' or even 'politic' behaviour did not make the leap on any significant scale into what we might call practical politics. The word 'politicus' appears only late in chronicles or in documents issued from the royal administration. The *Dictionary of Medieval Latin from British Sources* cites no examples of 'politicus'

---

[2] Nicolai Rubinstein, 'The history of the word *politicus* in early-modern Europe', in A. Pagden (ed.), *The Languages of Political Theory in Early-Modern Europe* (Cambridge: Cambridge University Press, 1987), 41–56, at 41.

[3] Hugh of Saint-Victor, *Didascalicon de studio legend*, ed. C. Buttimer (Washington, DC: Catholic University Press, 1939), II. 19, p. 37.

[4] John of Salisbury, *Policraticus I-IV*, ed. K.S.B. Keats-Rohan (Turnhout: Brepols 1993); John of Salisbury, *Policratici sive de Nugis curialum et vestigiis philosophorum libri VIII*, ed. Clemens C. I. Webb, 2 vols (Oxford: Clarendon Press, 1909); English translation: John of Salisbury, *Policraticus*, ed. and trans. C.J. Nederman (Cambridge: Cambridge University Press, 1990).

[5] For the dating of this translation see Nicole Oresme, *Le Livre de Politiques d'Aristote*, ed. A.D. Menut (Philadelphia: American Philosophical Society, 1970), 25.

[6] Matthew Kempshall, *The Common Good in Late Medieval Political Thought* (Oxford: Clarendon Press, 1999).

[7] Oresme, *Le Livre de Politiques d'Aristote*, ed. Menut, 3.

[8] Elodie Lecuppre-Desjardin and Anne-Laure van Bruaene (eds), *De bono communi: The Discourse and Practice of the Common Good in the European City (13th-16th c.)*, (Turnhout: Brepols, 2010), esp. Eberhard Isenmann, 'The notion of the Common Good, the concept of politics, and practical policies in late medieval and early modern German cities', in Ibid., 107–48, and Franck Collard (ed.), *Pouvoir d'un seul et bien commun (VIe-XVIe siècles)*. Special edition of Revue française d'histoire des idées politiques, vol. 32 (2010).

in chronicles or administrative documents.[9] The first example of use in such documents given by the *Anglo-Norman Dictionary*[10] and the *Middle English Dictionary*[11] relates to the same petition (in Middle English) and subsequent statute (in French) of 1429 which seeks to promote the 'good politique governaunce and supportation' of the Calais Staple.[12] This, indeed, is the first use of 'political' in the text of the digitised *Parliament Rolls of Medieval England*, which begin with the reign of Edward I.[13] This impression is confirmed when we extend the search earlier in the period with such resources as are now freely available in searchable digital form. A rough test corpus of Latin chronicles from the reign of Henry III, which takes in the contemporary chronicles of Roger Wendover (1216–1235: 339 pages),[14] of Matthew Paris until his death in 1259 [2043 pages],[15] and those chronicles published in the Rolls Series as *Annales Monastici* whose contemporary sections mostly concern the thirteenth century (2905 pages),[16] reveals no use of 'politicus'. A similar search of the Close Rolls, whose published Latin text is available in searchable digitised form from 1227 to 1251,[17] and the Patent Rolls, published in the original Latin from 1216 to 1232, yields a similar result.[18] No examples of 'politicus' are found in a search of the 'royal letters' of Henry III published by Shirley, which add letters to the king, now preserved in Ancient Correspondence (SC 1), and a sample of letters on the Close Rolls and Patent Rolls to 1272 (958

[9] *Dictionary of Medieval Latin from British Sources* (Oxford: Oxford University Press, 1975–2013).

[10] *Anglo-Norman Dictionary* consulted online at http://www.anglo-norman.net/gate/.

[11] *Middle English Dictionary* consulted online at https://quod.lib.umich.edu/m/mid dle-english-dictionary/dictionary.

[12] Parliament of September 1429 in *Parliament Rolls of Medieval England*, ed. C. Given-Wilson et al. CD ROM. Leicester: Scholarly Digital Editions, 2005, item 60 (Punctuation modified. It is clear from comparing the petition and the statute that 'politique' is an adjective in both). *Statutes of the Realm*, London: Record Commission, 1810–1825, vol. II, 254. No earlier example is found by searching the Michigan *Corpus of Middle English Prose and Verse*, consulted online at https://quod.lib.umich.edu/c/cme/.

[13] *Parliament Rolls of Medieval England*, ed. Given-Wilson et al.

[14] Roger of Wendover, *Chronica sive Flores Historiarum*, ed. H.O. Coxe, vol. IV (London: Sumptibus Societatis, 1842).

[15] Matthew Paris, *Chronica Majora*, ed. H.R. Luard, vols III–V [1248–1259], (London: Longman, 1876–1880).

[16] *Annales Monastici*, ed. H.R. Luard, 4 vols (London: Longman. 1864–1869).

[17] *Close Rolls of the Reign of Henry III*, ed. H.C. Maxwell-Lyte 6 vols [covering 1227–1251] (London: HMSO, 1902–1922). It was not possible on this occasion to continue this test to the end of Henry III's reign, since the texts for 1252–1272 are only available in closed form on British History Online. After 1272, the full texts give way to Calendars, and so terminological searches of this kind can no longer be carried out. Search for the Close Rolls, Patent Rolls, and the letters edited by Shirley was performed on roughly digitised (OCRed) texts, searching for the string of characters 'pol', so it is possible that some occurrences may have been missed.

[18] *Patent Rolls of the Reign of Henry III*, 2 vols [Covering 1216–1232], (London: HMSO, 1901–1903).

pages).[19] This corpus is admittedly early, and pre-dates the translation and commentary of Aristotle's politics, or the diffusion of such early translated and widely circulated 'mirrors for princes' as the *De Regimine Principum* of Giles of Rome (c. 1280), which was divided into three books dealing with Ethics, Economics (meaning the household) and Politics. But much the same is seen in thirteenth- and early-fourteenth-century chronicles in the vernacular, such as the chronicle of Robert of Gloucester (877 pages) and the version of the Middle English *Brut* chronicle to 1333 published by Brie (286 pages).[20] Neither the section of Ranulph Higden's *Polichronicon* covering the period 1135 to 1352 nor its continuations (587 pages) reveal any use of 'politicus', although, as we shall see, it is used in the earlier, discursive sections of this work.[21] It is always possible, indeed likely, that an instance of 'politicus' or its vernacular equivalent will be found by a more extensive search of chronicles and administrative documents, printed or unprinted. But it has to be said that its absence from this scratch corpus of thirteenth- and fourteenth-century documents dealing with precisely what we habitually consider to be 'politics' is in itself telling.

On the other hand, although the words 'politics' and 'political' seem to be absent from the discourse of what we would call practical politics, the form of reasoning which Aristotle's *Politics* and those who took it up were most inspired by—that rule ought to be for the profit and benefit of all, and that this overruled even the legitimate individual interests of individuals and groups— was absorbed early on in these same contexts. Indeed, this absorption occurred considerably before the translation of the *Politics* into Latin or its diffusion in 'mirrors for princes'. Moreover, this discourse did not only take the form of the invocation of powerful concepts in the abstract, but was manifested much more frequently in a form of reasoning which sought to establish mutual interest through the establishment of common profit and, just as importantly, common damage.

Early examples of this reasoning are to be found in the documents created by the struggle between Henry III and his critics which first came to a head in 1258. So, for example, in the royal letter of 2 May 1258 which announced the king's intention to create a council of twenty-four by whom 'the state of our kingdom will be ordained, corrected and reformed' this was to be done 'according to what they see best to do for the honour of God and for our faith and for the utility of our kingdom'.[22] Although none of the twenty-eight articles which were then presented to the king invoke the common

---

[19] *Royal and Other Historical Letters Illustrative of the Reign of Henry III*, ed. W.W. Shirley (London: Longman, 1862–1868).

[20] Robert of Gloucester, *Metrical Chronicle*, ed. W.A. Wright, 2 vols (London: Longman, 1887); *The Brut*, vol. 1. Early English Text Society, original series, 131, ed. F.W.D. Brie (New York: Schribner, 1906).

[21] Ranulph Higden, *Polychronicon*, ed. J.R. Lumby, vol. VIII (London: Longman, 1882).

[22] *Documents of the Baronial Movement of Reform and Rebellion, 1258–1267*, ed. R.F. Treharne and Sanders (Oxford: Clarendon Press, 1973), 74: 'ordinetur, rectificetur et

'utilitas', 'bonum' or 'commodum', a number of articles in this document do make a slightly different argument. They argue that certain practices result in damage to 'the land', to 'many' or to specific groups whose interests are linked to that of the king.[23] They protest, for example, that because the king almost never pays for the 'prises' raised for the needs of his court 'many merchants of the kingdom of England are impoverished beyond measure', and foreign merchants do not come to the kingdom 'by which the land suffers great damage'.[24] Another article protests that 'many are impoverished and destroyed' by price-manipulation by Cahors money-lenders in London which causes both 'great loss to the merchants and all the people of that town' and also 'great damage to the lord king'.[25]

These arguments in specific cases attempt to create a mutuality which will persuade the royal government to act. The rhetoric behind this implies that because something is in the interests of all then it should be done, and it is because it is in the interests only of individuals and particular groups, threatening specific common goods, that it should be undone. Even when, on a more emphatic level, oaths were sworn in 1258 for 'the reformation (*reformacioni*) and utility (*utilitaci*) of the king and the kingdom', and demands were made that the kings hated half-brothers quit the kingdom 'until the state of the realm be reformed' (*usque dum status regni reformaretur*) we see the same desire to create a mutual interest remains.[26] In these cases, the moral charge is sometimes clearer than it was in the complaints of the merchants, for example, when the Provisions of Oxford declares that the knights chosen to consider the reform of the kingdom do not have the right to refuse, because this service is 'for the common utility of the whole kingdom' (*pro communi utilitate tocius regni*).[27] But this common utility resists abstraction through the variety of ways it is expressed, and the fact that many of these expressions return to the mutual profit of the king, the kingdom and various sub-groups within it. When the newly appointed Justiciar swore to carry out his office, and to hold to justice to all people, this is 'for the profit of the king and kingdom', not the one without the other.[28]

Arguments in these terms gained in strength under Henry III's successors. Edward I, who had been an active agent on both sides of the controversies of this father's reign, was to make use of similar arguments for his own ends. When Edward tried to go to war in 1297 without the consent of a broad assembly which his practices in recent years had led his subjects to expect, he

---

reformatur status regni nostri secundum quod melius uiderint expedire ad honorem Dei et ad fidem nostram ac regni nostri utilitatem'.

[23] Ibid., 71–72.

[24] Ibid., 86, item 23.

[25] Ibid., 86–89, item 26.

[26] Ibid., 92.

[27] Ibid., 98, item 1.

[28] Ibid., 102, item 6.

justified himself in the name of the profit of all. In an open letter, the king argued that he had crossed the sea not only 'to recover his right inheritance' but also 'for the honour and the common profit of his kingdom'.[29] He denied having seen the complaints which he heard had been addressed to him, which were said to have been presented as being 'for the common profit of the people and of the kingdom'.[30] Aware of the power of such arguments, he asks that no one believe rumours that he refused such articles or did 'anything else against the common profit of the kingdom to shame and destroy his people', recalling how great discord had earlier occurred by such words being spread in the kingdom, 'and the damages which came from them'.[31] He prayed to all the good people of the kingdom that it was 'for the honour of God, and himself, and them, and the kingdom, and for lasting peace, and to put in good estate his kingdom' that he had undertaken this voyage.[32] By the reign of Edward II, the king's government was accustomed to thinking in these terms. Thus in the 'Stamford Articles' presented to the king in the parliament of April 1309, a set of petitions whose proper consideration was the condition of a grant of taxation, the king was first asked 'to have regard for his poor people, which feels very much hurt'.[33] Each article then presented the sufferings of the people under the pressure of the king's demands, although they do not refer to the common good. The royal government, however, did use this language, replying to one article that an ordinance of Edward I should be observed, which is 'convenient for the king and profitable for his people' (*covenable pur le roi et profitable pur son poeple*), and accepting that a tax on wine, cloth and other merchandise should be suspended until it has been established 'what profit and what advantage' will come of it 'for him and his people'.[34]

This form of reasoning in terms of mutual profit, and the need to avert common damage, was found whether the king acted voluntarily or whether his hand was forced. Thus the 'Ordinances' imposed on Edward II during the summer of 1311 were presented in royal letters as being 'to the honour of God' and also 'for the good of us and our kingdom', notably in seeking to restrain the expenses of the king's household, keeping in mind 'our [i.e.

---

[29] *Documents illustrating the Crisis of 1297–8 in England*, ed. M. Prestwich, Camden 4th ser. 24 (London: Royal Historical Society, 1980), 125: 'pur recoverir sun dreit heritage, dunt il est par graunt fraude deceu par le roi de France, e pur le honur et le commun profit de sun reaume'.

[30] Ibid., 127: 'pur le commun profit du pueple e du reaume'.

[31] Ibid., 128: 'ou autre chose contre le commun profit du reaume pur son pueple honir e destruire'.

[32] Ibid., 129: 'al honur de dieu, e de lui, e de eux, e du reaume, e pur pardurable pees, e pur mettre en bon estat son reaume'.

[33] *Select Documents of English Constitutional History, 1307–1485*, ed. S.B. Chrimes and A. Brown (London: A. & C. Black, 1960), 6: 'prient a nostre seygneur le roi qil voille, si lui plest, aver regard de son povre poeple, qe molt se sent greve'.

[34] Ibid., 7: 'pur saver quel profit et quel avantage accrestera a li et a son poeple par cele suztrete, e puis aura le roi consail selonc lavantage qil y verra'.

the king's] honour, and our profit and the profit of our people'.[35] Nor were such arguments restricted to moments of heightened tension. By the time the English Parliament had reached the form it would keep for the rest of the Middle Ages early in the reign of Edward III, petitions deemed to be of general interest and potentially furnishing a basis for future legislation were adopted by the Commons and enrolled together in the 'common petition' on the grounds that served the common good, in contrast to the 'singular petitions' which touched only particular interests.[36] This centrality of the difference between common profit and individual profit was not merely procedural: it is seen throughout the discourse of these petitions in their habitual use of the opposition between various forms of profit shared between the king, the kingdom and the people to recommend the need to action, and opposed to the common damage which would result if current abuses were allowed to persist.[37] In these contexts, into the fourteenth century and beyond, the mobilisation of the mutual profit of the king and kingdom was an essential element of what we would call 'politics'.

And yet, until the fifteenth century, the term 'politicus' remained largely confined to scholastic discourse in the Latin language and was not used to discuss specific examples of English contemporary 'politics'. As we have seen, no vernacular equivalent seems to be attested in Anglo-Norman or Middle English before the fifteenth century, even after Nicole Oresme's French translation of Aristotle's *Politics* in 1370–1377. It has been suggested that this was because, in scholastic usage, the word 'politicus' acquired, especially with William Moerbeke's Latin translation, an association with the government of a town or city, as opposed to a kingdom, and by one who is both ruler and ruled, in opposition to a king.[38] Thus Brunetto Latini, in his *Tresor*, glossed 'politique' as 'c'est a dire des governemens des cités'.[39] For Robert Holcot (d. 1349) the 'political' arts were the same thing as the 'civil' arts,[40] and for William of Ockham (d. 1349) 'principatum ... politicum' was one in which

---

[35] Ibid., 11.

[36] Doris Rayner, 'The Forms and Machinery of the 'Commune Petition' in the Fourteenth Century', *English Historical Review*, Vol. 56 (1941), 549–70; W.M. Ormrod, 'On – and Off – the Record: The Rolls of Parliament, 1337–1377', *Parliamentary History*, vol. 23 (2004), 39–56; Gwilym Dodd, *Justice and Grace: Private Petitioning and the English Parliament in the Late Middle Ages* (Oxford: Oxford University Press, 2007) 126–55.

[37] Christopher Fletcher, 'What makes a political language? Key terms, profit and damage in the Common Petition of the English Parliament, 1343–1422', in J. Dumolyn, J. Haemers, H.R. Oliva Herrer and V. Challet (eds), *The Voices of the People in Late Medieval Europe: Communication and Popular Politics* (Turnhout: Brepols, 2014), 91–106.

[38] Rubinstein, 'The History of the Word *Politicus*', 43.

[39] Brunetto Latini, *Li Livres dou Tresor*, ed. F.J. Carmody (Berkeley and Los Angeles: University of California Press, 1948), 391.

[40] *Super Sapientem Salomonis* [1336], Basel, 1586. Cited in the *Dictionary of Latin from British Sources*, sub. 'politicus': 'prime ... sunt artes civiles sive politice'.

'many rule'.[41] That said, even Brunetto Latini continued that, although he was only going to deal with the rule of the city, 'politics includes generally all the arts that are needful for the community of men',[42] and even though he was not going to consider those places, like France, whose kings ruled by a perpetual title, 'nevertheless any lord, whatever lordship he has, could take very good teachings from it'.[43] Ockham, too, uses this language in an effort to qualify an excessive contrast between monarchical, aristocratic and political rule. In this passage in his *Octo Quaestiones de Potestate Papae* (c. 1340 × 1342), he argues against those who maintain the absolute authority of the pope by invoking the contrast between monarchical rule (*principatus regalis*), in which one alone 'shines above all' (*praefulget*), and 'aristocratic and political rule, in both of which many command, dominate and excel'.[44] Instead, notes Ockham, the best rule occurs when charity, peace, friendship and concord flourish amongst subjects, and discord is prevented, which is best obtained when the prince rules in accordance with the common good.[45]

Long before John Fortescue argued that because England, unlike France, was not simply a *dominium regale* but a *dominium politicum et regale*, and that as a result the English king could not 'rule his peple bi other lawes than such as thai assenten unto' nor 'sett upon thaim non imposicions without thair owne assent',[46] politic rule was associated with good rule, which meant rule for the common good, established by reason and counsel. Walter Burley could remark as early as the 1320s that in order to contract important business the king needed to assemble parliament, and by that stage this had become an unavoidable rule of English 'political' life.[47] Similar connotations can be detected, for example, in the one use of 'politicus' by Ranulph Higden (d. 1364) at the start of his *Polichronicon*, in a discussion of the kinds of persons whose deeds are remembered after them: a prince in his kingdom, a knight in battle, a judge

[41] William of Ockham, *Opera politica*, ed. J. G. Silkes et al., 2nd edn. (Manchester: Manchester University Press, 1974), 109, cited in the *Dictionary of Latin from British Sources*, sub. 'politicus'.

[42] *Li Livre dou Tresor*, 391: 'politike compregne generaument tous les ars ki besoignent a la comunité des homes'.

[43] Ibid., 392: 'et neporquant tot signour, quel signorie k'il aient en poroient prendre mains bons ensegnemens'.

[44] William of Ockham, *Opera politica*, 109: 'tam principatum aristocraticum quam politicum, in quorum utroque, praesident plures, superat et praecellit'.

[45] Ibid.: 'Propter hoc enim est omnis principatus bono communis expediens principaliter institutus, et ista summo conatu plantare debet princeps et fovere in sibi subiectis'.

[46] Sir John Fortescue, *The Governance of England*, ed. C. Plummer (Oxford: Clarendon Press, 1885), chap. i, 109–10. Cf. Fortescue, *De Laudibus Legum Anglie*, ed. and trans. S.B. Chrimes (Cambridge: Cambridge University Press, 2011), 24–27 and Fortescue, *De Natura Legis Nature*, c. 16, cited at length in Fortescue, *De Laudibus*, ed. Chrimes, 152–53.

[47] Cited in Nicole Oresme, *Livre de Politiques*, 26. For the development of this requirement see G.L. Harriss, *King, Parliament and Public Finance in Medieval England to 1369* (Oxford: Clarendon Press. 1975).

in his seat, a bishop amongst the clergy, a 'politicus' amongst the people, a 'oeconomicus' in the house and a 'monasticus' in church.[48] Translators of this work into Middle English had difficulty rendering the first of these, even though they corresponded to the well-known Aristotelian division between politics, economics and ethics. John Trevisa's late-fourteenth-century translation of Higden rendered them as 'lawefulman in the peple, housbond in hous, religious man in chirche'. Being a 'politicus' was thus associated with having the standing of a trustworthy, law-worthy man of sufficient standing to act as a juror.[49] Only in the mid-fifteenth century was this translated as 'off a politike man in the people, of a howsebonde man in a house, of a contemplatif man in the chirche'.[50]

The 'political' concerned not just a kingdom but many different groups of human beings under some kind of authority and some form of law. In any context it involved rule over many according to established laws or conventions, in accordance with reason, often involving some form of consultation or counsel. As Ockham's use of these terms already implies, this did not just apply to lay rule. In Reginald Pecock's *The Repressor of Over Much Blaming of Clergy* (c. 1449), 'politik gouernauncis' refers to the rule, both spiritual and worldly, which churchmen have over other men, clergy and laity. Pecock seeks to demonstrate that this cannot be wrong in itself, but only when the officers who wield it, be they priests or dukes or any ruler, fall into sin.[51] For Pecock, 'politik gouernaunce' is simply rule of some over others, and a resulting hierarchical relationship of 'ouerte and netherte'.[52] These arrangements are specific to particular times. Just because the Old Testament Jews had only one bishop in 'thilk oold politik gouernaunce' does not mean that we should only have one now.[53] Such arrangements are man-made, in the past, and both 'bischophode and archbischophode, clekenhode and religiose mannys lawis' and also 'othere politik mennys lawis ben noon othere than mennys ordinaunscis and mennys tradiciouns reuling men forto do this or that, to which as bi Goddis pleyn lawe tho men weren not bifore bounde'.[54] That these laws were 'civil' did not make them 'republican' in the sense that they were determined by an authority other than the monarch. Rather, 'it is

---

[48] Higden, *Polichronicon*, vol. I, 34.

[49] *MED*, 'laueful', adj. James Masschaele, *Jury State and Society in Medieval England* (Basingstoke: Palgrave Macmillan, 2008), 37–38, 128–30.

[50] Ibid., 35.

[51] Reginald Pecock, *The Repressor of Over Much Blaming of Clergy*, ed. C. Babington (London, Longman, 1860), e.g. 429, 431 ('the synne and yuel cometh not fro and bi the seid iiij^c. gouernaunce had and vsid by the clergie, but fro and bi mannys natural passiouns and freelnesis and fre wil, aghens which is not mad sufficient fight and bateil'), 433, 435.

[52] Ibid., 424, 432 (for quote).

[53] Ibid., 437.

[54] Ibid., 453. See also, ibid., 464.

leeful to princis with hir comounalte forto make politik and cyuyl lawis and ordinauncis for the better reule of the peple'.[55]

In England, this was not a strictly 'ascending thesis' in Walter Ullmann's sense, in which power came up from the people not down from divine right, but it did involve rulers in the exercise of persuading their subjects that they were ruling for their mutual benefit, and not to their damage, ruin or impoverishment.[56] Persuasion by argument or by threats was an essential part of monarchical rule in England, just as it was in the pope's rule of Christendom or the bishop's of his diocese, in a way that brings us to the question of the 'public' and 'publicity'. Latinate writers with minimal exposure to Roman law would have known that: 'Those things which pertain to human right are either public or private. Public things are considered to be nobody's property for they belong to all (*universitatis*). Private things are things which belong to individuals (*singulorum*)'.[57] This could mean things which were common property, notably roads, bridges and watercourses. In the mid-thirteenth-century Close Rolls, 'public' denoted things that were the property of everybody, and thus which involved the special concern of the king as the guardian of the common good, such as the 'public road' or 'public street' (*via publica, strata publica*).[58] Or it could mean information: that which was 'publicly' proclaimed was consequently common to all. One important function of the network of royal officials at different levels in the kingdom of England and beyond was not just to execute orders but to relay information. In the mid-thirteenth-century Close Rolls, officials in England, Ireland and Gascony, bishops, bailiffs and sheriffs, were ordered 'that you should have publicly read', 'that he should publicly proclaim' or 'that in your whole county you should publicly read'.[59] They were also ordered to 'publicise' (*publicari*) particular proclamations or letters, or their 'publication' (*publicacionem*) was invoked.[60] Public protests and public appeals were made, and matters were publicly prohibited.[61] Brazen criminals went about 'publicly' in parts of the

[55] Ibid., 454.

[56] Walter Ullmann, *A History of Political Thought: The Middle Ages* (Harmondsworth: Penguin Books, 1965).

[57] *Digest*, 1.8.1 cited by Eberman 'The notion of the Common Good', 109, n. 14: 'haec autem res, quae humani iuris sunt, aut publicae sunt aut privatae. quae publicae sunt, nullius in bonis esse creduntur, ipsius enim universitatis esse creduntur privatae autem sunt, quae singulorum sunt'.

[58] *Close Rolls, 1231–34*, 44, 387, 399; *1234–37*, 462 (twice); *1247–51*, 498.

[59] *Close Rolls, 1227–31*, 45, 59, 392 for these citations. Reading and proclamation 'publice': *Close Rolls, 1227–31*, 45, 59, 392, 430; *1231–34*, 326, 542, 544; *1234–37*, 329, 512, 532; *1237–42*, 22, 133; *1242–47*, 127, 319, 357, 360, 472, 536, 547; *1247–51*, 108, 283, 320, 358, 424, 492, 504, 529, 549, 559 (29 instances). *Royal Letters of Henry III*, ed. Shirley, 102 (Ancient Correspondence: 1254), 300 (Close Rolls: 15 March 1266).

[60] *Close Rolls, 1227–31*, 93, 464 (twice), *1242–7*, 478; *1247–51*, 358 (twice). *Royal Letters of Henry III*, ed. Shirley, vol. II, 272 (Close Rolls: 21 Aug. 1264), 300 (Close Rolls: 15 Mar. 1266), 394 (Close Rolls: 12 October 1259).

[61] *Close Rolls, 1231–34*, 73; *1242–47*, 424, 242.

kingdom, and must be repressed.[62] 'Public indignation' was to be feared in 1260 if the king allowed his half-brother Aymer of Lusignan to return.[63] 'Public rumours' flew about, and it was reported to the king that subversive words were 'publicly ... said' in Gascony.[64] The 'public whores' of the clerks of Oxford, or the outlaw whose 'crime is publicly confessed', were to be dealt with in accordance of common knowledge of their status and dispositions.[65] The rebels still holding out at Kenilworth Castle in 1265 were threatened with being reputed as 'public enemies': enemies to all known by all to be enemies.[66]

Medieval 'politics' was understood as the art of ruling a broad variety of human groupings, but an art which relied especially on the mastery of communication within that group, with the aim of securing assent, and determining a course of action or a form of regulation which corresponded with reason and mutual benefit. This could and did involve the exercise of violence, symbolic or physical, whether the unit of rule was a kingdom, a manor, a town, an abbey or a diocese. But each of these units was best ruled when agreed conventions were respected, and mutual goods were seen to be the purpose of rule. Still, it is telling that although Aristotle's distinction between good and bad forms of rule was supposed to be found in rule for the common good as opposed to rule for the ruler's own interests, when this was illustrated in one manuscript of Oresme's translation of the *Politics*, what distinguished the good from the bad was calm discussion on the one hand, and the use of violence and cruelty, equipped with instruments of torture, on the other.[67] The ideal was communication, ideally face-to-face, to find the common good and persuade by reason, not violence: that was the difference between heaven and hell. In reality, however, not all these units were the same and not all were face-to-face communities as the medieval vision of 'politics' imagined them. Many indeed were characterised as assemblages of units geographically and socially dispersed. Not all the members of that meta-unit knew one another or had even met one another. In a kingdom, a diocese or the extended affinity of a great noble, a minority would have known the ruler well, some would have talked to him, some simply seen him or heard him speak. Most would only have dealt with their ruler's officials, or even those who had contact with those officials. In a town or a village, although hierarchy and degrees of closeness and distance persisted, rulers were accessible to differing degrees. Mayors and bailiffs, aldermen and worthy members of the merchant gild or inner council

---

[62] *Close Rolls, 1237–42*, 137.

[63] *Royal Letters of Henry III*, ed. Shirley, vol. II, 152. From Close Rolls, 18 January 1260.

[64] Ibid., 41 (1244), 183 (1261?). From SC 1.

[65] Close Rolls, 1231–34, 568, 570 (three times) (*publice meretrices*); 1237–42, 146.

[66] *Royal Letters of Henry III*, ed. Shirley, vol. II, 289 (1265). From SC 1.

[67] Brussels, Bibliothèque Royale MS 2904, ff. 1v, 2r reproduced in Oresme, *Livre de Politiques*, 6–7.

were still citizens of the town.[68] Manorial officials were closer, as active in the royal and seigneurial administration as at movements of sedition and rebellion.[69] A distant lord of a manor or town looked more like a king, seen less often (if at all) than his bailiffs and stewards. Recent historians have made good use of 'brokerage' in understanding the interaction between local formations of social power and the 'state', and recent work on ecclesiastical rule, too, stresses the local effects, in the parish, of bishops' search for groups of trustworthy men with whom to govern.[70] The forms of politics which characterised these assemblages were not the same as those which characterised the rule of a simple group of human beings, as medieval theorists imagined it. Perhaps that is why 'public', more than 'political', and specific assemblages of mutual benefit as much as an abstract common weal, provided the most cogent vocabularies for describing its workings.

HISTORIANS' CONCEPTS OF THE POLITICAL

So much for medieval vocabularies of politics: What of those of historians and how have they evolved? 'Politics' and 'political' in modern English usage have two distinct referents, which we might call the 'narrow' and 'broad' conceptions of politics. Over the last century, the 'narrow' definition, focussed on the state, has come to be challenged by various 'broad' conceptions, both explicitly in political science and implicitly in the use that historians make of the words 'politics' and 'political'. 'Politics' in the narrow sense is most easily understood with reference to *Politik* as famously defined by Max Weber in a lecture delivered in 1919, published in English as 'Politics as a vocation'.[71] Although his original German elides what in English would be separated into 'politics' and 'policy', Weber's characteristically clear and incisive discussion builds on what was then also a commonplace of liberal political thought in the Anglophone world: that politics is above all concerned with the state and

---

[68] For a development of this observation, see Christian Liddy, *Contesting the City The Politics of Citizenship in English Towns, 1250–1350* (Oxford: Oxford University Press, 2017).

[69] Christopher Fletcher, 'Justice, meurtre et *leadership* politique dans la Révolte anglaise de 1381', *Cahiers de recherches médiévales et humanistes*, no. 34 (2017), 61–86.

[70] Michael Braddick, 'State Formation and Social Change in Early Modern England: A Problem Stated and Approaches Suggested', *Social History*, Vol. 16 (1991), 1–17; Braddick, *State Formation in Early Modern England, c. 1550–1700* (Cambridge: Cambridge University Press, 2000); Masschaele, *Jury State and Society*; Ian Forrest, *Trustworthy Men: How Inequality and Faith Made the Medieval Church* (Princeton: Princeton University Press, 2018); Hilde De Weerdt, Catherine Holmes and John L. Watts, 'Politics, c. 1000–1500: Mediation and Communication', *Past and Present Supplement*, no. 13 (2018), 261–96.

[71] Max Weber, 'Politics as a Vocation', in *The Vocation Lectures*, trans. R. Livingstone (Indianopolis and Cambridge: Hackett, 2004 [1919]).

competition for control of its resources.[72] This choice of definition was given extra sharpness by the purpose of his lecture: he had been asked to discuss 'politics' as one of a series of 'vocation lectures' discussing different careers for an audience of students. Weber thus began by setting out a series of different uses of *Politik* in the 'broad' sense.[73] He defined *Politik* in a phrase as 'any kind of independent *leadership* activity', before clarifying this usage through a series of examples: the *Reichsbank*'s interest rate policy, for example, but also the *Politik* of a trade union in a strike, the policies of the board of management of an association 'and even of the political manoeuvrings [*Politik*] of a shrewd wife seeking to influence her husband'. But Weber then drastically narrowed the range of inquiry, excluding the vast majority of these 'broad' usages: 'Today we shall consider only the leadership, or the exercise of influence on the leadership, of a *political* organization, or in other words a *state*'. Much of the rest of this essay concerned the nature and development of the state as it was in 1919. Weber was interested, with his audience of student careerists in mind, in the process by which state officials come to direct but not to possess the means at their disposal. Politics was the business of trying to secure control over this 'means of administration'.[74]

Is it possible or useful to apply this 'narrow' concept of 'politics' and the 'political' to medieval conditions? What about the 'broad' sense of 'politics' which Weber puts to one side—the tactics of securing power in any human grouping? Is this useful, or is it too broad to teach us very much? The answers, usually implicit, which historians of late medieval England have given to this question have changed over time and have seldom commanded unanimity. On the one hand, there is a long tradition of studying the expansion, roughly between the mid-twelfth and the mid-fourteenth century, of the machinery of royal government in England.[75] This has been continued more recently as part of the broad comparative project of studying the emergence of the 'modern state' in a variety of contexts in late medieval and early modern Europe, notably under the aegis of the European Science Foundation in the 1990s, published by Oxford University Press in the *Origins of the Modern*

---

[72] For a critique, still valid as an attack if not in terms of the alternative it proposes, and despite its author's subsequent career, see Carl Schmidt. *The Concept of the Political*, trans. G. Schwab (Chicago: Chicago University Press, 1995 [1932]), 20: 'One seldom finds a clear definition of the political... In one way or another "political" is generally juxtaposed to "state" or at least brought into relation with it'. For a more congenial and more recent critique, see Pierre Rosanvallon, *La contre-démocratie: La politique à l'âge de la défiance* (Paris: Seuil, 2015).

[73] Ibid., 32.

[74] Ibid., 36–38.

[75] T.F. Tout, Hilda Johnstone and Margaret Sharp, *Chapters in the Administrative History of Mediaeval England*, 6 vols (Manchester: Manchester University Press, 1920–1933); William A. Morris, Joseph R. Strayer, James F. Willard, William H. Dunham (eds), *The English Government at Work: 1327–1336*, 3 vols (Cambridge, Mass.: Medieval Academy of America, 1940–1950); A.L. Brown,. *The Governance of Late Medieval England* (London: Edward Arnold, 1989).

State series, and more recently in the European Research Council project *Signs and States* (2010—14) headed by Jean-Philippe Genet. More recently still a number of historians, working on early modern as well as later medieval history, have taken a slightly different approach to 'state building', considering the different ways in which local 'brokers' put their social power at the disposition of various forms of royal administration, both increasing their power at a local level and increasing the range of action of the 'state'.[76] One might conclude that it would be perfectly legitimate to define competition over the control of royal fiscal, judicial and administrative apparatus as unimpeachably 'political' in a narrow sense. There were developed means of government, they were becoming more so and they were the focus of different kinds of appropriation or contestation. Still, it is interesting to note that movements in this direction amongst historians of late medieval England have been more hesitant, even though there has been a great expansion in recent years in the study of phenomena—petitioning, office holding, justice, direct and indirect taxation, jury inquests, representation—which historians of different periods and different regions have no problem in labelling as 'political'. In fact, there are good reasons for this in the historiography of late medieval 'politics', ones which have long been known to historians, but which are seldom discussed explicitly.

It was in the years before and after Weber's lecture that the view of medieval English political history as concerning rivalry for the control of the state apparatus reached its apogee. T.F. Tout (1914) and J.C. Davies (1918) both argued on the basis of detailed study of the king's administration that Edward II's reign was a key moment in the development of the royal government.[77] For Tout and Davies, the struggles between the king and his baronial opponents were struggles over the control or restraint of what Weber would call the 'means of administration'. For Tout, Edward's reign was a 'turning point' in the development of the royal governmental machinery, thanks to the administrative reforms which took place during his reign.[78] For Davies, the barons stood opposed to this 'royal system of administration' in a 'conflict of principles, contradictory and irreconcilable'.[79] Nothing could be more 'political' than that, even in a narrow sense.

In the mid-twentieth century, however, this approach suffered a devastating critique, to a great extent through the inspiration of the influential Oxford historian K.B. McFarlane. For McFarlane, over-concentration on the

---

[76] Braddick, 'State Formation and Social Change'; Braddick, *State Formation in Early Modern England*; Masschaele, *Jury State and Society*; De Weerdt, Holmes and Watts, 'Politics, c. 1000–1500'.

[77] T.F. Tout, *The Place of Edward II in English History* (Manchester: Manchester University Press, 1914); J.C. Davies, *The Baronial Opposition to Edward II Its Character and Policy: A Study in Administrative History* (Cambridge: Cambridge University Press, 1918).

[78] Tout, *The Place of Edward II*, vii.

[79] Davies, *The Baronial Opposition*, v.

machinery of royal government, together with a belief that there was inherent competition between the king and the higher nobility to control it, had fundamentally distorted the understanding of 'real politics' in late medieval England.[80] In his lectures in the 1950s and 1960s, now most accessible in his posthumously published Ford Lectures of 1953, he instead sought to examine the priorities of the English nobility to understand 'the character of fourteenth-century political activity' which an over-concentration on Parliament, in particular, had obscured.[81] It was not competition over some Weberian 'means of administration' that motivated the nobility, but the habitual concerns of their class: namely war, land and family, lordship and service, revenue and expenditure and only finally 'politics'.[82] It is telling, however, in terms of what was to come, that McFarlane was sparing in his use of the vocabulary of 'politics'. In his Ford Lectures he invokes the 'social and political consequence' brought by land, the consequences for a noble family of 'political miscalculation' leading to death and forfeiture; he talks of the limited effect of 'political disturbance' on agriculture, and of the importance of hospitality for 'building up and maintaining a political connection'.[83] But that is all: 9 uses in 121 pages, or 0.07 per page. Since McFarlane was trying to liberate late medieval history from the tyranny of an excessively institutional approach, this makes sense. It is even ambiguous in his usage whether 'political' is in the 'narrow sense' or the 'broad sense' since the nobility's political activities took place in the face-to-face community made up by them and the king. This is both the politics of the state (although McFarlane was specifically trying to assert that this was not its most important characteristic) and the politics of a particular human grouping.

As a new generation of historians took up the call to study the nobility as a means of understanding what was still called late medieval 'politics', the language of politics and the political crept back. For Edward II's reign, the two key works were the studies of J.R. Maddicott (1970) and J.R.S. Phillips (1972) on two prominent nobles: the king's foremost opponent, Thomas, earl of Lancaster, and one of his most loyal supporters, Aymer de Valence, earl of Pembroke.[84] Both concluded that Tout's and Davies' account of a 'baronial opposition' concerned to limit or control the royal machinery of government did not accord with a close analysis of the careers of these two key players. They were late medieval nobles and they acted according to the values and the

---

[80] K.B. McFarlane, *The Nobility of Later Medieval England: The Ford Lectures of 1953 and Related Studies* (Oxford: Clarendon Press, 1973), 120.

[81] Ibid., 120.

[82] Ibid., 6.

[83] Ibid., 10, 15 (twice), 58, 101.

[84] J.R. Maddicott, *Thomas of Lancaster, 1307–1322: A Study in the Reign of Edward II* (London: Oxford University Press, 1970); J.R.S. Phillips, *Aymer de Valence, earl of Pembroke 1307–1324: Baronial Politics in the Reign of Edward II* (Oxford: Clarendon Press, 1972).

interests of their class in the particular iteration represented by their landed holdings, their networks of association, their personal hatreds, rivalries and friendships, and the way the king's actions affected all of these. They wanted the king to get on with his job, and they only intervened positively or negatively when he did it badly. They did not act out of an active desire to secure control of the royal machinery of government, even if they might promote or oppose particular programmes to reform the administration of the royal government, notably the Ordinances imposed on Edward II in 1311.

Did this mean that the 'politics' of Edward II's reign were 'politics' only in the broad sense which might equally well denote struggles for power and authority within any human grouping: a factory, a school, an office or a family? In fact, although Maddicott and Phillips argue in essence that a state-centred account of the struggles for power which marked Edward II's reign was distorting, these historians nonetheless thought of themselves as studying 'politics'—and not in the 'broad' sense outlined above. Phillips' study of Aymer de Valence is subtitled 'Baronial Politics in the Reign of Edward II', and opens by objecting to Tout's and Davies' oversimplification of 'the very complex nature of political life during the reign', whilst still drawing a contrast between 'the politics of the reign' and the structure of Pembroke's retinue and land-holdings.[85] Politics, here, as it was for McFarlane, is a separate sphere from a noble's rule over his own men. Maddicott concurs in arguing that 'early-fourteenth-century politics cannot be interpreted in these terms' and asserting that his aim is to 'demonstrate the complexity of political life'.[86] Indeed, a more systematic analysis reveals that on the 64 occasions that Maddicott uses political (51), politics (8), politically (3) or politician (2) in 334 pages, or 0.19 uses per page, the unit in question is the politics of the kingdom.[87] Maddicott contrasts Lancaster's landed resources with both the implicitly national 'politics' which they allowed him to intervene in, and with the 'political ambitions' and 'political schemes' they enabled him to pursue.[88] 'Political life', 'political power', 'political influence', Lancaster's 'political career', 'political activities', 'political success' and 'political ventures' all concern interventions in an overtly 'political' sphere which, when one tracks them one by one, starts to seem strangely unmedieval, especially since, as we have seen, contemporaries would not have regarded them as more 'political' than the administration of a town or of a diocese.

Telling here is Maddicott's use of the word 'politician' to describe barons in general and Thomas of Lancaster in particular in a way which seems to

---

[85] Ibid., vii.

[86] Maddicott, *Thomas of Lancaster*, vii.

[87] This and subsequent counts of the use of words in secondary material have been performed manually, so a degree of error is not unlikely.

[88] Ibid., vii, 14, 18, 22.

undercut the attempt to de-centre our understanding of late medieval 'politics'.[89] One of Maddicott's recurrent concerns is to observe when Lancaster seemed to be acting according to 'his political principles', meaning his attachment to a particular programme: the enforcement of the Ordinances, possibly as part of a commitment to intervention in the politics of the kingdom stretching back to Simon de Montfort's opposition to Henry III.[90] From this point of view, what makes something political is the fact of directing ones actions, not just towards the interests of oneself or one's group, but towards the achievement of a specific programme. A comparable approach is found in J.C. Holt's *The Northerners* (1961), where he argues that fighting the king for the application of a charter of liberties, Magna Carta, marked a fundamental break from what had come before.[91] What makes something political, then, is a 'political programme', on the implicit analogy of a political party advancing a manifesto.[92] A comparable approach was advanced more recently by the French historian of late medieval England, Jean-Philippe Genet, in a long review article of J.R. Maddicott's *Simon de Montfort* (1995), which began by posing the question of whether Simon de Montfort was a 'baron' or an 'homme politique'.[93] This article sought to explore whether de Montfort was a 'baron comme un autre'—which here means seeking to advance himself, his family and his associates—or whether he was an 'homme politique', meaning that he sought to defend a specific programme. That there is more to this distinction than might first appear (why could he not be both?) becomes clearer in Genet's monograph *La génèse de l'État moderne: Culture et société politique en Angleterre* (2003).[94] According to Genet, '... politics does not exist outside of the State, and more precisely of the modern State; in feudal society, it was brute social relationships which founded the relationship to power...'.[95] We are thus back to Weber's definition: true 'politics' is narrow-sense 'politics', the struggle to control the state. It seems that, without the

[89] Ibid., vii, 333.

[90] Ibid., 238, 318, 319.

[91] J.C. Holt, *The Northerners: A Study in the Reign of King John* (Oxford: Clarendon Press, 1961), 1.

[92] Maddicott refers to the *Modus Tenendi Parliamentum* as a 'political broadside', although at one point he doubts that Lancaster's attachment to the Ordinances can be seen as commitment to 'a vital part of a political manifesto': Maddicott, *Thomas of Lancaster*, 259, 312. Cf. D.A. Carpenter. 'Chancellor Ralph de Neville and Plans of Political Reform', in P.R. Coss and S.D. Lloyd (eds) *Thirteenth Century England II* (Woodbridge: Boydell, 1987), 69–80.

[93] Jean-Philippe Genet, 'Simon de Montfort: Baron ou homme politique?', *Médiévales*, no. 34 (1998), 53–68, reviewing J.R. Maddicott, *Simon de Montfort* (Cambridge: Cambridge University Press, 1994).

[94] Jean-Philippe Genet, *La génèse de l'État moderne: Culture et société politique en Angleterre.* (Paris: PUF, 2003), 203.

[95] Ibid., 263: 'le politique n'existe pas en dehors de l'État, et plus précisément de l'État moderne, dans la société féodale, c'est le rapport social brut qui fond le rapport de pouvoir'.

state, all we have is broad-sense 'politics', the search for influence or authority as might be found in any human grouping.

Although this was nowhere made explicit, in the studies of the English nobility which emerged in the 1970s, the 'politics' under study were not treated simply as struggles for power which could take place within any group or community. This was arguably because nobles were actors who were in the same face-to-face community as the head of the royal government, the king. From this point of view, the study of the nobility becomes the history of 'politics' the moment a noble actuates his political potential by involving himself directly with the king. Thus nobles are judged to act 'politically' when they interact with the king, when they are active in his administration or engaged in activities against his projects. They are judged to be 'politically unimportant' if they limit themselves to the rule of their lands and the localities in which their landed resources were based. For Maddicott, the earl of Oxford was the 'least politically conspicuous' of the earls, was 'too obscure and politically unimportant a figure to need comment', and joins the earl of Richmond amongst the 'political nonentities'—meaning those who did not intervene in the politics of the kingdom.[96] In a comparable fashion, one influential study of the nobility of Richard II's reign, published in the early 1970s, remarked that the 'political importance' of Edmund of Langley, earl of Cambridge and subsequently duke of York, had perhaps been underrated, noting that he had avoided 'political extremism', and placing him together with the earl of Northumberland as one of 'the honest brokers of politics in 1388 and 1389'.[97] Another remarked that the king's uncle, Thomas of Woodstock, earl of Gloucester, once he became involved in politics could not escape, unlike Sir Peter de la Mare, who 'could fade into political obscurity as a Herefordshire gentleman', since as the king's uncle he was inevitably trapped in what, to modern eyes, appears to be the quintessential political realm.[98] It is telling that when work on the nobility reached the level of synthesis in the 1980s, they were by now considered to be identical to the 'political community',[99] and conflict between crown and nobility was self-evidently 'political conflict'.[100]

Things become more complicated when we consider how the political history of late medieval England subsequently developed. Being the king's uncle made one inevitably political, being the king even more so. Other nobles could choose to be political or withdraw to their 'country', leaving the king

[96] Maddicott, *Thomas of Lancaster*, 8, 68, 316.

[97] Anthony Tuck, *Richard II and the English Nobility* (London: Edward Arnold, 1973), 8, 141–42, 142.

[98] Anthony Goodman, *The Loyal Conspiracy: The Lords Appellant under Richard II* (London: Routledge, Kegan and Paul, 1971), 14.

[99] Christopher Given-Wilson, *The English Nobility in the Late Middle Ages: The Fourteenth-Century Political Community* (London: Routledge, Kegan and Paul, 1987).

[100] Anthony Tuck, *Crown and Nobility, 1272–1461: Political Conflict in Late Medieval England* (London: Fontana, 1985).

to himself and attending to the management of his estates. But wasn't their country political also? At first this question might seem to be one of our own definitions: in the broad sense of politics, yes, in the narrow sense, no. But the development of gentry studies which first appeared in print in the 1980s and 1990s problematized this situation. The dealings of knights and esquires with one another in the county were 'political' in the broad sense—they were 'local politics'—but they might also be 'political' in the sense that their collective interests also impinged on the narrow-sense politics of the kingdom. Thus although, for example, Nigel Saul's thesis on the fourteenth-century Gloucestershire gentry was avowedly 'mainly social and economic' in theme, it nonetheless brought 'politics' and the 'political' into question in a way which destabilised earlier certainties about what 'politics' was.[101] Thus although Saul uses these words a total of 34 times in 262 pages, or 0.13 per page, his usage moves between national politics (9 uses), local politics ('the politics of the shire', 'county politics', etc.) (9 uses), one ambiguous use (it is not clear if the '[p]olitical leadership in the shire'[102] wielded by magnates of second rank concerned the politics of the kingdom or of the county) and senses which concerned the interaction between the politics of the kingdom and the politics of the county (15 uses). When 'political factors', 'national political considerations' or simply 'political considerations' affect appointment to county office, when a 'political flavour' or 'political significance' is detectable or 'political affiliations', 'political influences' or 'political partisanship' are in play, the word 'political' denotes the influence of the politics of the kingdom (which is more perfectly political to the modern mind) on the politics of the shire (which is perhaps political only by extension). But when the concerns of county politics come to influence the gentry's attitudes to national politics, when they applied 'their ideas not only to local but also to the King's government', then an important slippage is introduced.[103] Is the 'increasing political self-consciousness of the gentry' their consciousness of the politics of the kingdom, or their consciousness of how that politics might impinge on their local concerns?[104] Although, for Saul, 'county politics' is still clearly less politics than the politics of the kingdom, something is starting to give. By the time Simon Payling published his study of *Political Society in Lancastrian England: The Greater Gentry of Nottinghamshire*, the semantics of the historiography of late medieval English 'politics' had moved further.[105] Thus whereas Payling uses 'politics' or 'political' 49 times in 220 pages, or 0.22

---

[101] Nigel Saul, *Knights and Esquires: The Gloucestershire Gentry in the Fourteenth Century* (Oxford: Clarendon Press, 1981), vi.

[102] Ibid., 4.

[103] Ibid., 167.

[104] Ibid., 259.

[105] Simon Payling, *Political Society in Lancastrian England: The Greater Gentry of Nottinghamshire* (Oxford: Clarendon Press, 1991).

times per page, 24 of these occurrences refer to 'shire politics' or 'Notting-hamshire politics', and in the remaining 25 cases, it is rarely clear if 'national politics' can be separated off from its organic relationship to the local. After all, was the office-holding greater gentry of Nottinghamshire 'political society' as opposed to 'county society' because of its political dominance of the shire or its role, collectively, in national politics? This indeed is Payling's central point: 'late medieval politics in general' cannot be seen 'solely in terms of the relationship between the crown and the nobility'.[106]

If the nobility easily became 'political' when they came into contact with the king in person, this was less obviously so of the gentry. Nonetheless, the underlying focus of most work on the late medieval gentry was how their ideas and interests affected the aims, interests and room for manoeuvre of the king, the nobility and the royal administration. This is the central theme, for example, of the work of Christine Carpenter and those of her students who have followed her down the road of analysing the 'political and social world in the localities' in order to understand the politics of the kingdom—the inter-action between locality, which is one thing, and polity, which is another.[107] In the 1990s and early 2000s, research into 'political culture' expanded further to seek to deduce the consequences of the values and activities of peasants and townsmen in the politics of the kingdom.[108] In much of this work, historians tend to start with the assumption that groups under study became interested in the 'politics' of the king and kingdom insofar as the latter impinged on their own lives, conceived of as originally local and self-sufficient. Thus the narrow-sense 'politics' of the kingdom is affected by a series of values, interests and concerns in a variety of social settings which are conceived of as 'local'—the county, the town, the village. These ideas include the broad-sense 'politics' of these settings (the competition for influence and authority within each of them), but also all the other concerns, economic, social or religious, for example, which animate these milieus. But it is worth noting that in many approaches which consider 'political culture' or 'political society' what makes a given culture or society 'political' is the effect which it has on the narrow-sense 'politics' of the king and kingdom. This becomes clear, for example,

---

[106] Ibid., 220.

[107] Christine Carpenter, *Locality and Polity: A Study of Warwickshire Landed Society, 1401–1499* (Cambridge: Cambridge University Press, 1992).

[108] David Carpenter, 'English Peasants in Politics, 1258–67', *Past and Present*, no. 136 (1992), 3–42; Michael Hicks, *English Political Culture in the Fifteenth Century* (London and New York: Routledge, 2002); John L. Watts, 'The Pressure of the Public on Later Medieval Politics', in L. Clark and C. Carpenter (eds), *The Fifteenth Century IV: Political Culture in Late Medieval Britain* (Woodbridge: Boydell, 2004), 159–80; John L. Watts, 'Popular Voices in England's Wars of the Roses, c. 1445-c. 1485', in J. Dumolyn, J. Haemers, H.R. Oliva Herrer and V. Challet (eds) *The Voices of the People in Late Medieval Europe* (Turnhout: Brepols, 2014), 107–22; Lorraine Attreed, *The King's Towns: Identity and Survival in Late Medieval English Boroughs* (New York: Peter Lang, 2001); Christian Liddy, *War, Politics and Finance in Late Medieval English Towns: Bristol, York and the Crown, 1350–1400* (Woodbridge: Boydell, 2005).

in terms such as 'infrapolitics' which, like the terminology of 'subpolitics' as used by modern political scientists, implies that the only true 'politics' is the narrow-sense 'politics' of the state.[109] For Christine Carpenter, indeed, this is almost a criteria of the acceptable use of 'political culture': if such a concept cannot be used to understand 'politics themselves and political narrative' then it ought to be discarded as lacking explanatory utility.[110]

There is, of course, something self-fulfilling about the present analysis. It is not surprising that historians interested first and foremost in the politics of the kingdom—explaining the events of Edward II's reign or the Wars of the Roses—will continue to centre their efforts on politics in Weber's narrow sense. Outside of this field, historians continue to use 'politics' in a way which cuts between different levels without necessarily impinging on the interaction of the king and nobility, or even the king and the gentry. Cordelia Beattie, for example, subtitles her thesis on medieval single women, published in 2007, *The Politics of Social Classification in Late Medieval England*.[111] In this work, a political act is 'an act of power', which might lead one to suspect that it is simply broad-sense politics which are at issue. But in fact this is not the case: Beattie is concerned with politics in terms of the efforts of central government to react to the crisis of labour supply in the aftermath of the Black Death.[112] Such an account is certainly political even in Weber's narrow sense, but it has little to contribute to understanding the interaction between the nobility and the 'political narrative' constructed around them. Is it thus not about politics? Mark Ormrod's *Political Life in Medieval England* (1995) deals with a range of contexts, notably judicial, in which the points of interaction between government and different groups of subjects are far more varied.[113] Work on the politics of the village, meanwhile, suggests contexts which involve the intervention of various forms of actors that historians are accustomed to regarding as 'political', notably royal and seigneurial officials, but which reveal how strange it would be to divide such matters from broader issues particular to a village context such as the management of resources, manorial legal and

[109] Simon Walker, 'Rumour, Sedition and Popular Protest in the Reign of Henry IV', *Past and Present*, no. 166 (2000), 31–65.

[110] Christine Carpenter, 'Political Culture, Politics and Cultural History', in L. Clark and C. Carpenter (eds) *The Fifteenth Century IV* (Woodbridge: Boydell, 2004), 1–19, at 5.

[111] Cordelia Beattie, *Medieval Single Women: The Politics of Social Classification in Late Medieval England* (Oxford: Oxford University Press, 2007).

[112] Ibid., 1 (for quote), 3, 11, 14, 31, 37, 94, 98, 144, 147.

[113] W.M. Ormrod, *Political Life in Medieval England, 1300–1450* (Basingstoke: Palgrave Macmillan, 1995).

judicial structures, and internal social and economic stratification.[114] Christian Liddy's work on late medieval English towns explicitly challenges the dichotomy we have been wrestling with between seeing politics everywhere and thinking only of politics in terms of 'the machinery of government'.[115] His characterisation of a particularly urban form of politics based around issues such as access to common land, the annual mayoral election and the control of the circulation of information seems a long way from the king and the nobility even if, when the latter sought to make use of the former, they were obliged to negotiate these concerns.[116] In Ian Forrest's recent study of the use of local juries to facilitate the rule of bishops over the laity of their dioceses, 'politics' and the 'political' are omnipresent, occurring some 69 times in 353 pages, or 0.20 occurrences per page, not as much as Payling, but more than McFarlane, Maddicott or Saul.[117] Forrest's 'politics' is a matter of power relations within parishes ('local politics') and of office holding ('political inequalities' did not necessarily correspond to 'economic inequalities') and only very occasionally of national politics (when 'political stability' permits economic recovery in the late fifteenth century).[118] Is this just 'broad sense' politics? In this case that framework seems more clearly anachronistic. Parish officers and parish jurors are clearly part of a continuum with manorial, seigneurial, urban and royal officers and jurors. All of these activities would have been regarded by medieval observers as part of 'politics', of 'common' or 'public' life: forms of rule by counsel and by reason justified by mutual benefit, dealing with that which was not private property, but which belonged to no one and to all.

CONCLUSION

Thanks to a century of empirical research, historians of late medieval England have ample means to avoid the stark choice between defining politics on first principles either as being about the state, the king and the nation, or else as simply being competition over power and influence in any human grouping. Late medieval English politics now has much more content than that. Historians' concepts have evolved more organically than hard, theoretical

[114] Christopher Dyer, 'The Political Life of the Fifteenth-Century English Village', in L. Clark and C. Carpenter (eds) *The Fifteenth Century V* (Woodbridge: Boydell, 2004), 135–57. More recently discussed by Chris Briggs, 'Identifying the Political in the Late Medieval Village', paper delivered at *Pratiques politiques quotidiennes. Journée d'étude at IRHiS*, University of Lille, 21 September 2017. For a comparable argument applied to the sixteenth and seventeenth centuries, see Andy Wood, *Riot, Rebellion and Popular Politics in Early Modern England* (Basingstoke: Palgrave Macmillan, 2002), 5–17.

[115] Liddy, *Contesting the City*.

[116] For an approach more centred on the consequences for the politics of the kingdom, see Christopher Fletcher, 'News, noise and the nature of politics in late medieval English provincial towns', *Journal of British Studies*, 56 (2017), 250–72.

[117] Forrest, *Trustworthy Men*.

[118] Ibid., 203, 208 for the last two quotes.

definitions allow, and this is fitting, since the phenomena they are describing are organic phenomena, not the crystalline structures of holistic theory. The themes brought to the fore by recent work on the politics of bishop and parish, town and village reveal enough common themes for it to be clear that the old binary is not as compulsory as it once was. They supplement rather than replace earlier work on the nobility and gentry, as well as the mighty volume of work on the English parliament and royal governmental and judicial institutions which preceded it. Important themes in the present state of the art intercut with the range of medieval concepts which included politics: the importance of officials and of different kinds of inquest jury; the importance of information—both information projection, information gathering and controlling common talk and rumour; the importance of accounting and being held to account; the importance of public resources and their management—common fields, common roads, common spaces, but also money, water supplies, labour supplies and even access to competent priests.[119] Breaking down the boundaries imposed by an early twentieth-century concept of politics need not lead to an excessively general notion of politics. Instead it can help to reconceptualise where we place the boundaries of politics today as much as in the middle ages. Once we abandon the implicit mental analogy, reinforced by our casual use of language, between late medieval politics and eighteenth- or nineteenth-century British political institutions, we might tentatively suggest that medievalists have a head start on colleagues working on more recent periods, who are currently trying to establish an approach to politics which is not just limited to what seems, before we stop to think, self-evidently 'political'.[120]

[119] In addition to works cited above, see John Sabapathy, *Officers and Accountability in Medieval England, 1170–1300* (Oxford: Oxford University Press, 2014); Christopher Fletcher, 'De la communauté du royaume au *common weal*: Les requêtes anglaises et leurs stratégies au XIVᵉ siècle', *Revue française d'histoire des idées politiques*, Vol. 32 (2010), 135–49.

[120] Jonathan Parry, 'Educating the Utopians: Review of *The Oxford Handbook of Modern British Political History, 1800–2000*', *London Review of Books*, 41:8 (18 April 2019), 10–12.

Part III

Afterword

CHAPTER 10

Reflections on Using Concepts

John Watts

Pope Innocent III was apparently fond of quoting Jeremiah 1.10: 'we … are set by God over the nations and kingdoms to root out and destroy, to build and to plant'.[1] It is a nice metaphor, both for the role of analytical concepts in history and for the task of the historian when faced with them: every 'tyrannous construct' is also—or at least once was—'a tool of the trade', exposing something even as it led away from other things; equally, it is the task of all historians to unpick the concepts they inherit, and recreate them in the light of the evidence, as read from the changed perspectives of their times. And, as far as this volume is concerned, perhaps the metaphor works in a third way, drawing together the conceptual world of a medieval pope, in which a combination of Scripture and divine prerogative were the prescriptions for revision of the temporal landscape, with the conceptual world of the academic historian, in which a combination of historiography and disciplinary norms drive the revision of the written past. Perhaps we can learn something about Innocent's situation and predicament by thinking about our own.

That is, perhaps, the most ambitious and original purpose of these essays—not just to question 'analytical categories', as the editors put it; nor simply to explore 'historical ideas'; but to set these two ways of working with 'concepts'

---

[1] Christopher R. Cheney, 'The Letters of Pope Innocent III', *Bulletin of the John Rylands Library*, 35.1 (1952), 23–43, 28, 40; Colin Morris, *The Papal Monarchy: The Western Church from 1050 to 1250* (Oxford: Clarendon, 1991), 431.

J. Watts (✉)
Corpus Christi College, University of Oxford, Oxford, UK

J. W. Armstrong, P. Crooks and A. Ruddick (eds), *Using Concepts in Medieval History*, https://doi.org/10.1007/978-3-030-77280-2_10

alongside each other.[2] Historians have been re-thinking analytical categories since at least the time of Augustine, and it has been a central activity of academic practitioners since the creation of scholarly journals in the late nineteenth century. Similarly, historians have worked with 'historical ideas' in an explicit way since at least the eighteenth century, and more implicitly or indirectly for far longer. But putting these enterprises together is a more recent and unusual phenomenon—apparent, perhaps, in the inaugural era of *Begriffsgeschichte*, when recovering the birth of modern conceptual language in the so-called *Sattelzeit* seemed so essential to understanding the contemporary era; apparent too in the post-colonial concerns of medievalists in North America; but not common in Britain and Ireland, and especially not in ways that are intended to prompt new understandings of the past itself.[3] It is a very attractive feature of this volume that its contributors are asked to do much more with analytical categories than 'ditch and switch', or 'plough on regardless', as Andrea Ruddick neatly puts it.[4] Rather, they are to consider what might be learned from scrutinising key critical concepts in dialogue with the medieval concepts to which they most obviously relate.

The experiment works. Ruddick's own piece shows how the slipperiness of modern concepts of identity is equally apparent in the medieval past. Would she have been prompted to think so flexibly and penetratingly about the interaction of external and autonomous identifications, or about the relationship between the act of identification and the state of identity, if she had not engaged in a deconstructive analysis of today's critical apparatus? And the takeaway is considerable—a perspective on medieval people that is much more sophisticated than the kind of casting we are used to, in which the objects of our study are often either 'pre-national' or lumped together in *gentes*, bounded by language, law and real or imagined ties of blood. Ruddick's medieval subjects felt ties and allegiances but also had to make their way in a world that was structured by arbitrary regulations and hostile neighbours; this makes them more 'real' to us, but it also helps us to understand more about the textures of society and culture in the later medieval British Isles.

Similarly, Peter Crooks' exploration of the notion of the colony allows us to re-balance our understanding of those topics that are approached through the lens of 'colonialism', liberating concepts and practices of cultivation and settlement from an automatic implication in imperial oppression. His chapter opens up the possibility of a different, less fraught and less ethnicised history of medieval Ireland. Of course, the establishment of towns and farms involved conflict in Ireland—just as it did everywhere else—but it must have involved

---

[2] For these terms, see above, pp. 8–9, 13–14.

[3] W. Steinmetz and M. Freeden, 'Introduction. Conceptual History: Challenges, Conundrums, Complexities', in W. Steinmetz, M. Freeden and J. Fernández-Sebastián (eds), *Conceptual History in the European Space* (New York and Oxford: Berghahn, 2017), 1–46, 2, 5; Kathleen Davis and Nadia Altschul (eds), *Medievalisms in the Post-Colonial World: the Idea of 'The Middle Ages' Outside Europe* (Baltimore, MD: JHU Press, 2009).

[4] Above, pp. 113–14.

opportunities and synergies too, and neither its agents nor its victims came exclusively from particular ethnic groups.

So it is with the other essays: deconstruction of a modern critical term provokes new insights on its conceptual counterparts in the medieval world. We learn from Chris Fletcher that, notwithstanding the absence of the term *politicus* from pre-fifteenth-century political discourse, the key components of that term—rule in the common interest and communication between rulers and subjects—were widely reproduced across society. Recognition of this social fact, he argues, has helped to guide an organic expansion in the reach of English political history. Jackson Armstrong argues for the constructive benefit of making explicit the friction between the concept of 'frontier' and the historical terminology available in our sources. The interrelatedness of this concept with others like lordship and sovereignty becomes important when specific terms describing historical 'frontiers' are variously thick, thin or absent, as they were in different regions of fifteenth-century Scotland. We learn from Eliza Hartrich that thinking critically about 'networks' quickly exposes the limitations of our sources and the problems we create if we assume the kinds of boundaries the term implies; if we switch from noun to verb, from 'networks' to 'networking', we get closer to both the practices and the situation of later medieval urbanites. Carl Watkins considers the historiographical legacy of 'crisis' as applied to late-medieval social change, and reviews how the concept can take on a rhetorically powerful, and powerfully distorting, interpretative force. This need not, he argues, require us to abandon the concept as a tool of explanation, but we may stand to gain from adopting more 'de-dramatised' language when interpreting the period. Finally, Sophie Page shows how the freighted analytical approaches through which medieval magic is approached—histories of religion, histories of witchcraft, histories of science and medicine—map uneasily on to medieval representations of the craft, which were themselves highly tendentious: we are dealing, then, with a social practice which was never treated neutrally, and that exposes something quite fundamental about its lived experience. Time and again, the unpacking of our own concepts exposes something novel about the way medieval people thought and acted.

Perhaps too, in a more general way, the exploration of 'analytical categories', or historiographical concepts, helps us understand the nature and operation of 'concepts' in the past. The 'tyrannous constructs' we decry in the present are not ontologically different from the concepts we typically try to unearth and understand in the past. The 'slipperiness' of modern critical repertoires, representing as stable and unified what is often disparate, protean, contested, is much the same as the slipperiness of historical concepts. Each has an aggregative tendency; each borrows and copies across the aura of legitimacy or authority from one constituent sector to another; each exists in conversation with other concepts—indeed, they are devices for conversation: sometimes for signalling disagreement, sometimes for concealing it. Importantly, in my view, they are positioned somewhere between thought and language; or, to put it another way, they are neither wholly linguistic, existing only in words, nor wholly ideal, existing only in thought. As we know intuitively from our revisionist efforts, we can think outside the terms of a given concept, even as its wording encourages us to think in certain ways—or not to think at all, but simply to mumble its incantations. But equally, from the other perspective, the instantiation of concepts in language is an important part of their utility—at the very least, they allow 'cognitive ease', as Peggy Brown puts it, borrowing from Daniel Kahneman; typically, they are also implicated in the prevailing rhetorics and discourses of our communities; and they change relatively slowly, as language changes relatively slowly—relatively, at least, to thought, which can move lightning fast before it has to find the means of verbalisation.[5] These generalisations about how to understand concepts, common enough in the literature on 'conceptual history', are also intuitively clear in our reflections on historiography. They may be less clear to us when we turn to 'historical ideas', but this book offers us a useful way of thinking about past concepts— as facilitative, rather than all-controlling; as misleading in their simplicity, but significant in their social traction—and it does that by setting *our* conceptual operations alongside those of the people we study. We struggle to be critical and knowing, and we sometimes (often?) fail; many of our subjects may have been less self-conscious than we are—few of them were academics, after all— but they may have sat in the same partly critical, partly passive, partly pragmatic relationship to concepts as we do.

This is certainly the way concepts have seemed to work in my own research. Over the last thirty years or so, I have been concerned with 'kingship' and 'common weal', 'counsel' and 'the commons', with the relationship between concepts and political practice, the relationship between language, thought and action, and the influence of linguistic changes on political behaviour.[6] At the outset, a major aim of my work was to bring ideas back into a political history which seemed to ignore them, and I was greatly helped by two 1970s essays above all: Quentin Skinner's 'Principles and Practice of Opposition', and the introduction to John Pocock's *Politics, Language and Time*.[7] Skinner's piece offered a powerful argument why every analyst of politics must be

---

[5] Above, p. 25.

[6] For examples, see *Henry VI and the Politics of Kingship* (Cambridge: Cambridge University Press, 1996), esp. chs 1 and 2; '"Common Weal" and "Commonwealth": England's Monarchical Republic in the Making', in Andrea Gamberini, Jean-Philippe Genet and Andrea Zorzi (eds), *The Languages of Political Society* (Rome: Viella, 2011), 147–63; 'Counsel and the King's Council in England, *c*.1340-*c*.1540', in Jacqueline Rose (ed.), *The Politics of Counsel in England and Scotland, 1286–1707, Proceedings of the British Academy* (Oxford: Oxford University Press, 2016), 63–85; 'Public or Plebs? The Changing Meaning of "the Commons", 1381–1549', in A. Huw Pryce and John L. Watts (eds), *Power and Identity in the Middle Ages: Essays in Memory of Rees Davies* (Oxford: Oxford University Press, 2007), 242–60.

[7] Quentin R. D. Skinner, 'The Principles and Practice of Opposition: The Case of Bolingbroke versus Walpole', in Neil McKendrick (ed.), *Historical Perspectives* (London: Europa, 1974), 93–128; John G. A. Pocock, 'Languages and their Implications', in *Politics,*

interested in the ideas invoked by politicians (on the basis that those ideas limit the range of acceptable actions open to them). Pocock's introduction demonstrated the nature and power of political languages, their shapes and their claims on the imaginations of politicians, on their debates and on their actions. Quickly, then, 'ideas' became things embedded in, and testified by, languages—and sometimes they were 'languages' in themselves (these days, I prefer Tilly's concept of 'repertoires', because it is more open-ended and allows more self-consciousness to the user, but I did not know it then).[8] At the same time, however, it was clear that action outside the sphere of one idea or language was always possible, and while some of that action might be conducted under the sway of another idea or language, not all of it was— some of it was creative and independent; there really was an '*hors-texte*'. It was also clear that other collective factors besides ideas and languages influenced political action—I focussed on a number of institutions, some governmental, some social: 'kingship' and 'counsel', for instance, were ideas, languages *and* institutions, and, while these three aspects were influenced by and related to each other, they did not map on to each other precisely and each ramified in many different ways. It was certainly possible to demonstrate that political behaviour was conditioned and structured by those partly ideal and partly linguistic phenomena that we are calling concepts, but it was also clear that the vague boundaries of concepts and the pressures and complexities of the real world also created space for politicians to behave flexibly, innovatively or indeed badly. Of course, I have only focused on some of those pressures and complexities, and my work is both better and worse for that, but if I had to single out one form of pressure which I think is particularly interesting to the political historian, it is the kind of squaring the circle that working with concepts demands. Politicians were and are very often trying to smooth over the gaps between what they see as authorised and what they see as necessary; in parallel, they are trying to smooth over the gaps between thought and sense-perception on the one hand, and ideas, principles and discourses on the other. It is this instinct towards order and tidiness, however pragmatic or cold-blooded it may be, that above all justifies the effort to reconstruct and understand the concepts of the past. And historians too are squaring the circle, of course—trying to induce and apply models and patterns to make sense of the mess of the past, using and refining 'analytical categories' to make their work comprehensible and drawing on 'historical ideas' to interpret and clarify past actions. There is a parallel here, which is central to this book.

The book is about the possibilities—'the pay-offs and pitfalls'—of working with concepts. Is that work something that historians can choose or avoid? Can we 'do history' without attending to concepts, whether those of our

Language and Time: Essays in Political Thought and History (London: Methuen, 1972), 1–41, esp. 11ff.

[8] Charles Tilly, *Regimes and Repertoires* (Chicago, IL: University of Chicago Press, 2006).

times or those of the past? The answer is surely no. If history is an attempt to understand the past from the perspective of the present, we must be forever examining our conceptual vocabulary, because what we inherit is full of anachronisms—words and ideas born in different times from the past we study and the present we inhabit. How useful it is to unpack the development of those terms—their intellectual archaeology—is a moot point: this is a project in itself, and quickly becomes an intellectual and literary study of intervening periods. But having some sense of the past trajectory of our terminologies can be eye-opening and suggest directions for the kinds of re-thinking we want to do. Crooks' point about the nineteenth-century shift in thinking about colonialism, from the perspective of colonisers to the experience of colonised peoples, is a case in point: discovering the shift opens up a different way of thinking.[9] And what of the study of past concepts? 'Conceptual history', in the sense of 'the history of concepts', may not be everyone's cup of tea— it has a well-developed and ever-advancing methodology, but it is clearly a branch of the discipline and not an approach that all historians have to engage with. But can we ever write history that sidesteps the concepts of the periods we study? The answer during the long hegemony of the linguistic turn has been no, but perhaps change is again underway. The increasing interest in the spatial, the visual and the material opens up some non-conceptual possibilities. Much of it has certainly been concerned with culture—cultures and concepts of space and looking, touch, ownership and so on—but some of it is experiential: about the un-conceptualised or under-conceptualised responses of individuals and groups to external pressures.[10] Similarly, the rising concern with climate and the environment, or with disease, or with DNA all promise to shift the agenda away from concepts, even if much of the work in these fields is still interested in the relationship between phenomena and consciousness.[11] Even so, the salience of communications technology in our lives, alongside less

[9] Above, pp. 55–6.

[10] Ian Gregory, Don DeBats and Don Lafreniere (eds), *The Routledge Companion to Spatial History* (London and New York: Routledge, 2018); Martin Jay, 'In the Realm of the Senses: An Introduction', *American History Review*, 116.2 (2011), 307–15, and accompanying 'AHR Forum' on 'The Senses in History'; Tony Bennett and Patrick Joyce (eds), *Material Powers: Cultural Studies, History and the Material Turn* (London and New York: Routledge, 2010); Dan Hicks and Mary C. Beaudry (eds), *The Oxford Handbook of Material Culture Studies* (Oxford: Oxford University Press, 2010).

[11] Bruce Campbell, *The Great Transition: Climate, Disease and Society in the Late Medieval World* (Cambridge: Cambridge University Press, 2016); Bruce M.S. Campbell and Francis Ludlow, 'Climate, Disease and Society in Late-Medieval Ireland', *Proceedings of the Royal Irish Academy*, 120, C1 (2020), 1–91; Monica Green, ed., *Pandemic Disease in the Medieval World: Rethinking the Black Death* (Kalamazoo, MI: Arc, 2015); Ronnie Ellenblum, *The Collapse of the Eastern Mediterranean: Climate Change and the Decline of the East, 950–1072* (Cambridge, 2012); Elke Kaiser, Joachim Burger and Wolfram Schier (eds), *Population Dynamics in Prehistory and Early History: New Approaches Using Stable Isotopes and Genetics* (Berlin and Boston, MA: De Gruyter, 2012).

verbal trends like climate change, ageing and advances in robotics, may mean that an interest in concepts has some time to run yet.[12]

A final concern of the book is with the practice of medieval history and how it sits in relation to the study of concepts. Are medievalists more resistant to concepts—whether critical or historical—than historians of other periods? Do we handle them in distinctive ways? Are we net importers of 'analytical categories', rather than exporters, and are we unusual in that? It is hard to feel that British and Irish medievalists have departed from the global trends in the historical discipline over the last century or so: the essays in this book reflect much the same set of concerns that one might expect to find in any historiographically alert collection written by specialists in one field or another (the absence of religion in a book on the Middle Ages may be an ironic exception, but it is surely adventitious, rather than deliberate). The modalities of the medieval world might encourage us to approach concepts in particular ways—the relatively exiguous and distorted evidence-base, the wide distribution of power and authority, the inevitability of translation between historic and authoritative languages and vernacular ones, the relative emptiness of the world and the relative simplicity of the tools for exploiting its riches. These familiar norms surely guide us down some paths and not others, but there does not seem to be anything to worry about. It seems to me that medievalists—once so powerful in the academy, and now surviving in much smaller numbers and with more explicit protection—suffer from a particular kind of cultural cringe. We worry about our influence. But the subject matter of our work seems full of relevance in an unmanageable world of warring faiths, asymmetric conflicts and existential dangers. We cannot any longer look out with the confidence of Innocent III, but we can still do our share of rooting-out and destroying, building and planting.

---

[12] Jamie Susskind, *Future Politics: Living Together in a World Transformed by Tech* (Oxford: Oxford University Press, 2018), is an eloquent statement of how ancient political perspectives continue to have relevance amid today's conditions.

INDEX

The manufacturer's authorised representative in the EU is Springer Nature Customer Service Centre GmbH, Europaplatz 3, 69115 Heidelberg, Germany. If you have any concerns regarding our products, please contact ProductSafety@springernature.com

Printed and bound by CPI Group (UK) Ltd, Croydon, CR0 4YY
24/04/2026
02096342-0001